VENTURE
INWARD

VENTURE
INWARD

Edgar Cayce's Story
and the
Mysteries of the
Unconscious Mind

Hugh Lynn Cayce

With a Foreword by Charles Thomas Cayce

ARE
PRESS

ASSOCIATION FOR
RESEARCH AND
ENLIGHTENMENT

A.R.E. Press • Virginia Beach • Virginia

A.R.E. Press
215 67th Street
Virginia Beach, VA 23451-2061

Library of Congress Cataloging-in-Publication Data
Cayce, Hugh Lynn, 1907-1982.
    Venture inward : Edgar Cayce's story and the mysteries of the
unconscious mind / by Hugh Lynn Cayce; with a foreword by
Charles Thomas Cayce.
        p.   cm.
    Originally published: New York : Harper & Row, 1964.
    Includes bibliographical references and index.
    ISBN 0-87604-354-6
    1. Cayce, Edgar, 1877-1945. 2. Subconsciousness. 3. Parapsy-
chology. I. Title.
BF1027.C3C3   1996
133.8—dc20   95-43166

Cover design by Richard Boyle

For Sally,
whose patience and encouragement
made this book possible

Contents

Foreword

WHEN *VENTURE INWARD* was published in 1964, it was described by Daniel A. Poling, editor of *Christian Herald*, as "an invitation to the unexplored world of the unconscious." "It is," he said, "a sane and sensible guide to the powers and perils of psychic experiences. In my opinion it is the number one book in its field." Although there has been a good deal written about the unconscious mind and psychic experiences in the past twenty years, we still have barely begun the exploration. This book in my opinion is still the best of its kind—a resource in plain language, illustrated with fascinating case histories, for those of us struggling with questions or experiences in this area.

In addition to discussions of psychic experiences, such as telepathy, clairvoyance, and mediumship, and altered states of consciousness such as drug-induced states, hypnotism, and meditation, this book serves two other purposes. It is an account of the perceptions and understanding of the man who worked and lived most intimately with Edgar Cayce, the greatest American psychic of this century. The author, his son, draws on his over fifty years of experience with his father and the psychic information that came through him, as well as on the elder Cayce's work with hundreds of others with psychic ability, to help us with our venture inward. The Edgar Cayce story is told here as no one else could tell it—by his oldest son who spent a lifetime with his father in the field of psychical research.

Also, in the final chapters of the book the author provides a safe, systematic approach to a venture inward. He does a fine job of summarizing and clarifying the information in the Edgar Cayce readings on this subject. For those looking for "safer doorways to the unconscious," they are described here.

For me and perhaps many others, an important aspect of the book has to do with the unique character of the author, who died in July 1982. His psychic research was always firmly rooted in his deep and strong convictions about the spiritual nature of human beings and his Christian faith. He knew that a personal relationship with Jesus was a source of inspiration for many, and he saw such a relationship transform the lives of some he came in contact with.

I have heard virtually every major figure in the field of psychic research in this country express his or her respect for and affection for him. I have heard the same from famous people and regular folks. Several years ago I saw a high school classmate for the first time in many years. He was a successful dentist who had been a member of a Boy Scout troop led by Hugh Lynn Cayce. He asked about Cayce and quietly said that the man had changed his life. He said that his experiences in the Boy Scouts with Cayce had been important to him. Later in high school he began to run with a rough crowd that got into lots of trouble with the police, and he appeared headed for more trouble of his own. One night at a high school sports event he found himself drunk and standing next to Cayce. Cayce "smiled and seemed to look deep inside me—all the way through me and I felt both hurt and relieved. It was an unbelievable experience. I never drank again. I think I owe my life and career to him." I've heard a number of such stories about the author's role in changing lives. This book reflects the personal philosophy that played a major role in influencing people in such a deep way, and the book can itself help people change.

As president of the Association for Research and Enlightenment, Inc., I see hundreds of people each year with fascinating stories and questions about who we *really* are, what life's purpose *really* is, and what happens to us when we die. To these people, I most frequently recommend this book.

I consider it a privilege to introduce this book to you. It is a privilege to be the author's son.

Charles Thomas Cayce

Preface

BEING THE SON of a highly publicized American clairvoyant has seemed difficult at times; however, it has always made for an interesting life. This book is the story of my experiences, not as a scholar or as a laboratory technician recording experimental data, but rather as an intimate observer of day-by-day activity of what surely seemed to be helpful clairvoyance for several thousand people over a period of forty years. If you have never met Edgar Cayce through any of the numerous books or magazine articles about him, I welcome this opportunity to introduce him.

In trying to understand the ever-present mystery of my father, I have worked through the years with a number of people who seemed to have a variety of extrasensory experiences. My efforts to study and help both my father and these people—many troubled in mind, body, and emotions—have resulted in some unusual experiences. Also, I have had to look at some startling and what I consider to be helpful concepts about the nature of man and his life in the earth. I would like to share these experiences and lay these ideas in front of you.

All of my observations are expressed against the background of information which poured through my father's unconscious mind in daily sessions. As the unconscious spoke it revealed, it seems to me, depths of the mind and pathways to these deep areas which are worthy of consideration and further investigation.

Some people who read this book will see it as an attempt to justify the psychic work of my father. Others may question the wisdom of spending so much time, energy, and money in examining what came through a sleeping man. A few people may point out that there was no controlled study on which to base statistical data as evidence for extrasensory perceptions. All of these are legitimate questions and points of view, but you must judge for yourself.

Actually, you may disagree or be disturbed by many of the ideas which are examined. The records of Edgar Cayce's unconscious expressions are uniquely voluminous. This is only my admittedly inadequate appraisal. It may be possible for others to go much further. Certainly, I will continue to try to do so.

For this present volume, it is my hope that this effort may prove of interest to many, helpful to some, and even inspirational for a few who read it.

Hugh Lynn Cayce

Venture Inward

As man begins his conquest of space, he is vaguely aware of the vastness of the universe. He believes that he is on, or really in, a small globe of matter of various density called the earth. As a tiny speck of matter resting on the hard surface of this globe, he is moving several hundred miles per hour as the surface turns around the axis. By his computations this earth is circling the sun at the rate of 70,000 miles per hour, and the sun, at the edge of the vast galaxy called the Milky Way, is turning around the center of the galaxy at the inconceivable speed of a million miles per hour. Light traveling at 186,000 miles per second takes 60,000 years, he figures, to go from one side of this galaxy to the other. At present, man has no way of knowing if there are still other movements of which he is unaware.

Looking out through his telescopes man is now able to estimate that his galaxy (the one in which his sun, moderate in size, is moving) contains, like other galaxies, from a hundred million to ten billion stars. There are at least a hundred million galaxies in sight.

Equally awesome are the intricacies of the structure of the physical body in which man's consciousness seems to be housed. Its cell structure alone is as bewildering as the complexities of form in outer space. The cells in a human body are like the population of an enormous anthill. Various cells have special work to do and they go about their business in an orderly, systematic manner. There are three major parts to each cell—the nucleus, the cytoplasm, and the outer membrane. The nucleus, the directive part, controls structure so that a cell always produces an exact duplicate of itself. Each nucleus contains forty-eight chromosomes. The minute chromosomes contain at least thirty thousand genes, the plans of inheritance.

There are many kinds and shapes of cells. Some are tiny blobs, others have tentacles, and some nerve cells have tails more than two feet long. Cells are momentarily dying by the millions, and others are being born to replace them. In the blood, for example, there are twenty-five to thirty thousand billion red cells and approximately fifty billion white cells. There can be as many as twenty thousand million red cells in a teaspoonful of blood.

The life of the smallest cell in the male body, the sperm cell—spermatozoon—is even more amazing. In a lifetime one man produces approximately 400,000 billion sperm cells. Though they are so small that it takes hundreds of thousands lying side by side to cross the diameter of a human hair, the total number produced in a lifetime, if lined up touching each other, would extend twelve-and-a-half million miles into space.

If a particle of matter called an atom were enlarged to a pinhole size, a corresponding pinhole in comparison would grow to be over a mile in diameter. In an atom, its component parts—the proton and electron—are relatively as far apart as two balloons if one were placed in the center of a football field and the other in the top seats of the stadium. Yet man has witnessed energy released from these tiny particles, atomic explosions, so incredibly destructive that his boldest imagination cannot measure them. With the Psalmist it is easy to say, "What is man, that thou art mindful of him? and the son of man, that thou visitest him?" (Psalm 8:4)

How are we related to this complex world of matter, or, rightly we should say, to this complex world of energy? Is consciousness—the depths of our hates, fears, suffering, and confusion, or heights of our longings, dreams, desires, and loves—born wholly of this world we call matter? Are we merely physical organisms, more complex, but like all other animal forms, which begin at physical conception and cease to exist at death?

Let us put this another way. Can man know anything of time-space-energy except through the physical senses of his body? Do we dare think of ourselves as possessed of spiritual energies which might constitute something called a soul? Perhaps the direction of our search has brought us to this impasse. Our concern with the outer world of houses, automobiles, washing machines, airplanes, rockets, and bombs has led us to depend on physical stimuli for the answers to all of our questions. Is there another direction for our search? Do we dare venture inward?

Introduction

Beyond Consciousness

SARAH MARTIN PAUSED outside her eleven-year-old daughter's bedroom door. Again she heard a sob, a moan. She opened the door and went in quickly. Margaret was sleeping, but from the corner of her eye a tear was squeezed out and trickled down her cheek. Mrs. Martin shook her daughter. The girl sat up, rubbed her eyes, and suddenly burst into tears.

"He's dead!" she cried. "He's dead!"

"Who's dead? What do you mean?" Mrs. Martin asked.

"Brownie's dead!" wailed the girl. "He's been run over. He's dead."

"Nonsense," said her mother. "He just ate a pound of meat. He is very much alive."

The girl smiled weakly. "I must have dreamed it," she said. "I heard you tell me Brownie was killed by a car. It was so real. Please don't let him out of the yard today."

Two days later when Margaret returned from school Mrs. Martin did tell her daughter of Brownie's death. He had been struck by an automobile.

What appears to be a psychic warning of the dog's death in this strange little dream can possibly be explained by checking the habit patterns of the family and coincidence. At times Brownie may have barked at cars. The family probably had talked about the danger of the dog's being killed. Mrs. Martin could have been heard expressing concern over the dog. Margaret's dream therefore may have reflected only her unconscious worry. It just happened to be brought to consciousness when Mrs. Martin awakened her daughter. However, the dream, like all dreams, is an indication that the mind is more active on an unconscious level than we are generally aware.

As a Sunday school teacher for fifteen years in an orthodox Protestant church and as a scoutmaster for twenty-five years, I have had an opportunity to observe and record a great many spontaneous cases of dreams, premonitions, apparent telepathy, and religious experiences of young people which seem to be rather normal and frequent actions of the mind beyond consciousness. Persistent observation always ends with the disturbing thought that the regular psychological explanations of memory patterns and coincidence do not adequately explain *all* these occurrences.

Rather early in my life I had the opportunity to observe a distinct group of people whose mental activities were even more startling. During seven summers of my childhood and adolescence I visited a Kentucky farm adjacent to a large State mental institution. My cousin's father was a very popular physician at the institution. He frequently took us from ward to ward as he talked with the patients. With two other boys of our own age, sons of the superintendent, we had the freedom of the extensive grounds where hundreds of the less disturbed inmates spent endless hours sitting in the sun or moving restlessly about in restricted areas. During many long summer afternoons my friends and I listened to these patients talk. There were times when their conversations were quite normal. Then suddenly one of them would open a door into another world peopled with angels, devils, and weird animals. Some of these men and women frightened us. Others were gentle and kind. Obscenity, beauty, imagery, and fear were mingled in a kaleidoscopic outpouring from their distorted minds.

With a few of the less disturbed patients, the "trusties," we went swimming and blackberrying. Sometimes we stole watermelons and, while eating them in the shade of a convenient haystack, our peculiar friends gave fantastic accounts of impossible happenings from their early childhood.

Years later with a little background in abnormal psychology it was possible to identify some of the types and their problems. Daniel and Ezekiel's visions were no more symbol filled than many we heard described. I will never cease to wonder about the man who, after pledging us to secrecy, would accurately and instantaneously tell exactly how many small rocks were in a pile or how many blackberries were in a can or bucket. Each day when he was able to join us provided a new opportunity to challenge him. He was right so frequently that we lost interest after a few rounds. There was another man who would stick pins in himself, apparently without experiencing pain; and an older teenage boy could imitate any sound he heard. We became acquainted with a very interesting group of people.

From these troubled individuals, as from the more normal young people, I learned that the mind beyond immediate consciousness was filled with strange patterns, capable of unusual feats of memory and remarkable control over the body.

More than any other experience or observation, it was the day-by-day examination of the words pouring out of one unconscious man which brought me face to face with a world about which we know very little in normal consciousness. When I was born my father was already attracting local attention through his ability to speak from a self-induced unconscious state. By the time I was three years old the accuracy of the psychic content of his unconscious speech had become the subject of national newspaper publicity. My earliest memories include fragments of discussions about the value and dangers of, as well as how to handle, this peculiar ability. Throughout the years a great many people came to ask for help, question, study, test, and sometimes ridicule and persecute my father. It was natural that my interest in psychic subjects would grow. And it is understandable that in considering the activity of the unconscious mind I must draw heavily on my experiences with him and the information which he gave during his unconscious states.

I have become acquainted with an enormous, and frequently

confusing, mass of writings by and about people who had experiences beyond normal consciousness. More exciting and rewarding have been the years of investigations and comparative studies of contemporaries who, like my father, spent considerable parts of their lives in unconscious states. I have visited mediums, talked with people who claimed to have had visions, read thousands of pages of automatic writing, and been involved in various types of experiments with hypnosis.

In considering any type of unconscious state, questions always occur far faster than they can be answered. How does the mind work beyond physical awareness? How valuable is the information which comes through or from the unconscious? What can an understanding of this area of the mind tell us about the dimensions of ourselves? Through various doorways—hypnosis, the use of drugs, trance, automatic writing, meditation, spontaneous experiences, religious ecstasy, and the everyday, universal experience of sleep—people slip away from physical consciousness. In twenty-five years I have observed the weird and grotesque, the amusing and the filthy, as well as the beautiful and complicated, the profound and challenging, aspects of this hidden mind. Perhaps here we can find some answers to questions about the nature of our being.

The type of the outpourings from an unconscious is governed to some extent by whose unconscious is being explored and by who is doing the exploring. It must have been an exciting experience in olden times to watch the unloading of a ship returned from the Orient laden with exotic and beautiful treasures. When slave ships docked, however, excitement must have changed to morbid fascination. Just so the material from an unconscious can be stimulating or disturbing. Obvious tensions, conscious fears, dreams, and repeated mistakes in speech are only a few of the psychological indications of unconscious mental activity. Psychology and psychiatry have made great strides in tracking such material to its source, at times in some deep-hidden memory bank. When exploring the unconscious, we are like children walking at night through familiar woods, imagining trees to be wild animals and waving bushes to be ghosts and dragons. In the unconscious, as in the woods a little light can be most helpful. Reports are sometimes so incongruous that it is not recognized that explorers are describing small sections of the same labyrinth.

It is obvious that much of the furnishings of the unconscious are memories of forgotten conscious experiences. Some memories are beautiful; some are unsightly; and there is a considerable mixture. Childhood recollections of the old swimming hole can be pleasant—unless the individual almost drowned there. Or a war experience which contains many painful reminiscences may also include thought patterns of friendships which remain strong and positive.

In attempting to discover just where our memories are located, it is logical to begin the search in one of the most remarkable components of man—the fifty ounces of pulpy, gray mass in his head—the brain. This is a world in itself, made up of millions of cells. Though the functions of some groups of these cells are known—sight controlled through the occipital lobe, hearing through the temporal—the activity of a large part of the brain is unknown. Man knows far more about the surface of the earth than he does about his brain.

I have tried visualizing the earth and attempting to locate the various continents and countries in them. Then, I have tried to think of the brain. My knowledge of even the areas from which the control of activities of the body stems is woefully limited. A few years ago I learned of the discovery of a new country in the brain.

Dr. Wilder Penfield, until 1960 director of the Montreal Neurological Institute, speaking before a 1957 meeting of the American National Academy of Sciences, described experiments with tiny electrical currents which when applied to an area in the fine tissue covering the brain, stimulated memories of forgotten experiences. Apparently details of consciousness are physically recorded and can be recalled when activated. The brain seems to contain a very efficient tape recorder. Patients, numbering almost a thousand, reported vivid recall more real than remembering. One patient not only heard a forgotten song again but also recognized it as being heard in the present. The interpretative process seemed to work simultaneously with remembering. This discovery locates at least a part of what is known as the unconscious mind of man. However, the memory of conscious action, as complicated as it may be, does not seem to account for all of the strange discoveries being made by many "inward" explorations.

When the North American continent was sighted, the first landing crews penetrated only a few hundred yards inland. Most of the observations were made as the ships sailed along the coast. Later, better-organized expeditions returned, bringing explorers and settlers who kept records and journals. The discoveries of areas of the mind have been like this. First explorations skirted around its edges; then more trained scientists led expeditions into the interior. Their findings have become the basis for many of our psychological theories. Psychiatrists like Freud, Jung, and many of those who followed them would have been the first to acknowledge that their discoveries only began to measure the dimensions of the unconscious mind. Comparable to vast forests, rivers, and mountains or ore deposits of a new-discovered continent, there are areas of the mind which lie unexplored and undeveloped. Like the urges which drove our early American pioneers, feverlike in their intensity, there seem to be similar impulses in our modern society to explore the unconscious. Popular motion pictures, plays, television and radio programs, wide-read books, newspaper and magazine articles, reflect a trend of interest which amounts to fascination, as man begins to unlock doors leading off the dimly lighted corridors of his mind.

Even at the risk of oversimplifying the profound concepts of some of the first modern discoveries about the mind, it seems to me that a few brief definitions will help us move forward in our thinking about the unconscious. Sigmund Freud, perhaps the best known of the early explorers, described it as that part of our mental life of which we are unaware. Unconscious material is shut off from consciousness when it is not needed or is unacceptable. He concluded that the unconscious holds infantile instinctual material with all its inherent amorality. The "id," according to Freud, is that part of our mental personality which clings to all primitive cravings and instincts.

C.G. Jung, for a time a student of Freud's, spoke of the unconscious as having two layers—the personal and the collective. He said that the personal layer includes the earliest memories of infancy, but the collective layer comprises the preinfantile period, that is, the residues of ancestral life. Jung explained that our consciousness floats like a little island on the boundless sea of the unconscious. In describing the help which can come from it, he suggested that the unconscious gives us all the encouragement and help that a bountiful nature can shower on us. He points out, "It holds possibilities which are locked away from the conscious mind, for it has at its disposal all subliminal psychic contents, all those things which have been forgotten or overlooked, as well as the wisdom and experience of uncounted centuries which are laid down in its archetypal organs ... the unconscious can serve man as a unique guide, provided he can resist the lure of being misguided."[1]

The direct approach to the unconscious, which allows it to speak for itself under controlled conditions, has provided some of the best material for study. The worth of this approach, like the worth of a garden, may be judged by its fruits, and the fruits have been good. An outstanding historical example was Sigmund Freud's early studies of Anna Q., a patient of Josef Breuer. In a conscious state and under hypnosis she was allowed to talk about her symptoms and each in turn disappeared. Freud visited Professor Jean Baptiste Charcot to observe his work with hypnosis. Later Freud turned from hypnosis to dream analysis and free association as ways of exploring the unconscious. The discovery that this hidden area of the mind to some extent could "explain itself" led to the development of Freud's monumental work in the psychiatric field.

As already mentioned, one of the major approaches to the unconscious mind which will be considered in this book is the mass of data which came from the unconscious of one man. Of special interest will be the material which seems to involve clairvoyance, telepathy, precognition, and descriptions of other than three dimensions. All of these subjects lie in the province of psychical research, which explores the unconscious as it attempts to measure and evaluate mental and spiritual powers apparently operating beyond the five senses. My personal experiences involve many of the different approaches which are used. Among the most widely publicized are hypnotism, experiments with mediums, drugs, card guessing and matching, spontaneous cases of extended perception such as warning dreams, hunches, visions of the dead, etc., investigations of so-called haunted houses, and automatic writing. As will be seen, such invasions of the unconscious frequently awaken "a sleeping giant" like the ogre in *Puss in Boots,* capable of becoming an elephant, a lion, or a mouse.

Obviously this book can be only a very limited examination of the psychic phenomena I have observed. Some brief historical ref-

---

[1]C. G. Jung, *Two Essays on Analytical Psychology,* Bollingen Series II (New York: Pantheon Books, 1953, p. 114).

erences have been included in order to make comparative reference to my father's experiences and data. This book is not a psychiatric study, though it deals frequently with abnormalities in mental activity. It is not an examination of the vast and complex world of symbology, so obviously associated with the language of the unconscious mind, though the stories related here contain much symbolism. Nor can this be a psychological analysis of complexes and frustrations, interpreted through various tests and measured evaluations of responses to either individual or group stimuli. It is not a documented laboratory study. If there seem to be contradictions and confusing explanations, it is because of my inadequate observations. There is no pretense here that all the answers have been discovered. I will be content if the importance of the direction of the search is suggested.

This is a compilation of my studies and observations of people who through psychic experiences have found themselves in touch with this seemingly boundless unconscious. In spite of the dangers, the fraud, the self-deception, the ever-present question of insanity, my conviction has grown through the years that in or perhaps through this unconscious lies a thread of light, hard to find and harder to follow, which leads to higher realms of mental and spiritual awareness.

This book is addressed to thousands of people who have had spontaneous psychic experiences which seem to transcend normal sense perception—hunches, warning dreams of coming events, and flashes of telepathy. It is also directed to the many individuals who are confused because of having dabbled in some psychic experiment. They have attended a seance, or tried automatic writing or a Ouija® board. The directions given them have been just exciting enough to lead them on. Can it actually be a dead grandfather, an East Indian guide, or a Space Man who spoke so flatteringly of one's place in the New World Order? Also there are within orthodox churches many sincere people who are asking questions about the many psychic abilities and experiences described in both the Old and New Testaments. Can modern psychic research offer helpful explanations of such happenings? Are these same kinds of events taking place today? And last, there is a small but important group of students of the paranormal who may find here a few bridges from one area of mental and spiritual phenomena to another. The searching of this last group is not so much concerned with the magiclike powers of the unconscious exhibited through psychic phenomena, but rather with achieving some small insight into the true nature of man. Through focus on controlling matter, we have acted like a person who has entered a small room, shutting himself away from the grandeur of the stars, the majesty of the forest and mountains. Plato described this as being chained in a dark cave, forced to observe only flickering shadows on a wall. William Blake puts it in those haunting words from "The Marriage of Heaven and Hell": "If the doors of perception were cleansed everything would appear to man infinite. For man has closed himself up till he sees all things through the narrow chinks of his cavern."

Mystics, sages, and philosophers of many ages have directed us to move outward through love, service, and sacrifice. It is these very people who have simultaneously ventured inward beyond the barriers of individual and mass fears and conflicts to find the indwelling source of inspiration and energy from which direction and control for outer expression may be achieved. This book is predicated on the belief that a better understanding of the functioning of the inner world, the unconscious mind, can bring insight into the true nature of humankind. And further, that such understanding can be clarified through examining some of the historic and contemporary practices of venturing inward.

1

THE EDGAR CAYCE STORY

1

A Helpful Unconscious

"SON, THE DOCTORS are going to have to operate on your eyes." It was Dad's voice breaking through dark, aching layers of bandages on my head and face. For a seemingly endless number of pain-filled days I had been lying in bed suffering from burns, shock, and the blinding flash from a part-filled box of flashlight powder into which I had dropped a lighted match. As a six-year-old boy, I was undergoing my first experience with real physical pain.

The silence seemed to press down. Someone coughed nervously.

"Dad, you're a good doctor when you're asleep," I answered; "why don't you tell them what to do?"

A story I had heard told many times by members of my family came back to me. My mother had contracted tuberculosis. She had suffered terrible pains in her chest and had begun to grow frail and weak. Her brother had died of this disease, and the doctors had expected her to die. Dad, who had no medical training, had given "a reading" which included directions for inhaling brandy fumes. The inroads of the disease on the lung had been stopped. A special diet had helped restore her health. The story always ended, "Edgar told the doctors what to do in a reading. There has never been any trouble with the TB since then."

I knew about readings. My father would lie on a bed or couch and seem to go to sleep. Gertrude, my mother, would sit near him and when he began to breathe slowly and regularly, as a sleeping person does, she would give him the name of someone who had asked for help. The individual might be there in the room or off in a far part of the country or even abroad. It was important, though, for the individual to be in the place agreed upon at the time the reading was being given. Gertrude would ask my father to look over the individual and report the physical condition, making suggestions for curing whatever might be wrong. This he would immediately do, describing any deviation from health. A stenographer would write down exactly what my father said so that a transcript could be given to the individual or to his doctor. These reports were called *readings.* Ever since I could remember, all kinds of people had been coming to Dad seeking help.

My father gave a reading on the condition of my eyes. Medicine to be taken internally, a special diet, and new solutions for the external bandages were recommended. From the time the dressings were changed I began to feel better. When the bandages were removed several weeks later, I could see. That personal experience with Edgar Cayce's psychic power has remained my most vivid impression of "a reading."

When this incident occurred in Selma, Alabama, in 1913 Edgar Cayce was already famous as a man who spoke like a doctor when he was in a self-imposed, hypnotic-like sleep. Several thousand people had already sought his help. The reading on the injury to my eyes was only one of a series of family readings which influenced him in trying to use his gift to help others when they asked. My mother, Gertrude Cayce, had appendicitis. Dr. Gay, the family physician, recommended an operation. A reading from the sleeping husband advised a combination of drugs in three capsules. The operation would not be required, it was stated. Dr. Gay followed the directions. It was not necessary to operate. On the other hand, when

Edgar Cayce himself suffered with intestinal pains in the general area of the appendix, the doctor did not advise an operation. A reading described an appendix wrapped around the intestine and about to burst. An immediate operation was urged with the warning that my father might die. Dr. Gay operated and found the appendix in exactly the condition described.

For me the scope of the medical clairvoyant power grew more and more impressive through the years. For a woman in Washington, D.C., a reading described the cause of a serious physical condition as arising from poisoning from a depilatory agent she had used. The treatments which were outlined restored her health. The correspondence requesting the reading made no reference to the depilatory cream. Nevertheless, it proved to be the source of the trouble. As early as 1910 an Edgar Cayce reading described for a man, hundreds of miles away, an ulcerous condition of his stomach. The treatments suggested were not unusual, but in the reading a final succinct sentence was added: "This will relieve the condition but know that this distress will return unless this entity changes his attitude toward his wife." Psychosomatic studies, the mental and emotional influences on body conditions, were not so well known then as they are today. Edgar Cayce apparently knew not only how the man felt toward his wife, but also what this was doing to his body.

The clairvoyance at times seemed to reach beyond the individual who requested help. In an Eastern city a woman complained that an inhalant prescribed for her in a reading had irritated her throat and nose rather than producing a soothing effect. A subsequent reading explained that the druggist who filled the prescription had substituted another ingredient for one recommended. When confronted with the question, the druggist admitted the change. He explained that since it was not a doctor's prescription and was not to be taken internally, he substituted what he believed was a better ingredient for one he did not have in stock. When compounded according to the directions in the reading, the inhalant proved very helpful. Here is distant perception of a compound and/or the mind of the druggist.

A great many "emergency" readings were given which brought immediate help, such as the following cases. For a girl in a Midwestern city suffering from a serious intestinal infection, a reading suggested poultices of crushed grapes and castor oil packs as part of the treatment, which produced almost immediate results. A telephone call to Edgar Cayce asked for an emergency reading. A man was suffering severe gallstone pains. A reading given the same night included an outline of treatments which provided relief and made an operation unnecessary.

Distance from the subject of the reading did not appear to be a barrier. A man in London was given a detailed, checkable analysis of his physical condition. The suggestions were followed with excellent results. The same reading contained a brief reference to what the man was doing as the reading was being given thousands of miles away.

Here is a fair example of a complete reading, which shows accuracy in diagnosis. The suggested treatments brought good results without involving overdramatic circumstances.

On May 30, 1934, in Virginia Beach, Virginia, the following information was given by Edgar Cayce, in an unconscious state, for a woman forty-eight years old, several hundred miles away in Raleigh, North Carolina. The woman's sister and a friend were present at the reading. Neither of them talked with Edgar Cayce prior to the time the information was given.

Now, as we find, while there are many physical conditions in this body that are very good, there are those conditions that with the correction would make a much better body physically and mentally for the activities in the mental, spiritual, and material body.

The disturbances, as we find, have to do with some minor conditions respecting functionings of organs, and little or no organic disorder. While many portions of the system are involved at one time or another, the conditions are such that they may be easily corrected in the present.

These are the conditions as we find them with this body.

First, in the BLOOD SUPPLY: here we find the form of an anemia, or the lack of a proper balance in the numbers of the red blood cells and the white blood cells. This condition exists now. Later we may find an alteration in just the opposite direction. This arises from nervous conditions that disturb the circulation, and the assimilation of what is taken as food values for the body. The nerve disturbance arises, as we shall see, from two—yea, three—distinct causes, making a combination of disorders contributory—as will be seen—one to another. Hence there is not only the variation in the red and white blood supply, or the form of anemia, but the character of the disturbance in other portions of the body, as we shall see.

As to the characterization of the blood itself—that is, the hemoglobin, the urea, the activity in its coagulation and in the blood count—this varies, not so much as to cause what may be termed an unbalanced metabolism but the very character of the nervous condition makes low blood pressure and at times disturbances to the heart's activity and its pulsation. Dizziness arises at times from distinct causes, during the periods of the menstrual activity, in elimination and during the periods when there is overexhaustion by excitement to the nerve forces of the body, or at other times we may find it arising purely from gases that form from nervous indigestion. These changes and alterations in the pressure cause changes in the character of the blood itself, though the body may not be said to have a blood disturbance—but the functioning of the organs themselves and their activity upon the system through the nerve supply makes the disturbance, though the character of the blood so far as carrying poisons or any character of bacilli in same is lacking; for it is very good in these directions.

In the NERVE FORCES of the body we find much that is a cause, and much that is an effect. So, it is not altogether nerves; though the body is nervous naturally from those conditions that have existed and do exist in the body, but under stress or strain no one would call the body a nervous person; for she would be very quiet and very determined and very set in what she would do, and she would do it!

In the cerebrospinal system we find there has been a relaxation in the third and fourth dorsal area that has tended to make for a relaxing in the *position* of the stomach itself, or the organs or the nerve tendons and muscular forces through the hypogastric and pneumogastric plexus, as to allow the stomach itself to tilt to the lower side, or the pyloric end up and the hypogastric or the cardiac end lower than normal, you see. This makes for a tendency of easy fermentation in same, and is a natural strain on the nerve system. The muscular reactions cause the condition, but the effect is in the nerve system. And as those plexuses in the upper dorsal are in close connection or association with the sympathetic and sensory nerve reactions through the ganglia near the first, second, and third dorsal area, this makes for a slowing of the circulation to the head, you see, sympathetically. Hence organs of the sensory system *sympathetically* become involved, as at times there is the tendency for a quick drying of the throat—and the body feels as if it would spit cotton often! At other times we have a thumping or drumming in the ear. At others there are the tendencies for the conditions to produce irritations and burnings in the eyes, especially if there has been an eyestrain either by being in the wind, poor light or strong light; any of these will produce an irritation through the necessary energies used and the lack of supply of nerve energy from the depletion in the area as indicated.

From this sympathetic condition, both as to the nerve supplies to the organs of digestion and as to the activities in the eliminations of the body during the periods that should be natural or normal, the reactions also produce an irritation again which causes the secretions from the vagina in such measures or manners as to make irritations so that the body is irritable in manner; and until the flow has begun there are pains produced in top of head, dizziness, lack of appetite, and an excess activity of the kidneys or bladder. These are purely reflex and are sympathetic conditions, as we have indicated, from a subluxation in the third and fourth plexus area.

As to the activities of the ORGANS themselves?

In the brain forces the reactions and activities are near normal.

The organs of the sensory system, as indicated, are disturbed through reflex conditions arising from the upper dorsal and reflexly through the cervical area.

Lungs, bronchi, larynx: only at periods when there are irritations to the hypogastric area is there any disorder of a nature which is not normal, but this will be corrected when the corrections are made throughout the system.

The digestive system, as indicated, shows disturbances; not only as to the position of the stomach itself but as related to the digestive activities and reflexly to the heart's activity through poor circulation impoverished by the inactivity of that assimilated being properly directed in the system, and sympathetically also for the organs of the pelvis in their activity.

The liver, spleen, pancreas, as we find, would function near normal when there is a normalcy from the position or the activities of the body. When there are those changes that may be brought about by the addition of those properties necessary for creating a balance in the system, these will make for proper activity throughout the body.

Then in making the corrections for this body we are speaking of:

First we would begin with making the proper adjustments osteopathically, especially—or specifically—in the upper dorsal area, *coordinating* the rest of the ganglia and the activity of the organs with same as these corrections are made. As we find, this would not require more than sixteen such adjustments and treatments.

Begin immediately, when the body rests, with having the feet very much higher than the head; and after much rest there should be the holding of the abdomen better in position by the use of bandage or belt about the body. Not so tight as to cause discomfort, but as the manipulations and adjustments are made let these be of *sufficient* activity as to *hold* the position of the stomach, that the activities through same may be kept in their proper relationship with the rest of the system.

For those disturbances that have been produced by the nerve reaction to the other organs of the system, so as to make that incentive for the corrections being made to coordinate with the activities of the glands and functioning of the organs, we would take a compound put together in this manner, adding the ingredients in the order named:

To 16 ounces of distilled water, we would add, stirring in, beating fine or powdering each ingredient:

> Dried Wild Ginseng Root (rolled together or
> beaten very fine) .... 1 ounce,
> Indian Turnip .... ½ dram,
> Wild Ginger (now this isn't wild ginseng, but gin-
> ger, which is a different root entirely) .. 1 dram.

Boil slowly until it, when strained, will amount to 12 ounces. Then add to the solution 2 ounces pure grain alcohol and 1 ounce Syrup or Essence of Wild Cherry. See? The dose would be ½ teaspoonful twice each day, morning on arising before the meal and when ready to retire. And continue taking until the whole quantity has been taken, you see.

Keep the manipulations about twice each week, making corrections specifically in the upper dorsal area and the *general* conditions throughout the body made to coordinate with same.

This would be an outline for the diet, though it may be altered as the seasons change, you see:

Mornings—citrus fruit or dry cereals with fruit or berries and milk, but do not use the citrus fruits *and* the cereals at the same meal, or quantities of milk with the citrus fruit. Very crisp bacon with browned bread, coddled egg or the like may be taken at the same meal. These may be altered at times to fresh fruits or stewed fruits, stewed rhubarb or the like, which are well, but change them from time to time.

Noons–either a liquid diet or a green fresh-vegetable diet; such as juices of vegetables, juices of meats, but do not combine the green vegetables and the soups, or the liquid diet *with* the green or fresh vegetables. Include all the vegetables that may be eaten in a salad. And if there is to be taken any pastry, pie, cake, cream or the like, eat it at the noon meal, not in the evening or morning meals.

Evenings—preferably well-cooked vegetables, with at least one period each day (either morning or evening—and well that it be altered) of beef *juices;* not the meats but the beef juices made fresh every few days, not large quantities, but that we may change the activities in the system as to the correction in the blood supply. The meats should be rather those of fowl, liver, tripe, pigs' feet, or the like. Any of these should be included as to meats, but the greater portion should be of vegetables—with meats such as these taken at least three times each week.

Do these and, as we find, in thirty-six to forty days we will have a body quite a bit changed and near normal.

Ready for questions.

(Q) What causes pains and weakness around heart?

(A) As indicated, the straining on the system, the tendency of the dropping or falling of the stomach itself, and the gases that form which make pressures through the alimentary canal and in the stomach itself, you see. Reflex; not an organic condition.

(Q) Do I have astigmatism?

(A) More in one eye than in the other. Everyone has it in some form or another. This will be much corrected, or very much changed, with the correction in the upper dorsal as indicated, and through the cervical region.

(Q) Are the pills I am taking harmful?

(A) They *are!*

(Q) Can she get the proper osteopathic treatments in Raleigh; if so, whom would you suggest to give them?

(A) C— or C—, one or the other.

(Q) Would a belt manufactured for the purpose of holding the stomach in position be suitable?

(A) As we find, this may be best fitted or adjusted; but a belt may be made by using the heavy cloth that is of the nature that would hold the stomach in better position, you see, and much easier, and not cost so much either!

(Q) In what minerals am I deficient, and how may they be supplied?

(A) Not so much deficient in minerals as in the blood supply, as we have indicated, being deficient in the ability of the system, in its present condition and nervous state, to *assimilate* that taken. With the corrections osteopathically, and following the diet outlined, or in that direction, we will supply the proper minerals.

(Q) To what colors do I vibrate?

(A) Shades of red.

(Q) Please give mental and spiritual advice.

(A) When individuals have been under such nerve strain as has existed with this body for some time, spiritual advice is often rather aggravating than satisfying; though at times the body has sought such in its activities. With a change in the physical conditions, the outlook of the mental body will be entirely different.

Each soul should gain this as its basis for activity:

The *mental* IS the builder. Hence the mental attitude has much to do with the physical conditions of the body, but it does not set broken bones, neither does it strengthen ligaments that have been stretched through activities that have gradually drawn on a body.

But the attitude of mind, if it is from the spiritual forces and desires, will bring that which will build a life and an experience of peace, harmony, and happiness.

Follow that. 565-1*

There are fourteen checkable points given in this reading—anemia; low blood pressure; dizziness at times brought on by the menstrual period, and overexhaustion; nervous indigestion; characteristics of determination, set opinions; third and fourth dorsal condition; position of stomach, which was checked by X-ray; drying of throat; thumping and drumming of ears; irritations produced by excessive burning in eyes; secretion from vagina; lack of appetite; excessive kidney activity; and the heart's reactions which were described as a sympathetic activity. The treatments were specific and could be administered by a local physician.

The woman was so impressed that she decided to follow the suggestions in the reading. She went to a prominent doctor in Raleigh. He wisely refused to follow the suggestions until he had checked to confirm the conditions described. She was given a thorough examination including a series of X-rays. The reading was corroborated.

The doctor stated in writing his amazement in being able to confirm details of the information which had been given by Edgar Cayce without his ever having seen the woman. She made excellent progress and returned to normal health.

This is one of an estimated 16,000 such psychic readings given by Edgar Cayce between 1901 and 1944. It is one of the 14,306 readings for over 5,000 different people of which there are copies in the archives of the Association for Research and Enlightenment in Virginia Beach. Thousands of request letters, reports, and other docu-

---

*Numbers appearing before or after case material designate documents on file in the archives of the Association for Research and Enlightenment, Inc. (A.R.E.), Virginia Beach, Va.

ments are filed with these readings. Of this number 9,604 deal with problems of the mind and the physical body. There are also 1,919 readings dealing with vocational, psychological, and human-relations problems. These have been called "life readings." In addition there are 956 miscellaneous readings. Copies of the earliest readings were lost. The oldest copy on file is dated 1902. Two-thirds of the readings were typed single space and they averaged three-and-one-half pages to a reading. Estimating at a conservative 250 words to a page, this totals more than twelve million words. There was never an indication that Edgar Cayce was conscious of a single word he uttered while in the self-imposed unconscious state. All of this material seemed to come through or out of his unconscious mind.

At this point it might be well for me to acknowledge my prejudice in favor of the conceivable accuracy and possible helpfulness of information coming from an unconscious mind. Living with Edgar Cayce conditioned me. Try to put yourself in my place as you follow this story. Perhaps, along with several thousand other people, I was fooled. Maybe this man wasn't unconscious when he gave these readings. Then, as I see it, the story is even more remarkable. For, it seems impossible to me that the conscious self I knew as a father, a Sunday school teacher, and a friend could have so split itself and kept up a masquerade before family, friends, and several thousand people for over forty years. It seems much more reasonable to postulate a trance, an unconscious state, as separate from the conscious self.

It should also be mentioned here that through the years, in observing what seemed to be accurate, checkable telepathy and clairvoyance, I have become more critical—perhaps too critical and careful at times—in expecting and continuing to search for the same kind of objectivity and exactness in dealing with other people who claim to possess psychic powers. This has not been a happy position to maintain. On one hand I find myself sympathetic to the many difficulties which any psychic person must face, and on the other I look for every possible explanation of any so-called psychic incident.

Before examining any additional data from these readings, it might be well to consider the circumstances under which they were given. Someone would request a reading by letter, telegram, phone, or in person. An appointment would be set for 11 A.M. or 3 P.M. on a specified day. The applicant did not have to be present with my father. It was necessary that Edgar Cayce be given the real name and · address where the person would be at the specified time. He could be anywhere in the world. Anyone could give the instructions and ask the questions. My mother was the "conductor" for most of them.

At the appointed time Edgar Cayce would come in from his garden or from fishing, or from working in his office. He would loosen his tie, shoelaces, cuffs, and belt and lie down on a couch. His hands, palms up over his forehead, were later crossed over his abdomen. He would breathe deeply a few times. When his eyelids began to flutter, it was necessary to read to him a suggestion formula which had been secured in a reading in answer to the request, "Give the proper suggestion to be given Edgar Cayce to secure a physical reading." It was necessary to watch the eyelids carefully. If they were allowed to flicker too long before the suggestion was read, my father would not respond. He might then sleep for a couple of hours or more and awaken refreshed without knowing he hadn't given a reading. Here is the opening suggestion:

Now the body is assuming its normal forces and will give such information as is desired of it at the present time. The body-physical will be perfectly normal and will give that information now. You will have before you the body of [name and address]. You will go over this body carefully, examine it thoroughly, telling us the conditions you find at the present time; giving the cause of the existing conditions, also suggestions for help and relief for this body. You will speak distinctly at a normal rate of speech, and you will answer the questions which I will ask.

When the reading was concluded and Edgar Cayce would say, "We are through for the present," the conductor would say:

Now the body will be so equalized as to overcome all those things that might hinder or prevent from being and giving its best mental, spiritual, and physical self.

The body physical will create within the system those properties necessary to cause the eliminations to be increased as to bring the best normal physical conditions for the body.

The mental will so give that impression to the system as to build the best moral, mental, and physical forces for this body.

The circulation will be so equalized as to remove strain from all centers of the nervous system, as to allow the organs of the system to assimilate and secrete properly those conditions necessary for normal conditions of this body.

The nerve supplies of the whole body will assume their normal forces; the vitality will be stored in them, through the application of the physical being, as well as of the spiritual elements in the physical forces of the body.

Now, perfectly normal, and perfectly balanced, you will wake up.

Instantly he was awake.

Who was the man Edgar Cayce?

In June, 1954, a child's color comic book, *House of Mystery,* described Edgar Cayce as "America's Most Mysterious Man." During this same year the University of Chicago accepted a Ph.D. thesis based on a study of his psychic readings. In this thesis he was called, among other things, a "religious seer."

Here is his story as recounted in newspapers and magazines from 1901 to 1959:

VOICE RESTORED
EDGAR CAYCE SUDDENLY RELIEVED OF A TERRIBLE AFFLICTION
VOCAL ORGANS PARALYZED A YEAR AGO MADE WELL AS EVER

On the night of April 18, 1900, young Edgar Cayce, a photographer in W. R. Bowles' gallery, suddenly lost his voice and for nearly ten months was unable to speak above a whisper.

Sunday night he recovered his voice as suddenly as he lost it. When he awoke Monday morning there was a feeling of relief about his throat and when he attempted to speak he saw he could speak as distinctly as ever.

Overjoyed, the young man hastily dressed and rushed into his mother's room to break the good news. All day yesterday he was on the streets talking to his friends and receiving congratulations.

Mr. Cayce is a son of Mr. L. B. Cayce, and is a very worthy and deserving young man. When he became afflicted he was a salesman in a Main Street store but had to give up this business and then secured a position with W. R. Bowles. His general health has continued good and he has worked regularly at his business.

It is supposed that his loss of speech was due to paralysis of the inferior muscles of the vocal organs. At times there was stifling sensation about his throat and occasionally a little soreness. The feeling was akin to that felt by persons suffering from asthma and it was the absence of this feeling that first brought the realization of the good fortune that came to him while he slept.

Mr. Cayce during the last ten months had been under the treatment of specialists in this city, Nashville, Louisville, and Cincinnati all without benefit. Many other doctors had also looked into his case. It had been a month since he took any sort of medicine and his power of speech was restored as suddenly and unexpectedly as it was lost.

This undated newspaper clipping from a Hopkinsville, Kentucky, paper must have appeared early in 1901. It was this throat paralysis which led Edgar Cayce to try hypnosis. After putting himself into a sleeplike state, Edgar gave suggestions for relieving his own throat paralysis. A friend, Al Layne, who was simultaneously studying osteopathy and hypnosis, tried asking the sleeping man about some of his most difficult cases. Edgar talked intelligently about them also. A strange partnership developed. When his voice failed, Edgar asked Layne to give him suggestions while he slept, which restored his voice; and when Layne needed help on a case, he sought advice from Edgar.

In 1902 my father took a job in a bookstore in Bowling Green, Kentucky. He became active in church work and for a group of young people invented a party game called "Pit." This event was noted in the local paper:

NEW PARLOR GAME
EDGAR CAYCE, OF BOWLING GREEN,
SELLS INVENTION TO MFG. CO.

Mr. Edgar Cayce, head clerk in the bookstore of L. D. Potter & Co., on State Street, is the author of a parlor game which will net him considerable money and bring him much fame. The name of the game is "The Pit," and is to be played with a deck of thirty-four cards. It is on the order of the famous game of "Bourse" but those who have played both games say that the one of which Mr. Cayce is the author is far superior to the other. The cards represent the various cereals, railroad, mining stock, etc., which are sold by the New York exchange. They are first dealt to the players and the object is to corner the market, on certain things. The one doing this is the winner. To play the game successfully requires considerable science, and luck of course plays no small part. Mr. Cayce has sold his game outright to the Parker Manufacturing Co., of Salem, Mass. He received a good price for it and is naturally quite elated over its success. The game will be placed on the market as soon as a copyright can be secured.—Bowling Green *News.*

On June 17, 1903, Gertrude Evans and Edgar Cayce were married in Hopkinsville, Kentucky. The following day the Bowling Green paper carried the story:

PRETTY WEDDING AT HOPKINSVILLE

Yesterday afternoon at Hopkinsville a very pretty home wedding was celebrated in which a number of Bowling Green people took part. The bride was Miss Gertrude Evans, the lovely daughter of Mrs. Elizabeth Evans, an old and prominent family of that city. The groom was Mr. Edgar Cayce, the popular salesman in L. D. Potter's book store, this city . . .

On the Sunday following the wedding Al Layne evidently needed Edgar's help and visited him and his new bride in Bowling Green. The Cayces must have had strange feelings when they read the Bowling Green paper on June 22:

IN A TRANCE BOWLING GREEN MAN IS ABLE TO DIAGNOSE HUMAN ILLS. HAS NO RECOLLECTION OF IT WHEN HE AWAKES, AND DOES NOT PRETEND TO UNDERSTAND HIS WONDERFUL POWER.

Dr. A. C. Layne, osteopath and magnetic healer, was in the city Sunday from Hopkinsville to have Edgar Cayce, the well-known salesman at L. D. Potter & Co., diagnose a case for him.

This sounds peculiar in view of the fact that Mr. Cayce is not a physician and knows nothing in the world about medicine or surgery. Since Mr. Cayce has been living in this city he lost his voice and was unable to speak a word. He returned to his former home at Hopkinsville and was there treated by Dr. Layne and had his voice restored. At this time it was discovered that Mr. Cayce possessed unusual mediumistic powers and since then he has discovered that by lying down, thoroughly relaxing himself and taking a deep breath he can fall into a trance, during which, though he is to all appearances asleep, his faculties are alert. Some time ago Dr. Layne had him go into a trance and diagnose a difficult case at Hopkinsville.

The diagnosis proved to be correct in every particular and it was not long until the patient had recovered.

The physicians had been unable to diagnose the case. Yesterday he came here to have Mr. Cayce diagnose another case and it was done in the presence of several people at Mr. Cayce's home on State Street.

The patient is not here, but is ill at his home in Hopkinsville. Cayce went into his trance and then the doctor told him that the patient's body would appear before him and he wanted him to thoroughly examine it from head to foot and tell him where the diseased parts were located.

In a moment more the doctor commenced at the head and asked Cayce minutely about every part of the body. He answered, telling of the location of blood clots, that one lung was sloughing off and detailed other evidences he saw of disease. It was as if the body was immediately before him and he could see through it and discern plainly every ligament, bone and nerve in it.

Dr. Layne was thoroughly satisfied with the diagnosis and when it was completed had Mr. Cayce diagnose several other cases of less importance, and then left for his home and will base the treatment of each case on the diagnosis as given by Cayce.

Mr. Cayce does not know what he is saying while in the

trance, nor when it is over has he any recollection of what he said. He does not pretend to understand it and is not a spiritualist in any sense of the word, but is an active member of the Christian church.—Bowling Green *Times Journal.*

During the following year several doctors in Bowling Green and Hopkinsville became interested in Cayce and Layne. There may have been other publicity but on March 29, 1904, the following story appeared in a Nashville, Tennessee, paper:

X-RAY NOT IN IT WITH THIS BOWLING GREEN MAN

EDGAR CAYCE STARTLES MEDICAL MEN WITH HIS TRANCES

HE DIAGNOSES DISEASES IN PERSONS FAR DISTANT
AND TELLS WHAT TREATMENT TO GIVE THEM.

Bowling Green, Ky., March 29.—(Special.)—Edgar Cayce, salesman in a book store here, has developed a wonderful power that is greatly puzzling physicians and scientific men. He is a quiet young man of the strictest integrity of character and thoroughly reliable in every way, and would not knowingly be a party to a deception. He some time ago discovered that he could relax himself and go into a trance and while in this condition could tell what people whom he did not know were doing miles away. This test was made some time ago when he told just what certain members of a family were doing at a certain time of the day. The physicians have been using his power to help them diagnose their cases. Several evenings ago one of the most prominent here, in company with one of the college professors of the city, tested Cayce's powers and are surprised and mystified at the result. Cayce lay down on the operating table and relaxed himself and in a few minutes appeared to be in a deep sleep. The physician told him that he was treating a little boy of this city, calling him by name, who at the time was on a sick bed in another part of the city and whom Cayce did not know and that he (the doctor) wanted him (Cayce) to describe to him the physical condition of the boy. At once Cayce began to talk and said that he saw that the boy's right lung was in very bad condition and that no air was going into it from below; that the left lung had also been involved but was nearly all right again. He also reported something wrong at the pit of the stomach. This, the physician says, was a perfect description of the boy's condition. He also described the condition of the professor's wife, telling of trouble with her eyes, which fact could not have previously been known to Cayce. He also told of the functions of the spleen and talked of the vertebrae and used medical terms in describing different parts of the body, whereas he knows nothing whatever of physiology or anatomy. In some cases he told the physician what particular medicine or treatment to use for certain derangements he found the bodies he examined in his mysterious way, but for others he gave no remedy, saying he saw no label for the medicine for that particular derangement. Where treatment was suggested it was what the physician says should be used.

In short, while in these trances, and while the patient is not in his presence, Cayce seems to look the body through and through and describe the anatomy to the minutest particular, and if there is any derangement, or any diseased or abnormal condition, he can point it out.

Cayce remembers nothing he has said when he comes out of the trance, and it is all a perfect blank to him. He does not pretend to account for his extraordinary power, does not understand it in the least, and is not using it to make money. Further tests will be made by our physicians who are deeply puzzled over Cayce's strange powers. Mr. Cayce formerly lived at Hopkinsville but has been here for several years.

During the ensuing years my father left the bookstore, became a photographer and opened his own studio. Interest in the readings increased. Edgar and the doctors avoided publicity. Two disastrous fires destroyed the photographic business. Edgar and Gertrude returned to Hopkinsville in 1909 with me, their two-year-old son.

One of the doctors who had visited Edgar in Bowling Green was Wesley H. Ketchum. On September 30, 1910, the following story was reported from Boston:

MARVEL DOCTOR DISCOVERED

ILLITERATE YOUTH IN HYPNOTIC CONDITION
DOES WONDERS, SAYS PHYSICIAN
[SPECIAL TO THE RECORD-HERALD]

Boston, Sept. 29.—A remarkable story of an illiterate young man living near Hopkinsville, Ky., who, while in a self-imposed hypnotic condition, is a physician of great power, was told in a paper prepared by Dr. Wesley H. Ketchum of Hopkinsville, which was read at the annual meeting of the American Association of Clinical Research here today.

According to Dr. Ketchum the "illiterate," whose name is not divulged, while in a state of autohypnosis drops into medical phraseology with the familiarity of a skilled medical man.

Dr. Ketchum says he has taken several patients to the young man, who diagnosed their cases correctly. He says he took to him the daughter of a prominent Cincinnati man whose case had been pronounced by several physicians as hopeless. The "illiterate" went into a trance, prescribed a course of treatment, and in three months, according to Dr. Ketchum, she was entirely well.

The Association was so impressed with Dr. Ketchum's statements that a committee probably will be chosen to investigate the "marvel."

Selections from the New York *Times* story of October 9, 1910, follow:

ILLITERATE MAN BECOMES A DOCTOR WHEN HYPNOTIZED
STRANGE POWER SHOWN BY EDGAR CAYCE PUZZLES PHYSICIANS

The medical fraternity of the country is taking a lively interest in the strange power said to be possessed by Edgar Cayce of Hopkinsville, Ky., to diagnose difficult diseases while in a semiconscious state, though he has not the slightest knowledge of medicine when not in this condition.

During a visit to California last summer Dr. W. H. Ketchum, who was attending a meeting of the National Society of Ho-

meopathic Physicians, had occasion to mention the young
man's case and was invited to discuss it at a banquet attended
by about thirty-five of the doctors of the Greek letter fraternity
given at Pasadena.

Dr. Ketchum made a speech of considerable length, giving
an explanation of the strange psychic powers manifested by
Cayce during the last four years, during which time he has
been more or less under his observation. He had stimulated
such interest among those present at the National Society's
meeting that one of the leading Boston medical men who
heard his speech invited Dr. Ketchum to prepare a paper as a
part of the program of the September meeting of the American Society of Clinical Research. Dr. Ketchum sent the paper,
but did not go to Boston. The paper was read by Henry E. Har-
rower, M.D., of Chicago, a contributor to the *Journal of the
American Medical Association,* published in Chicago. Its presentation created a sensation, and almost before Dr. Ketchum
knew that the paper had been given to the press he was del-
uged with letters and telegrams inquiring about the strange
case.

It is well enough to add that Dr. Wesley H. Ketchum is a
reputable physician of high standing and successful practice
in the homeopathic school of medicine. He possesses a classical education, is by nature of a scientific turn, and is a gradu-
ate of one of the leading medical institutions of the country.
He is vouched for by orthodox physicians in both Kentucky
and Ohio, in both of which states he is well known. In Hopkinsville, where his home is, no physician of any school stands
higher, though he is still a young man on the shady side of Dr.
Osler's deadline of 40.

Dr. Ketchum wishes it distinctly understood that his presentation of the subject is purely ethical, and that he attempts
no explanation of what must be classed as mysterious mental
phenomena.

Dr. Ketchum is not the only physician who has had opportunity to observe the workings of Mr. Cayce's subconscious
mind. For nearly ten years his strange power has been known
to local physicians of all the recognized schools. An explanation of the case is best understood from Dr. Ketchum's descrip-

tion in his paper read in Boston a few days ago, which follows:

"About four years ago I made the acquaintance of a young man 28 years old, who had the reputation of being a 'freak.' They said he told wonderful truths while he was asleep. I, being interested, immediately began to investigate, and as I was 'from Missouri,' had to be shown.

"And truly, when it comes to anything psychical, every layman is a disbeliever from the start, and most of our chosen profession will not accept anything of a psychic nature, hypnotism, mesmerism, or whatnot, unless vouched for by some M.D. away up in the profession and one whose orthodox standing is unquestioned.

"My subject simply lies down and folds his arms, and by autosuggestion goes to sleep. While in this sleep, which to all intents and purposes is a natural sleep, his objective mind is completely inactive and only his subjective is working.

"By suggestion he becomes unconscious to pain of any sort, and, strange to say, his best work is done when he is seemingly 'dead to the world.'

"I next give him the name of my subject and the exact location of same, and in a few minutes he begins to talk as clearly and distinctly as anyone. He usually goes into minute detail in diagnosing a case, and especially if it be a very serious case.

"His language is usually of the best, and his psychologic terms and description of the nervous anatomy would do credit to any professor of nervous anatomy, and there is no faltering in his speech and all his statements are clear and concise. He handles the most complex 'jaw breakers' with as much ease as any Boston physician, which to me is quite wonderful, in view of the fact that while in his normal state he is an illiterate man, especially along the line of medicine, surgery, or pharmacy, of which he knows nothing.

"After going into a diagnosis and giving name, address, etiology, symptoms, diagnosis and treatment of a case, he is awakened by the suggestion that he will see this person no more, and in a few minutes he will awake. Upon questioning him, he knows absolutely nothing that he said, or whose case he was talking about. I have used him in about 100 cases, and to date have never known of any errors in diagnosis, except in two cases where he described a child in each case by the same name and who resided in the same house as the one wanted. He simply described the wrong person.

"Now this description, although rather short, is no myth, but a firm reality. The regular profession scoff at anything reliable coming from this source, because the majority of them are in a rut and have never taken to anything not strictly orthodox.

"The cases I have used him in have, in the main, been the rounds before coming to my attention, and in six important cases which had been diagnosed as strictly surgical he stated that no such condition existed, and outlined treatment which was followed with gratifying results in every case.

"One case, a little girl, daughter of a gentleman prominent in the American Book Company of Cincinnati, had been diagnosed by the best men in the Central States as incurable. One diagnosis from my man completely changed the situation, and within three months she was restored to perfect health, and is to this day.

"Now, in closing, you may ask why has a man with such powers not been before the public and received the endorsement of the profession, one and all, without fear or favor? I can truly answer by saying they are not ready to receive such as yet. Even Christ Himself was rejected, for 'unless they see signs and wonders they will not believe.'

"I would appreciate the advice and suggestions of my coworkers in this broad field as to the best method of putting my man in the way of helping suffering humanity, and would be glad to have you send me the name and address of your most complex case and I will try to prove what I have endeavored to describe."

In further explanation, Dr. Ketchum give this statement as obtained from the young man himself while asleep, when asked to describe his own powers and the source of his mystifying knowledge:

"Our subject, while under autohypnosis, on one occasion, explained as follows:

"When asked to give the source of his knowledge, he being at this time in the subconscious state, he stated: 'Edgar Cayce's mind is amenable to suggestion, the same as all other sub-conscious minds, but in addition thereto it has the power to interpret to the objective mind of others what it acquires from the subconscious mind of other individuals of the same kind. The subconscious mind forgets nothing. The conscious mind receives the impression from without and transfers all thought to the subconscious where it remains even though the conscious be destroyed.' He described himself in the third person, saying further that the subconscious mind is in direct communication with all other subconscious minds, and is capable of interpreting through his objective mind and im-parting impressions received to other objective minds, gath-ering in this way all knowledge possessed by millions of other subconscious minds.

"In all young Cayce has given more than 1,000 readings, but has never turned his wonderful powers to his pecuniary advantage, although many people have been restored to health by following out the course of treatment prescribed in his readings while in a state of hypnosis."

Newspapers from one side of the country to the other reported this story:

—CHICAGO EXAMINER
PSYCHIST DIAGNOSES AND CURES PATIENTS
IGNORANT OF MEDICINE, TURNS HEALER IN TRANCE
KENTUCKIAN NEW PUZZLE FOR PHYSICIANS
ADMITS HE CAN REMEMBER NOTHING
THAT OCCURS IN HYPNOTIC SLEEP
SOLVES MURDER MYSTERY
REMARKABLE AND SUCCESSFUL TREATMENTS ARE
SWORN TO IN AFFIDAVITS BY ROSWELL FIELD

—CINCINNATI TIMES-STAR
MAN'S STRANGE POWER
PUZZLING PHYSICIAN
WHILE IN HYPNOTIC SLEEP EDGAR CAYCE, KENTUCKY PHOTOGRAPHER,
DIAGNOSES COMPLICATED DISEASES ACCURATELY

—KANSAS CITY POST
    YOUTH IN TRANCE DIAGNOSES DISEASE

—THE OREGON SUNDAY JOURNAL (PORTLAND, ORE.)
    KENTUCKY FARMER EFFECTS CURES WHILE IN TRANCE

In 1912 Edgar attempted to stop giving psychic readings. He moved with his family to Selma, Alabama, and opened a photographic studio. In 1914 he went to Lexington, Kentucky, to give a reading for a Mrs. DeLaney, who was paralyzed with what may have been a type of arthritis. She recovered.

While in Lexington Edgar met some neighbors of the DeLaneys, Mr. and Mrs. Solomon Kahn and their eight children. This family, especially the mother, Fanny Kahn, and the oldest son, David, became lifelong friends and in many ways played an important part in Edgar's life and psychic pursuits. Mrs. Fanny Kahn recognized something of the significance of the phenomena which she witnessed. It was her interest, perhaps, which focused the interest of her eighteen-year-old son, David. Through the years he brought Edgar Cayce and his work to the attention of a remarkably diversified cross section of the American public, under circumstances which provided some of the best evidential clairvoyance in the history of psychical research.

David E. Kahn's interest was fired by the DeLaney case and early readings for members of his own family. Later while in the army his questions ranged into troop movements in which he was involved. According to him, the accuracy of the precognition of these readings enabled him to astound his superior officers on many occasions. He got the reputation of knowing more than his general about the division's movements.

When World War I ended David Kahn turned to an Edgar Cayce reading for advice. The reading which recommended that he leave his family grocery business and go into "wood and metal products" was only one of many personal readings which contained evidence of Edgar Cayce's strange insight into a business world completely unfamiliar to his conscious mind. The fact that radios were just being developed and were soon to be put into wooden cabinets in millions of American homes may have been coincidence. It may have been just hard work and coincidence that David Kahn for several years manufactured and sold more radio cabinets than any other man in America; but Mr. Kahn was and is more than willing to attest to the fact that the Edgar Cayce readings were important factors in his choice of vocation as a manufacturer of radio cabinets.

The files of readings given by my father contain the names of businessmen and their families all over America who were introduced to readings by David Kahn. From New York, Chicago, Los Angeles, Dallas, anywhere that David traveled, would come telephone calls and telegrams with names and addresses of business associates and their families who needed assistance. David Kahn wanted to help people. He also wanted to prove his friend's power. He was used to laughter and skepticism. Telegrams contained no leading questions, and telephone conversations in the presence of the man who was to secure the reading gave no opportunities to look up information. The results were a series of startlingly accurate and helpful psychic readings given frequently for critical, unrelated people scattered all over the United States.

One of David's most treasured pieces of correspondence is a letter from a physician in a Southern hospital admitting that his diagnosis of the physical ailment suffered by a superintendent of one of David Kahn's factories was not so accurate as Edgar Cayce's.

It is one thing to give psychic information on a man's health after talking with him or his family and quite another to work from a name and address hundreds of miles away. David Kahn knew this very well. He made effective and dramatic use of Edgar's gift. Yet, back of every request was the desire to help another human being. Perhaps it was this basic concern to serve others that enabled Edgar Cayce and David Kahn to use my father's power effectively.

In 1920 Edgar gave a reading for men in Texas who were drilling an oil well. The information was thought to be so accurate that they urged him to join them. For many years my father hoped to build a hospital someday where readings could be checked and the treatments outlined in them carried out exactly as given. Moved by visions of the money needed to build his "dream" hospital and the excitement engendered by the activity in the oil fields, Edgar began a Ulysses-like search for fortune and adventure. David E. Kahn returned from France and joined him in Texas. For three years Edgar and David followed readings that were frequently proved to be right but never brought lasting success.

The following heading appeared on an article in the Birmingham *Age-Herald* October 10, 1922. Edgar Cayce was in Birmingham at the time giving a series of readings.

"Peculiar Gift Has Been Mine Since Youth," Says Edgar Cayce

Mysticism, Psychism, or What You Will, Envelops Man Whose
Power in Healing Has Created Tremendous
Interest Among All Conditions of Men

He stayed on in Birmingham for several weeks, during which time he spoke for various groups, including:

Edgar Cayce to Speak to Psychologists Here

The regular meeting of the Birmingham Club of Applied Psychology, which meets at the courthouse every Tuesday night, Judge Smith's room, will be favored with an address by Edgar Cayce, psychologist and healer, now stopping here. He delivered an interesting address before the club at the last meeting and has kindly consented to speak again Tuesday night, at 8 o'clock. This meeting will be open to the general public and everybody is cordially invited to attend. At the close of the regular address, Mr. Cayce will be pleased to answer questions.

On returning to Selma for a short stay, Dad was interviewed regarding his plans.

Cayce Leaves to Promote Hospital

Great Million-Dollar Institution to Be Built by Selmian and
His Partner—Will Develop Psychic Diagnosis of Baffling Cases

Edgar Cayce, on the eve of his departure for Nashville and New York this afternoon, spoke with confidence of the work which lies before him, in raising large funds with which he and his associate, David E. Kahn of Cleburne, Texas, and Lexington, Ky., propose to build a great hospital or sanitarium where the invalids of the nation, rich or poor, whose cases have baffled science, may receive treatment.

In this humanitarian work, Mr. Cayce will associate himself with a corps of able surgeons and physicians, who have complete charge of administering the hospital. His work is to consist exclusively of diagnosing the troubles of those who have sought long and hopelessly for relief.

RECORD OF CASES

Substantiating the claims of Mr. Cayce, as a discoverer of elusive and undreamed-of ailments, whose treatment alone is necessary to cure seemingly hopeless cases, are records and affidavits from many reputable men and women, who testify to the benefits received, when physicians followed Mr. Cayce's diagnosis.

As has already been pointed out, the dream of raising money for the hospital through readings on oil failed.

When my father returned to Selma from Texas and began pulling together the pieces of his photographic business, his heart was not in it. Behind him was a twisted path of failure. The psychic information which he gave in the unconscious state seemed to be only partly accurate when dealing with the location of oil wells. He found that men who dealt in oil leases did not follow the rules laid down in Sunday school books. His friends had lost time and money backing him. For months on end he had been separated from his family. His photographic business was disintegrating.

On the positive side of the ledger was a conviction that people wanted readings, that people needed him. As he had traveled about the country attempting to raise money for the oil ventures, he gave hundreds of readings on health problems. The recipients and their doctors had been amazed at the accuracy of the analyses and the results obtained from the suggested treatments. People continued writing for help and began coming to Selma to hear readings. And the friendliness he found in Selma was no small encouragement. In both business and church circles the Cayces were welcomed back.

With an equivocal confidence in his readings and a necessity to earn a living, my father decided to resume his photographic busi-

ness and at the same time offer whatever help he could to those
who asked for readings. He set aside one room of his studio for the
purpose and advertised for a secretary. The peculiar circumstances
of taking dictation from a sleeping man and the speed with which
the words were delivered so upset the average applicant that she
couldn't handle the job. One girl, when asked after a session to read
her notes, could only gasp, "I forgot to write anything."

One young woman, Gladys Davis, was more successful from the
beginning than any of the others. Each day my mother read old
readings to Miss Davis, who practiced recording them in shorthand
and transcribing her notes. From September 10, 1923, all readings
were recorded, transcribed, and filed along with the correspondence pertaining to them. Through the years Miss Davis continued
as the recorder and then custodian of these files. At a later date letters were written to the person who had requested the reading, asking for a report on its success. Similar requests for reports went to
the doctors who were consulted. All of the data were kept in the
case file. The files assembled through the years are far from complete and certainly do not constitute scientifically controlled experiments. However, they do contain a remarkably complete
day-by-day record of Edgar Cayce's psychic readings, consistent reports of evidence of accurate, distant clairvoyance, and thousands
of statements on the help received after following the suggestions
given in the readings.

In the fall of 1923 Arthur Lammers, a wealthy printer from Dayton, Ohio, came to Selma and had readings. He urged Edgar to give
up his photographic business and devote all his time to giving readings. Edgar visited Dayton to meet Lammers' friends and discuss
the matter further. Arthur offered to finance the family move to Dayton and open an office where readings could be given.

Mr. Lammers did not confine his questions to physical bodies.
He was curious about philosophical questions. He secured the first
of what were to become known as "life readings." Two books[1] have
been written about these readings.

The new sponsor became involved in business difficulties. He
was unable to continue his financial help and interest in the work.

_____

[1] *Many Mansions* and *The World Within*, both by Gina Cerminara (New York:
Wm. Sloane Associates, 1950 and 1957, respectively).

A difficult period of a year and a half ensued. Thomas Brown, a Dayton manufacturer, and M. B. Wyrick, a Western Union official in Chicago, introduced Edgar to many of their business associates. David E. Kahn, now a New York businessman, introduced Morton and Edwin Blumenthal to the readings. The Cayce family moved from Dayton in 1925 to Virginia Beach, Virginia, a place designated in the psychic information many years before as the best location for the hospital.

David E. Kahn, working with the Blumenthals, was primarily responsible for organizing a nonprofit association chartered in Virginia to study Edgar's work. In 1928 Edgar Cayce's dream of a hospital where his readings could be checked and followed became a reality.

In July, 1928, the Virginia Beach *News* carried the following story:

WORK STARTED ON HOSPITAL AT VIRGINIA BEACH

STRUCTURE OVERLOOKING OCEAN TO COST
$100,000 WHEN ALL UNITS ARE COMPLETED
BEING ERECTED BY NATIONAL
ASSOCIATION OF INVESTIGATORS

PSYCHIC RESEARCH
TO BE CARRIED ON

The National Association of Investigators has let a contract for the construction of a 30-bedroom hospital to be built at 105th Street, Virginia Beach. The building, already under construction, is the first unit in the project and other additions will follow, and the whole will be known as the Cayce Hospital for Research and Enlightenment. The building is to be concrete and shingle construction and will contain besides the 30 bedrooms, a large lobby, and dining room, lecture hall, doctors' and nurses' quarters, and large spacious porches.

The total cost of the investment, including ground, building and equipment will be approximately $100,000. Plans for the structure were drawn by Rudolph, Cooke and Van Leeuween, and the contract has been awarded to the United Construction Company, of Norfolk.

The site of the hospital will be one of the most attractive features. Rising from a high sand dune, probably the highest between Virginia Beach and Cape Henry, it will command a view of all the territory around with an unobstructed view of the Atlantic Ocean. The first unit will be followed by others as the occasion demands.

The Association of National Investigators was incorporated May, 1927, in the State of Virginia. Although the immediate basis of its foundation was to further foster and encourage the physical, mental and spiritual benefit that thousands are deriving from Mr. Cayce's endeavors in the psychic world, the larger and more embracing purpose of the organization was to engage in general psychic research, and also to provide for practical application of any knowledge obtained through the medium of psychic phenomena.

In the matter of specific application the association seeks to render aid to the sick and ailing through its hospital, and to disseminate and exploit for the good of humanity, knowledge obtained from its research work through the lecture halls, library and other educational channels.

The Association will furnish those who seek psychical readings and desire to secure treatments exactly as prescribed therein the opportunity to gain such treatment at the hands of competent and sympathetic physicians. The hospital is to be conducted along the most modern scientific and ethical lines. Every comfort and service for room, board and treatment will be given patients, and all money paid in, except for physicians' fees, will go into the maintenance of the institution.

With many ups and downs, including the loss of the hospital during the Depression years of the thirties, Edgar worked on through 1944. In 1942 Thomas Sugrue, a friend and classmate of mine at Washington and Lee University, who had become a newspaper and magazine writer, wrote *There Is a River*,[2] a sympathetic biography of Edgar Cayce.

The next year a *Coronet* magazine article entitled "Miracle Man of Virginia Beach" brought hundreds of letters daily to my father.

---

[2]New York: Henry Holt & Co., 1942.

Appointments for readings were set ahead for two years.

Work and pressure mounted during the war years. Following a stroke and several months' illness, Edgar Cayce died January 3, 1945.

The Association which had been formed to study his psychic work and preserve his readings began a program of cross-indexing under subject headings the data in the 14,306 documents. Studies of the correlated data on specific subjects, such as historical and geological information, life after death, and reincarnation, as well as experiments based on ideas in the readings, were instituted. Lectures, discussion groups, publications, and other activities, comprising a general educational program in psychic studies, were continued in Virginia Beach and in many large cities throughout the United States.

In September, 1953, *Pageant Magazine* carried an article on Edgar Cayce under the title "The Man Who Made Miracles." In interviewing physicians who had looked at some of the readings, the author quoted one of them as saying that none of the treatments recommended could do any harm but they didn't make any sense to him. Another M.D., a heart specialist, said that after studying the readings for a month he believed the medical information in them was not only true, but also far ahead of its time.

In 1956 Dell Publishing Company brought out a fifty-cent pocket edition of *There Is a River* under the title *The Edgar Cayce Story.*

Morey Bernstein, author of *The Search for Bridey Murphy*,[3] a study of hypnosis and reincarnation which grew out of an interest in the Edgar Cayce readings, wrote an article for *True Magazine* in May, 1956, in which he described his own investigation of many of the reports in the Cayce files. In the same year a new pocketbook life of my father, entitled *Edgar Cayce—Mystery Man of Miracles*, by Joseph Millard was published by Fawcett Publications. This book was recently translated into Japanese and published in Japan. A hardback edition appeared in England in 1961 under the title *Edgar Cayce—Man of Miracles.*

In 1959 *American Mercury* carried an article on Cayce, "In Slumber Deep," by Lytle W. Robinson, and the *American Weekly* told its several million readers about him in the April 12, 1959, issue. The article titled "The Mystery of Edgar Cayce" by Maurice Zolotow was

---

[3]New York: Doubleday & Company, Inc., 1956.

based on a New York physiotherapist's (Harold Reilly) several years' experience in following the Edgar Cayce readings.

NBC "Monitor," a national weekend radio program, carried thirteen interviews with people who had had Edgar Cayce readings and with members of the Association staff on May 15, 16, and 17, 1959.

What kind of person was this who spent part of each day for more than forty years in an unconscious state?

As a child, my father was described as quiet and secretive, almost a recluse. He was a dreamer, a very imaginative boy. At an early age he planned to be a preacher. Though he was never formally ordained, his talks both in and out of the church had the quality of sermons. The language of the readings was biblical in phrase and illustration, though by no means confined to the Bible. The quietness of the boy changed; for, as a man, Edgar Cayce loved people. His studios in Bowling Green, Kentucky, and Selma, Alabama, were meeting places for groups of young people.

Throughout his lifetime Edgar Cayce maintained active church interests: janitor at ten years of age in a little country church; teacher in Sunday school; leader of Christian Endeavor societies; deacon; and adult Bible class teacher. In Hopkinsville, Louisville, Bowling Green, and Selma, where Edgar was active in Sunday school classes, he was responsible for the members' work with people in prisons. Entries in his journal describe his Sunday school class in Selma, which at one time was reported to be the largest in Alabama. He also mentions the Bibles provided for, and the visits to, those in prison. He refers back to similar work in Louisville when members of his class met a young man who was jailed for selling "moonshine" whiskey. He helped teach the young man to read. During those years he was a member of the Disciples of Christ Church. There was no church of this denomination in Virginia Beach, so there we joined the Presbyterian Church.

My father spent some part of each day reading his Bible, praying, and meditating.

Dad was a man who enjoyed catching perch in a Kentucky pond or sailfishing off the Florida coast. He liked games—checkers, bowling, croquet, golf. He enjoyed card games only if they did not require too much concentration as in the case of bridge. About such games, he said it was too easy to read the minds of the players.

He was a man with many skills. As a photographer he made pictures, developed, printed, mounted, and framed them. He sponsored exhibits of good photography. He used models for some of his best photographs, but also took prizes with his picture of a cotton plant in full bloom. Parents brought children to him from all over Alabama as he gradually became known as an exceptional photographer of children.

He delighted in making preserves, jellies, and wines, provided he could handle them in quantity. After summer visits to Hopkinsville, my mother found every available shelf covered with jars of brandied peaches, jellies of all kinds, preserved figs, and vats of wine. During his lifetime he must have given away several thousand jars of jelly and preserves. Wherever we lived—Hopkinsville, Selma, Dayton, and Virginia Beach—there was a home workshop. Dad could mend anything. As soon as we were old enough, he taught my brother and me to work with tools (an accomplishment in itself). The family was always adding to or remodeling the house. Painting, concreting, plastering, etc., were frequently part of a day's activity. My father's early farm training was never completely forgotten. He was proud of his gardens, the variety of trees in our yard, and the cultivated berries on which he spent a great deal of time and work.

Money was the topic of considerable conversation in the Cayce household. There was either too little (long periods) or too much (short periods). My father spent money sometimes as if he had an inexhaustible supply. Then he worried over it. He would buy jars, fruit, and sugar for a big preserving spree, even if the family had to eat nothing but bread and preserves for several meals. If he happened to see a particularly attractive offer of a variety of trees for sale, the groceries might be light for a few days. He was generous with money, with his family, with people who worked for him, and with himself.

To say he was a sensitive person would be a gross understatement. I think he was constantly more aware of what went on in the minds and emotions of those around him than most people realized. This was actually painful to him, and he tried to shut these impressions out of his mind. To some degree, this sensitivity may have been responsible for his violent temper—which he worked hard all his life to control. This sensitivity may also have been at least partly the cause of his extremes of emotional reaction—very happy or very depressed—very talkative or very silent—very optimistic or very pessimistic. Often he functioned at one end of the emotional scale or the other. He was sentimental and moody. When he laughed his world was light and joyful; when he frowned his world was a very dark place. He trusted everyone and frequently moved with those around him in wrong directions. He could easily forgive others. He was harder on himself.

My father radiated interest in, as well as concern and love for, people. These attitudes showed in small ways, as well as through his desire to help people through his readings. He was kind to children and they were drawn to him. He was thoughtful of servants. His patience with young people was an important factor in his success with groups throughout his life. When he traveled he was soon on friendly terms with anyone he met. I can never remember my father's showing irritation with a waitress or waiter in a public place. People, all kinds of people, were drawn to Edgar Cayce.

This was the clairvoyant, the psychic, whose comments on the unknown powers of the mind have made the greatest impression on me. Whatever else his gift may have been, it was a window through which his mind could be seen functioning at an unconscious level.

In examining the content of this material there are a number of points to ponder. A respectable amount of the clairvoyance seemed to be accurate. Many people who tried suggestions in the readings reported they received practical help. Some insight was shown in areas of knowledge which later investigations proved to be correct. Of special interest are statements on endocrine gland functions, body currents, knowledge of prehistoric earth changes, archaeological discoveries, etc. It will be seen that a number of philosophical concepts about which Edgar Cayce had only vague conscious opinions were developed in some detail in his readings. Some of the most obvious of these are reincarnation and karma, the origin of the soul and its purpose in the earth, the causes of many specific diseases, life after death, and a world of thought forms. And though my father was a student of the Bible, his unconscious interpretations of many passages, as well as his comments on biblical history, were sometimes startling, to say the least. Accuracy in one area of his information did not require that any other statement be accepted without question. However, through the years, the evidence for extended perception in many directions accumulated rapidly.

Preservation and thorough examination of his psychic readings seemed warranted.

Certainly in the life and work of this man we find an example of an attempt to use a psychic gift for the benefit of those who sought his help. The measure of his success has not been completed.

Of considerable importance, it seems to me, is the examination and testing of any statements made from this unconscious mind as to how psychic abilities may be developed. Where are the rooms of the unconscious which contain the radio and television sets of the mind that reach beyond the five senses—and how does one get to them?

Finally, it seems reasonable to say that a study of my father's life and the mass of unconscious data of his readings might give us some insight into the nature of the unconscious—its activities and dimensions.

2

A Boundless Unconscious

THE LABORED, HEAVY breathing of the man on the bed could be heard outside the room in the hall. The doctor who had been listening with stethoscope turned away and spoke: "This man has one lung completely closed. The other is in bad shape. He must be moved to the hospital immediately. Pneumonia may have set in already."

Edgar Cayce was the man on the bed. It was I to whom the doctor had spoken. For days my father had suffered with a heavy cold. We were visiting with friends on Staten Island, New York. Day after day he had met people and given readings morning and afternoon. Finally he had gone to bed. Outside a heavy snow was melting.

The doctor went downstairs to call an ambulance. Dad motioned to me to come to the bedside. "What did the doctor say?" he croaked.

I touched his hand and head. They were hot and dry. I told him exactly what had been suggested.

"Shut the door," he said. "Don't let anyone in here until I wake up."

I obeyed him without question.

In a matter of minutes his eyelids fluttered; his breathing became deep, regular, and heavy. He rattled like the crackling of thick underbrush in a dry forest.

Within five minutes great beads of sweat broke out on his forehead and face and began to run down his neck. As I watched and listened, the sheet which touched his chest became wet, and the breathing grew heavier and more labored.

At the end of fifteen minutes, perspiration was running off the bed onto the floor where it stood in a little glistening puddle. The breathing was clearing and was more even now.

Someone knocked at the locked door. I tried to explain without opening it.

In a little more than twenty minutes Edgar Cayce opened his eyes, stretched, smiled, pulled back the covers, and asked for his robe. The sheets, the blankets, the mattress were soaking wet. His voice was clear; his head and hands were cool. The ambulance went away without him.

This is an example of the strange power of the subconscious to take suggestion and control automatically the internal functionings of the physical body.

Living would be difficult indeed if man consciously had to regulate his breathing, not to mention what regulating his digestive processes would entail. Just how would one plan the digestion of a carrot? What mind plans the distribution of the assimilated food? Different parts of the body need varying amounts of energy at different times. Extend this idea a little further. There is a truly magical power of the body to rebuild the tissue of an injury or a cut. The proper amount of the right kind of tissue is restored. Hair or bone does not grow where muscle tissue is needed. Such functions, along with breathing, blood circulation, much of eliminations, and hundreds of other automatic body functions are controlled from an unconscious level of the mind. This amazing control is accepted without thought until it is possible to observe a demonstration of the power of suggestion for someone in an unconscious state.

Throughout his life my father lost his voice at varying intervals.

As soon as he lost consciousness in order to give a reading, suggestions could be given him to increase the circulation through the
throat area to relieve the nerve tensions. Anyone watching his reactions could see the tissue of the throat change color. Generally he
would awaken able to speak again.

The amenability of the unconscious to suggestion and the power
of suggestion to affect the physical body are well known to anyone
who has practiced or observed hypnosis. The range and degree of
effects which can be produced apparently depend upon the skill of
the hypnotist and the susceptibility of the subject. A responsive
subject will weep over an apple if told he is eating an onion, or raise
a blister when touched with a piece of ice, if told he is being burned
with a match.

It is frightening, at times, to consider the range of the power of
suggestion. In a report on "subliminal projection" it was stated that
an invisible commercial was flashed on the screen of a drive-in the-
ater while the regular pictures were being projected. In *The Reporter,*
October 17, 1957, it was stated that over a period of six weeks 45,000
people were moved by the suggestion, which bypassed the conscious mind, to increase their popcorn purchases by 57.5 percent.
It is not generally recognized that the unconscious may contain a
record of every experience of consciousness, even though there is
no conscious awareness at the time of perception.

On several occasions Edgar Cayce demonstrated an ability to
read over material and then bring it accurately to consciousness
after sleeping for a few minutes. This occurred first when it was suggested to him that he could remember every word in a spelling
book. At a grade-school graduation he was reported to have memo-
rized a long political speech after one reading and a few minutes'
sleep. When he first began working for a wholesale stationery company, he learned the entire catalogue. As a walking information center on the company's products, he was in constant demand.

The completeness and complexity of this unconscious memory
play a far more important part in an individual's life than he is aware.
Literally, a man becomes what he feeds into his unconscious. This
idea is taking on more and more importance with the development
of psychosomatic medicine. Particular thoughts and emotions are believed to be directly related to specific diseases. The meaning of the
phrase "mind is the builder," repeated over and over again in the Edgar

Cayce readings, cannot be understood fully. However, it takes on new meaning as one begins to glimpse the depths of the unconscious.

Consciousness varies from moment to moment. It is like a mixing bowl into which various ingredients are being poured through sense perceptions—sight, hearing, taste, feeling, and smell. Other ingredients which appear now and then do not seem to come from sense perceptions. It is generally assumed that these "extra ingredients" in consciousness are from unconscious memories where previously recorded sense perceptions are stored. A few adventurers in the world of the mind suggest racial memories stored in genes and chromosomes, or a collective unconscious to which we are all connected. These areas of the mind are like the part of the iceberg below water or the invisible rays of the sun. Perhaps in following Edgar Cayce as he seemed to move into the unknown regions of this inner world it will be possible to observe some of the "reaches" of the unconscious.

In the words of the readings, mind partakes of both the material and the spiritual aspects of man. It is a spark of a force of the Maker, an active principle which governs man and expresses itself at many levels of consciousness. At the physical level mind manifests through the senses. It reasons with impressions from the senses. This is the conscious mind.

Two other large rooms of the mind may be called the subconscious and the superconscious, two broad divisions of the unconscious. The subconscious stores impressions from physical consciousness and, as has been pointed out, picks up far more than is consciously known. The readings suggest that this mind becomes the conscious mind, so to speak, when the physical body is laid aside at death. The superconscious mind might be said to be the part of the mind which has not come into physical expression at all. It is the original spiritual pattern. *Man's development depends on his being able to release spiritual energy from this higher area of the unconscious and bring it into conscious expression.* Mind is a part of the soul.

The Edgar Cayce readings describe the soul as a particular creation, an arrangement or pattern of energy. It might be considered to be made up of spirit, mind, and will. The spirit is the essence of the life force; the mind is the creative building quality; the will is the power of choice, the birthright of every soul.

It is only natural for man in three dimensions to think of the terms—soul, mind, will, spirit—as taking form in matter. As Edmund Spenser said,

> For of the soule the bodie form doth take:
> For soule is forme, and doth the bodie make.

In another room of the unconscious mind there seems to be at times a mechanism for establishing attunement with other minds. Some psychologists suggest that it is in a collective unconscious that such telepathic phenomena operate.

From the unconscious state Edgar Cayce described his own ability as a process of attunement with the subconscious of the person for whom he was giving information. The majority of his readings dealt with diseases of the body. The request for help seemed to set up a telepathic or clairvoyant bridge, enabling some area of his unconscious to blend with the subconscious of the seeker.

This activity of the unconscious was described in many readings. Here is one quotation:

> Then in seeking information there are certain factors in the experience of the seeker and in the channel through which such information may come. Desire on the part of the seeker to be shown. And, as an honest seeker, he will not be too gullible; neither will he be so encased in prejudices as to doubt that which is applicable in his experience. Hence the information must not only be practical but it must be rather in accord with the desires of the seeker also.
>
> This desire, then, is such that it must take hold not only on that which is primarily the basis of all material manifestation of spiritual things, but must also have its inception in a well-balanced desire for the use of such information not only for self but for others. Then there may come, as for this body in the present, that which if applied may be helpful in the present experience.
>
> On the part of that channel through whom such information may come, there must be the unselfish desire to be of aid to a fellow man. Not as for self-exaltation because of being a channel. Not for self-glorification that such a channel may be well-spoken of. But rather as one desirous of being a channel

through which the highest spiritual forces may manifest in bringing to the material consciousness of the seeker those things that may be beneficial in a spiritual and material sense to the seeker.

What, then, is the hypothesis of the activity that takes place during such an experience? It is not merely telepathy; neither does a beneficent spirit seek to do a service by giving advice, as some have suggested. For, if such were true at all times, there would never be a fault—if really developed spirits were in control. But rather in *this* instance is *this* the case:

The soul of the seeker is passive, while the soul of the individual through whom information comes is positive. As the physical is subjugated into unconsciousness the latter goes out, guided by suggestion, on the forces which are released to that individual place of the seeker. And the souls commune one with another. 531-2

It should be kept in mind that Edgar Cayce was never consciously aware of anything he said while giving a psychic reading. In other words, he was functioning at an unconscious level. Even more interesting is the fact that he was able to give information which was not consciously known by the individual who requested help.

The remarkable ability of the unconscious at times to provide helpful information about its own problems would be readily admitted by psychologists and psychiatrists. Parapsychological studies have uncovered a hitherto unsuspected way in which this helpfulness operates and can extend to others. It is the ability to establish communication between two unconscious minds, and seems to depend on rapport or attunement based on desire, directed by suggestion. Literally thousands of Edgar Cayce readings seem to be examples of this type of unconscious communication. The following impressed me and will illustrate the point.

786: Male, Age 1 year. Location: California. All the information known to Edgar Cayce was contained in a letter from the grandmother—December 18, 1934:

I now have two little grandchildren who are needing medical attention badly, but we are unable to obtain a correct diagnosis for them. Ruby, a little girl of two years, and John, age one year.

Reading: Yes. As we find with this body . . . the affectations are from the activity of not the stomach but intestinal infections . . . from a form of worms (1), that make for the irritations, for the lack of appetite (2), and at other times an overappetite (3), at times the belching up of foods and the spitting up (4), restlessness (5) at night, the inability of the body to be active (6), and tendency for the cold (7) and congestion through the system. These make for the quick pulsation at times, a little rise of temperature that comes at times (8), irritation in the throat (9), the irritation in the mucous membranes of the nostrils and face (10), the overactivity at times of the kidneys (11), the effect produced upon the eliminations and especially a peculiar color and odor that is indicated from the stool (12). 786-1

A report was received in a letter from the grandmother dated March 30, 1935:

So sorry not to have written sooner to thank you for the reading you sent my little grandchild. We started right in with the work as directed and have had very good results.

We gave the medicine to John as directed, and he had his first good night's sleep in months. But it did not seem to get the worms, as he showed the same symptoms soon afterward, so in three weeks' time we repeated the dose and got a quantity of pinworms . . .

There is absolutely no hint of the condition in the grandmother's letter. Edgar Cayce had never seen this child who was three thousand miles away when the information was given. Twelve checkable symptoms are given. Is it possible that the unconscious mind of this one-year-old child was capable of attunement with Edgar Cayce's unconscious, thus supplying the description of the body's condition and needs?

777: Male, Age 56. Location: New Jersey.
Information known to Edgar Cayce: Letter from the individual, December 29, 1934:
I would like a general reading as to the general state of my

health and whether you can help me.

Reading, January 4, 1935: In the *blood supply* we find evidences of a poor elimination as well as a distinct disturbance in various channels of the elimination, evinced by the rash that at times appears on the forehead ... Also we find a torpidity of the liver, the pressures or conditions that affect through the activities in the kidneys . . . As to the functioning of the organs themselves, as we find, there has been for some time back those pressures existent in the lower dorsal area—10th, 11th, 12th dorsal ... 777-1

Report: Letter, February 21, 1935: I know you will be interested to learn that the X-ray I had taken of my back showed the exact trouble in the 10th, 11th and 12th dorsal that your reading described. It seems almost unbelievable that a reading at a distance would be given so accurately ...

In this case the unconscious rapport of the two minds provided information which was checkable by X-ray. There are thirty-three spinal vertebrae. Edgar Cayce selected three. No information on the man's physical condition had been given prior to the reading.

Another remarkable activity of the unconscious mind which is reflected in the Edgar Cayce readings has to do with some kind of movement in time-space. This is hinted at in the reading quoted earlier, "goes out on the forces which are released." This activity seems to be illustrated by a variety of relatively unimportant but very interesting opening remarks in the physical readings. These indicate: a knowledge of actions as if he were viewing the body at the exact time of the reading; a descriptive knowledge of the surroundings of the individual who had requested the reading.

It should be remembered that at least two, generally four or five, witnesses were present for each reading. When remarks such as the following were made, the subject of the reading was never present. So far, more than seven hundred statements of this type have been indexed. Many were confirmed by return mail. Confirmation was requested from others when the reading was indexed. Each reading shows the names of those present and the exact time and date. It is easy to imagine the shock for some people when they received the typewritten reading through the mail and realized that Edgar Cayce several hundred miles away had known exactly what they had been doing at the time the reading was given.

> 4687-1: Yes, we have the body here. We have to let the body get still a minute. [pause]
>
> 3063-3: Yes, we have the body here [in undertone]; the body is just leaving, going down in the elevator now.
>
> 168-1: Is this body in bed? No, she is sitting in a large chair, talking to a man.
>
> 1713-1: Yes, we have the body here. We have had this before. She hasn't dressed yet, you see.
>
> 3433-1: She was in here and taken out. [For a patient in a certain room in a sanitarium.]
>
> 806-1: Yes, in the Gent's. We have the body here.
>
> 1683-2: Out for a walk and coming in now.
>
> 3546-1: Yes, it's about time you were waking up.
>
> 531-2: Yes, we have the body here, 11:47. He has just laid aside his paper he was reading.
>
> 3853-1: What is the body doing right now? Sitting in edge of window here, quarter of twelve o'clock.
>
> 1078-1: Yes, we have the body here—he's just finished keeping the time—went out!
>
> 1727-2: Yes, we have the body here. It would be better if he would keep quiet a minute. No use of bawling that man out.
>
> 1311-1: Yes, that's where he was yesterday, 418 Cedar St.; he's at 419 now.
>
> 930-1: Yes. He is on his way.
>
> 5339-1: Yes, we have the body. Kind of busy, clerking in a supermarket.
>
> 5078-1: Child's reading: Yes, we find the mother praying.

The following reading shows much more than observation of physical action at the period of the reading. In this case Edgar Cayce seemed to go back in time to events which had already taken place and to move forward to future actions already set in motion when he gave the information.

The sister of a friend of Edgar Cayce's had gone for a visit with a friend. After the time passed for her expected return, a call to the friend she had been visiting indicated that the girl had departed on time. Days went by without word or trace of her. The letter mentioned was received the next day. Details were confirmed.

> 4953: Information is desired as to the whereabouts of Miss X who was at her friend's home [address] on Wednesday night, July 7, 1920:
> We have had the body before. A message on the 8th to home was given someone else to post. It has been delayed. The message will reach home tomorrow. On way now. Delayed. She will separate from someone before she reaches home. There has been sickness to someone else, but she is all right. 4953-1

Other comments at the opening of physical readings indicate a knowledge of the surroundings of the person. In only rare cases did such information deal with places of which Edgar Cayce had any conscious knowledge.

> 2883-2: Benham Road, yes, this goes by the brook. Yes, we have the body.
> 3904-1: 1075 Park Avenue Apt.—very unusual in some of these halls, isn't it? What funny paintings!
> 1746-1: Yes, on the shady side—we have the body.
> 2969-1: Yes—right pretty rooster—we have the body.
> 599-10: Yes, keep quiet. They have an accident right in front of the house.
> 2185-4: On the edge of the hill.
> 3079-1: Yes, a little stream here.
> 4637-1: Yes, we have the body . . . smells much like a drugstore.
> 1951-1: Yes, fresh paint.
> 5499-1: Too much medicine about—it smells.

A rather amusing bit of information was given when Edgar Cayce once opened a reading by giving what was later confirmed as the childhood nickname of the person, "Nabisco."

Sometimes the internal conditions of the body were described along with body actions, such as, "complaining of a little headache this evening." (4576-1)

Practically every physical reading contained descriptions of internal functions of the body. Thousands of such readings were checked by the recipients and by physicians. Now and then the small details showed knowledge which was easily checked by the individual or those around him. The following are mentioned only as examples.

Case 313, in his fourth physical check reading, was given the exact location of a tooth which needed to be extracted, though there was no conscious problem with the tooth. Case 415 was warned of a splinter of glass in his knee. It was located and removed.

When present for their physical readings, it was a common experience for people to feel that Edgar Cayce was reading their minds. He answered questions before they asked them. The following are typical examples.

One man planning to ask the question, "What is causing the pain in my stomach?" had given up the idea, deciding instead to see what Edgar Cayce would say. Imagine his surprise when the reading mailed to him stated:

"We find these conditions arise rather from a form of swelling produced in the lower portion of the duodenum, rather than in the intestinal tract itself . . . " (257-242)

It is hard enough to admit that the unconscious can become sensitive enough to pick up telepathically a thought of a person in the same room. Distance, which does not seem to affect such communication, lends an additional air of mystery to such proceedings.

Mr. 257 had in mind to ask but had not submitted the questions: "Please review cause of the rash and itching, and tell me how to get rid of it."

His reading began:

Those disturbances, as we find, that have been aggravating to the body (Yes, he's coming in now) [11:05 to 11:10 A.M., EWT] these would appear if there would be the consistency in cleansing the body tissues, think what they would be if they were expressed in the alimentary canal—that has given the body so much trouble! . . .

When the portions of the cuticle or the rash or irritation under the skin become overaggravating, use the D.D.D. Prescription—preferably the cream, for this body . . . 257-245

An equally interesting bit of telepathy seemed to be involved in the following memorandum by Edgar Cayce's secretary dated February 15, 1939:

> Due to many interruptions we were late getting started with the reading. There were two other check readings to be given. Mrs. Cayce presented the first name on the list (920-13), which was a lady in New York. Mr. Cayce repeated the name and address as he always does in locating the body; then he said: "Better begin with [949]; he is going out!" So Mrs. Cayce then presented [949's] name and address in California, and his reading was obtained first. (11:20 to 11:30 A.M., EST)
>
> When asked about this, [949] answered:
>
> [March 3, 1939:] I was very interested in reading the note about the reading, saying to take me first as I was getting ready to leave. I usually do leave the apartment at about nine o'clock. Your being delayed meant that you started the readings at 8:30 (our time), so you see that it was a pretty close call. As always, I am very much interested in the sidelights of the readings.

There were times when those present for readings were startled to hear Edgar Cayce give information which had not been requested. In all such instances letters asking for readings were in the mail.

On April 17, 1940, Edgar Cayce was in New York. After the scheduled reading had been completed, this was given:

> . . . periods of anxiety have arisen recently regarding this weakness of [1465], those tendencies for the activities that cause almost a coma . . . 1465-10

A letter from 1465's brother requesting the reading was forwarded from Virginia Beach to New York and arrived several days later. It had been written on April 17, 1940.

During the late evening of January 17, 1925, Edgar Cayce gave a first physical reading before a group of more than seven people in an apartment in New York City. This reading was concluded at 12:15 A.M., January 18, 1925.

Immediately he began speaking again about a Mary Smith in

Eugene, Missouri. No one in the room had ever heard of her. He said in part:

> Now, in this condition that has arisen in the body from the disarrangement in the pelvic organs, especially those in the false pelvis, we find these need attention at once, through that condition as given, for the operation on the body, else there will be in nineteen days the setting up of an infection that will bring destructive forces to the whole system. The alleviation of the pressure has been effective to the body, but this attempt to lift that heavier than the body should have attempted under the existing conditions has brought about this condition, or falling more of the organs in the pelvis, and the rupture of the left Fallopian Tube, and these conditions should be attended to at once. 5700-6

On January 18, 1925, Mary Smith of Eugene, Missouri, addressed a letter to Edgar Cayce in Dayton, Ohio, asking the following questions:

> What should I be operated on for? Should my womb be taken? Just what should be done? Could the operation be done through the vagina? Should I take chloroform or ether? How long should I stay at hospital? Could I wait till about May or June to go for operation, then use the electric machine three or four weeks just before going? Would this operation make my nerves any worse than they are, and in what way would it make them worse?

The letter was not opened until Edgar Cayce returned to Dayton from New York several days later.

It would seem that this woman's request as stated in her unopened letter reached the sensitive unconscious of Edgar Cayce hundreds of miles away—actually before the request was put in writing.

In the unconscious state Edgar Cayce apparently was able to reach other rooms of both his own and others' minds. His explorations brought to light psychological and philosophical information so completely incongruous with his conscious ideas that it is hard for me to believe he picked this up from things he read or conversations. The outstanding example of this kind of information is the "life readings." They were considered by many people who secured them as being at least equally as accurate and helpful as the physical readings. Much of the philosophical comment contained in the Cayce psychic data is found in them. Thomas Sugrue's section on philosophy in his biography of Edgar Cayce, *There Is a River,* has attracted considerable attention, though some students of Edgar's readings believe this section is considerably colored by the author's background in Catholic mysticism.

My introduction to the life readings is associated in my mind with a disturbing experience. Perhaps this affected my reaction. For the first half of my junior year in high school I stayed with friends in Selma, Alabama. At Christmas time I joined my family in Dayton. Dad had given up his photographic business and was devoting all his time to giving readings. Letters from my mother and brief notes from my father had hinted at difficulties, but I was not prepared to face the actual conditions. The family was in financial straits. The rent was long overdue. Proper clothing and food were scarce. My train fare, I learned, had been paid with a gold piece my mother saved for years. At the conclusion of a homecoming dinner, at which we shared a very scrawny chicken, I was told that Dad had been giving a new kind of reading. They had gotten one for me. I read the typewritten pages with my name on them and at the same time half listened to the running conversation about past lives and odd historical characters. Slowly I began to wonder, "Were people right? Was my father crazy?" Never in all the ten years in his Sunday school classes had I heard my father mention past incarnations, other lives, from which talents and weaknesses could come over to influence the present life. As I continued to read what was written about me I began to get mad. Even then I sensed a kind of exposure. I thought my father had betrayed me. There was too much about my fears and feelings on these pages. He had no right to say these things where other people could see them, even if they were true. I fought back angry tears. I listened and retreated inside myself. For five long years I fought the ideas in that reading. Under different circumstances they might have been easier to consider with less prejudice.

In order to come to grips with these data let us examine one of the case histories of a life reading. The following was given August

29, 1927, for a fourteen-year-old boy living in a distant city. The request for the reading was made by the boy's sister. The parents did not accept the reading and did not let the boy see it or know about it.

The boy was a good student. He had been assisting with buying his own books and clothes for several years by working as a news boy. Aside from these facts and the knowledge that he was interested in stamp collecting, the sister, who lived in the same town as Edgar Cayce, had no special insight into his character.

Life reading suggestion: You will give the relation of this entity [Robert Moore] and the universe, and the universal forces, giving the conditions which are as personalities, latent and exhibited in the present life; also the former appearances in the earth's plane, giving time, the place, and the name, and that in each life which built or retarded the development for the entity; giving the abilities of the present entity and that to which it may attain, and how.

Reading: We have the entity and those relations with the universe and universal forces, which are latent and exhibited in the present earth's plane.

In the present experience we find more of those conditions as latent urges than those which have been manifested or expressed through the application of will—as yet—in the body. Yet the urges are definite, defined, and these are those as we find in this entity— and the urges which are seen through the sojourns in those planes wherein the various phases of development are experienced by the entity.

In entering the earth's plane we find the entity coming under the influence of Jupiter, Mercury, Venus, and the benevolent influences in the Sun and in Orion. We find the urge, then, for one strong of body, yet with those inclinations and tendencies toward those *physical defects or physical disabilities which afflict the body as tending toward the digestion*—or the internal system. Hence the body should be warned against indulging in any of those conditions which might tend to bring about troubles which would be afflictions in the physical, under the strain and stress of the digestive system.

Now, regarding influences seen in Jupiter, we find one extraordinary in mien. One with the disposition or turn that naturally makes friends, and is slow to anger—yet when wrath takes possession, the entity is mad—as it were—all the way through, and is not lacking in means of expressing same.

The entity is one, then, who—without respect [or consideration] of the will—finds these conditions as urges in the present experience:

One who will find the greater success, the greater development in the present experience, coming through the association with people—in the condition of the *businessman, especially in that pertaining to materials, clothing, or of such natures.* These will be the natural trend and bent of the entity in its relations with individuals and things. For with the ability to make friends, and of the turn that is seen in the nobleness of purpose, this [vocation] will offer the channel through which the greater development in the moral, physical, financial and spiritual way may come in this present experience. Hence the training which the entity should have, under such conditions and relations, should begin as soon as it may—either by the gradual development into the association of, or to get—as it were—the correct groundwork for such a development.

One who loves to know things for their ability to be applied in the betterment of conditions for self and for others.

One who will find that the keeping of himself in attune with the Divine—through the religious experiences of the entity—will bring the greater association for good in the life than can be found through any or all other spheres or phases of life's experience. Keep this [spiritual contact] well in the activities of the entity, then, through its creative period—or the period when the experiences mold the manner of thinking for the maturer man.

As to those experiences in the earth's plane and the urges seen from the sojourns, we find:

Before this the entity was in that period when the people in France were near to the rebellion, during the period of Louis XIII. The entity then was among those who were the escorts and protectors of that monarch; he was especially the *one who chose the dress or the change of apparel for that ruler*—though not in the capacity of the valet. Rather the entity was *one who set the styles for the people.* The name then was Neil, and the entity gained through that experience, giving of himself in service in the manner which was in keeping with the period, and not acting in any manner other than the correct in mien and in position. There is seen in the present the particular urge—or the urge to be particular with himself as to dress; *the ability to describe well the dress of a whole room full of people,* if he will set himself to think—as it were—concerning same.

Before that we find the entity was in what is now known as Salonica, during the period when there were changes in the land. The entity was *then among the tradespeople,* in the name Cohal, and the entity gained and lost through that period—*gaining* in the service to country and to the people whom the entity served—losing in the application of self when the entity was put in power or position. The present urge is seen in the ability to fit himself into any place or position, or among any people with whom the entity may find himself associated. Especially is the love of family and of those closely associated with same seen from that experience.

Before that we find the entity was in the land now known as Persia, when the people were divided in the service of the people who brought divisions in the land. Then the entity, as a physician in the court, gained and lost—or lost and gained. He lost through misapplication of himself to that for which the entity stood. He gained through the services rendered, even when persecutions came through the invading forces. The name was then Abiel. The urge seen in the present is the innate desire to know or to study chemical compounds, or the urge toward a desire to be a physician. Rather let this be replaced by that urge, as we have indicated, which comes from the experience *regarding the tradespeople,* than attempting a service in the limited field seen from the urge felt from the Persian experience.

Before that we find the entity was in the Egyptian land during the period when there was a division of the kingdom. The entity was among those people who were of the native folk, yet the one who brought much comfort to many people in providing for the application of truth which was given by those in rule—so that the native understood the intent and purpose. The entity acted then in the capacity of teacher, minister, or the go-between between the priests of the day and the common people. Hence the entity was among those who first in the land *took on especial class raiment or garments to designate self from other peoples,* being appointed or given this permission through those in power, both religious and political. Then in the name Isois, and there is seen yet among the Egyptian ruins or relics reference made to the entity's application of self to the peoples; becoming in later years—after the entity had entered again the spirit plane—among those who were worshiped by the peoples. The entity gained through that experience, and the urge seen in the present is the ability to apply himself to the *masses*—as well as to the individuals.

Before that the entity was in the Atlantean land when the floods came and when destruction ruled in that land. The entity was among those so destroyed from that experience, being among the people in power and the successor to the throne, had that land remained.

Gaining, and losing in that experience through the misapplication of self to the lessons or tenets which were in the way of being applied by the entity. The name was then Amiaieoulieb. The present urge is seen in the *abilities to know materials, especially that as applies to wearing apparel.*

As to the abilities of the entity, then, it is seen that many conditions arise which are to be met by the entity in the application of himself pertaining to will's force, in meeting the conditions through which the experiences have placed the entity in the environs of the present experience.

First, beware of those conditions which might bring detrimental forces to the *physical well-being through the digestive system.* Then, in this channel follow specific diets and the correct application of foods and food values for the physical well-being.

In the mental and the body building, the entity needs to apply himself first to that which will give the more perfect knowledge of his relation to Creative Energy, or to the spiritual lessons which may be gained from the study of the Master's experience in the earth's plane as the son of man.

In the material sense apply self toward *salesmanship* and to the abilities of meeting the needs of man as pertaining to business relations.

Keep self physically, mentally and spiritually fit—for in service the greater blessings are given; and in the application of self to meet the needs of every condition there is given the way of escape, if one will but rely upon those promises in Him who gave, "I have set before thee good and evil. Choose thou whom thou will serve, for no man can serve two masters."

And in the day when the sun goeth down, bring thy gifts to Him who said, "Come unto me, for I have prepared the place, that where I am there ye may be also."

Keep the law as is befitting to man's relations to God. Keep self unspotted from the world. Not as eye service, but as service of the heart to the Maker.

We are through for the present. 641-1

Italics have been used where the reading mentions the difficulties with the digestion. As clairvoyance this is not unusual when compared with medical information in the physical readings. Here, however, a physical difficulty is described as being a kind of inherited debility. The boy had a stomach weakness from birth. Later he was exempted from military service because of this condition.

In a subsequent reading given December 3, 1940, a specific question was asked about the problem:

(Q) What circumstances of a past sojourn brought about my present weakness of the digestive system, and why?
(A) The overindulgence through the French as well as the Persian experience, with too much of the activity of the acid-producing forces in the system. 641-6

By those who hold a belief in reincarnation the condition described would be called physical karma, the bodily weakness in the present life experience being a reflection of a misuse of the body in a former life.

On the positive side there are the frequent references to the abilities "to know materials, especially that as applies to wearing apparel."

The reports on this case indicate that the reading was eventually used:

August 22, 1934: At the age of twenty-one, Robert Moore was still working with the small-town newspaper. Although he had risen to the position of assistant circulation manager, he was making only a moderate salary and was then the chief support of his mother and a younger sister. He reported that he had not had the opportunity to get into the line of work suggested by the reading, and besides he could feel no special inclination or urge in that direction. It was hard for him to understand why the reading advised a lifework which had no appeal for him. However, he felt that he was at a standstill in his present position and saw no chance for advancement; consequently he was seeking a change of some kind.

Spring of 1940: Moore, while visiting in a large city, called on some friends of his sister who had first obtained the reading for him. These friends were in the clothing business; for three generations their family had manufactured uniforms. They knew of Mr. Cayce's readings from personal experience; their confidence in them was such that they took Moore on faith and offered him a job as a traveling salesman in a territory of several Southern states. His success in a year's time was phenomenal. Both partners of the firm admitted that Moore had a special knack for handling customers which their dozen or more other salesmen did not have, although Moore was the youngest and newest addition to the staff.

Because of gasoline rationing and traveling conditions it was necessary for him to give up his job on the road for the duration of the war. In 1943 he was made manager of an officers' clothing center in one of the large induction centers. Here fifteen hundred or more officers were outfitted each week.

September, 1946: At the age of thirty-three, Moore took charge of the retail sales business of the same uniform company with which he had been associated before the war, in and around the large city where the business is located.

Let us assume that a sleeping man who had never seen the fourteen-year-old boy guessed he would be successful in working with clothing. Why did he drag in reincarnation, complete with names, dates, and places, to explain the vocational analysis? Coming from the unconscious mind of an orthodox Disciples of Christ Sunday school teacher, this didn't seem reasonable. If Edgar Cayce had been a student of theosophy or Rosicrucian teachings; if he had read or studied Hindu or Buddhist writings; or if he had a library of occult books, this might be considered a fabrication of the subconscious. Any knowledge he had along these lines was kept a secret from his family and friends. In all the years I knew him I never saw my father read any book other than the Bible. He read it every day. Until I began to collect books on occultism, mysticism, psychology, and related fields, there were no books on these subjects in our home.

However, let us examine a few more cases before attempting to evaluate the range of the clairvoyant power operating through the unconscious in this kind of data.

In 1927 a life reading was given for a Florida businessman. The reading contained repeated warnings and considerable spiritual advice, including the following:

> ... with the greatest purport of self to accomplish the good, many at times speak evil when no evil intent or purpose is meant by the entity ... One that in the present plane found that often, on account of adverse conditions apparent when none meant, the entity tends to appear to others as secretive in actions, when to the entity such conditions present that as an element of safety, rather than that of attempting to be of the undermining or secretive nature ... In the abilities of the entity, and in the application of same, it is found that in the experience there comes, through this, much of the ability to counsel, and many of the privileges of monies under the control of the entity, of its own and of others ... 943-3

When this reading was given neither Edgar Cayce nor anyone present was acquainted with this man. The recipient put the information aside for several years. Situations arose where business associates accused him of being secretive, doubted his motives, and became severely critical. The possibility of a prison sentence arose over the handling of monies. Perhaps some of these conditions could have been avoided had the life reading been studied and the advice followed.

Consider another instance:

> ... the body becoming one-tracked toward one influence;

a theoretical and not a real, applicable, workable influence in a material world . . . In the application of will as respecting this condition, with influences in the active forces from the occult, it will be seen that—without balance—the individual may often be misjudged by associates and those related in active, material demonstrations of mental proclivities of a body; considered radical, and even radical to the extent of not being practical. 204-1

When this reading was given Edgar Cayce had not met this man, who a few years later became a public figure. This individual came close to being recognized as an outstanding "servant of the people." First, he was criticized for his radical attitude and interest in the occult. Next, he was charged with being too visionary. Finally, the public attacks charged, "Impractical!"

In another case, where the advice in a reading was followed, Edgar Cayce's clairvoyant ability appears to have helped the recipient unlock a specific talent. A young man working as an engraver was urged to escape the binding conventions of a possessive family and pursue the career of an artist. Here it was stated he could be an outstanding success, especially in work with modern friezes. The ensuing years have seen his transformation from a suppressed and relatively ineffectual young man to an esteemed and recognized artist of remarkable talent.

There were other instances in which complete changes in occupations were recommended. In one case a shift from the grocery business to wood and metal products, which later developed to be radios and television, brought phenomenal success. In another instance a young automobile salesman, thoroughly disgusted with life, was advised to go into housing. The latest report is that since he made the change he has never been happier and is intensely interested in his work.

Occasionally would-be musicians were advised that their efforts were misdirected and specific instruments were recommended. In one such case a young girl who resisted playing the piano was led to the harp. Here she seemed to have natural ability and found a deep sense of accomplishment. Today, years later, the harp under the skilled touch of the now mature woman brings joy to many.

On March 23, 1936, Edgar Cayce gave a life reading for J. D. which contained the following description of a colonial American incarnation:

> Before this the entity was in those lands of the present nativity or sojourn, during the period just following what is known as the American Revolution.
>
> The entity's activities were among the soldiery, and the soldiery of the British or the English activity, acting in the American land in what would be termed the Intelligence Service. Not as a spy was the entity, but rather among those who mapped out the plans for the campaigns by Howe, Clinton, and those in charge of those portions of the services in that particular portion of the land.
>
> However, the entity remained in the American soil after those activities, not as one dead, but as one alive in the very services of making for cooperation then between the peoples of the entity's native land of adoption. 1135-1

In 1956 a relative reported that Mr. D. planned a naval career during the war and sought a commission. Instead he was assigned to the Intelligence Service and helped train men dropped in France to assist the underground movement. The training was conducted at a Long Island estate.

With the onset of the war a cycle of activity having to do with Intelligence work seemed to unfold without any desire on the part of the person involved. The various tests taken as part of the application for work with the navy revealed these natural abilities which were accepted by the authorities as qualifications for the Intelligence work. Edgar Cayce seemed to have seen these talents years previously as the karmic pattern of activity from what must have been at least partly distasteful work in the Intelligence Service during the Revolutionary War. Even the place seemed to be part of the cycle.

The following passage is taken from a life reading given M. S. in 1937:

> The entity was then what would be termed in the present, in some organizations, as a Sister Superior, or an officer as it were in those of the Essenes and their preparations.
>
> Hence we find the entity then giving, ministering, encour-

aging, making for the greater activities; and making for those encouraging experiences oft in the lives of the disciples, coming in contact with the Master often in the ways between Bethany, Galilee, Jerusalem. For, as indicated, the entity kept the school on the way above Emmaus to *the way that "goeth down towards Jericho" and towards the northernmost coast from Jerusalem.* The entity blessed many of those who came to seek to know the teachings, the ways, the mysteries, the understandings; for the entity had been trained in the schools of those that were of the prophets and prophetesses, and the entity was indeed a prophetess in those experiences . . . thus gained throughout. 1391-1

The Dead Sea Scrolls were discovered in 1947. In 1951 excavations were undertaken on ruins near the coast of the Dead Sea, which were thought to be the remains of an old Roman fort. These ruins have since been identified as an Essene monastery (now called Kherbet Qumran) where the scrolls were written and studied before they were buried in the caves in the nearby hills.

Does the reference given eleven years prior to the discovery of the scrolls point to M.S.'s incarnation as an Essene at Qumran?

Josephus, the Jewish historian, refers to Essene communities as containing only men. Edgar Cayce described M.S. as having an incarnation in an Essene order as a woman. When the graves around Qumran were opened, skeletons of many women were found.

Here are two final reports on the life readings. The first is from an eighteen-year-old boy who had a life reading when he was four years old. Perhaps he was reminded too often of the responsibility of living up to it. He reported:

It is not easy to grow up with a Cayce reading being held over your head. I'd like to take time out and give parents some advice on how to use them. But let me get on with my own story . . .

The part of the life reading which interested me most, as early as I can remember, was a description of a past life in which I was a man about whom there is some historical record. Some of this record is good and some of it is not so good. I have figured out several ways in which I am very much like that man, but my first excitement over being able to learn a great deal about one of my previous lives has given way to the realization that knowing about my past faults and weaknesses may help me overcome some of my present problems.

You may be interested in knowing how accurately the reading described me. Here is the list of character traits mentioned in various places in the reading: "temper, hardheadedness, tendency to argue about everything, leadership, easily influenced by love (spiritual or purely carnal)." This may seem general to you, but I can think of many things he could have said which would not have fitted me as well as these traits, especially "tendency to argue" and "hardheadedness." And I guess you could say that my election to several offices in school and young people's activities shows some leadership. Mr. Cayce didn't see me at the time of the reading, but even if he had I was just four years old.

Probably one of the most unusual parts of my life reading was a prediction that came true. I was warned that between the thirteenth and fifteenth years anger would affect "the mental activities."

It was that period in my life when I began to have trouble with teachers in school and it ended up with my leaving school for a time in my fifteenth year. Naturally this caused my family considerable worry. Anger played a big part in all this trouble.

There are sections of the reading which fit me better than anyone else knows. I have just begun to realize how strong some of the urges can be. Being warned about them helps a great deal. It has enabled my family to understand and help me, and in the future I think it will continue to help me.

The second report comes from a young businessman:

. . . Then my reading came! And I knew that to some eye I had been an open book—a book read all the way through. Here were my shortcomings and my dreams, the unconfessed and hidden good and bad in me.

Here, for instance, was the rebuke to that old hesitancy of mine to go on with life—that recurring bugaboo of, "Why am I bothering about life at all—and is it real anyway?" No mere human being had ever guessed at that thought which had been at times an all-day consciousness in me.

Agnostic that I prided myself to be, I had spit mentally at many a church door (and curled my lip at many a church member). Yet this all-seeing eye had registered my bitterness and forgiven it—had known what I really meant when I had said so often, "That bunch wouldn't know Jesus if they fell over Him in the street" . . .

Here were comments on the work I had done and on the work I might do. Here were even the ways and manners for going about it.

Here was romance at its top. For here was a drama in which I was the star. I moved across the stage of life, according to this reading, and life had gone on for centuries. Did I feel important? Yes, and that feeling brought new hope, new courage and new power.

Yes, I have had a life reading.

My first objections to the idea of reincarnation were similar to those raised by anyone who runs into it for the first time. Why don't I remember past lives? The idea is fantastic; too many people think they have been kings and queens. There are not enough woodcutters and scrubwomen. Everyone will commit every sin in the book, believing he can escape to "another chance" in the next life. It can never be proved. These and many other familiar objections enabled me temporarily to ignore this phase of my father's work. The less I thought about it the better I felt. Gradually it dawned on me that there might be something wrong with this attitude. I began to look into the subject and at the same time tried to apply the same objective standards of measurement to the life readings as were being applied to the physical readings with doctors' examinations, X-rays, etc.

My first searching brought more questions. I discovered that some of the great Eastern religions held rebirth as a central part of their doctrines. Millions of people believed in various concepts of it. Nor was interest limited to primitive savages. A course in comparative religions disclosed reincarnation as not only one of the oldest but also one of the most widespread beliefs about the soul. It didn't help much either to find Plato, Plotinus, Origen, Spinoza, Schopenhauer, and many other philosophers apparently in agreement on the idea. A whole group of Jewish scholars considered it a valid system and early Christian mysticism was filled with ideas on it, I found. Too many stories of past-life memory seemed to exist to ignore them. And a re-examination of passages in the Old and New Testaments which seemed to suggest the rebirth idea disturbed me further.[1] Novels, poetry, short stories, and plays with a reincarnation theme added a bit of glamour to the whole idea. The water got "hotter and deeper."

It was possible to consider the whole subject abstractly until talks with investigators in the field of psychical research revealed that through hypnosis, free association, dreams, drug experiments, etc., past lives were repeatedly showing up. It was then that I turned to a serious study of the accuracy of the Edgar Cayce life readings. At this point I am forced to admit that the life readings are an even greater challenge to me than the physical readings, though plainly much harder to check. More thorough studies are obviously needed. Currently two approaches are being made. It is slow work.

Of the 1,919 life readings 166 were given for children from one day old to fifteen years. A study by an independent clinical psychologist of these young people (who have now become adults) to determine by psychological tests and interviews how accurate Edgar Cayce was in describing talents, weaknesses, faults, vocational aptitudes, in the light of what he called past-life achievements will be undertaken as quickly as funds are available for this work.

Another approach is being made through hypnosis, regressing those who had Edgar Cayce readings to a designated past life and attempting to secure from them *additional* data which may then be checked by archaeological and historical investigations. It is realized that this would not provide proof, but it would be disturbing evidence of *two* clairvoyant sources (one from Edgar Cayce and the other from the unconscious of the individuals) or suggest a past life at the specified time and place named.

Gradually from the 1,919 life readings I have pieced together partial answers to my first questions.

Why don't we remember past lives? We do remember but not in

---

[1]Job 14:14; Eccles. 1:11; Jer. 1:5; Matt. 17:9-13, 16:13-14; Mark 6:15; Luke 9:8; John 1:21, 25, 3:7; Col. 3:3; Jude 1:4; Rev. 3:12.

terms of physical consciousness. Talents and weaknesses, constructive attitudes and fears, some physical disabilities and healthy bodies, *are* memories of other lives.

The idea is fantastic—too many princesses and too few woodcutters. The highlights of periods of development and achievement
would naturally be picked up through deep personal memory or by
someone else. The Edgar Cayce readings contained descriptions of
both successes and failures in past experiences.

Won't people take rebirth as an excuse for sinning, looking forward to another chance? On the contrary, a serious study of the
theory of karmic law should act as a deterrent. "God is not mocked:
for whatsoever a man soweth, that shall he also reap." (Gal. 6:7) If
man could accept this idea he might change his thought and action
for the very selfish and powerful reason that he will be reborn into
the world he helps improve or destroy. What could be fairer?

For a more complete psychological study of the life readings one
should read *Many Mansions* and *The World Within* by Gina
Cerminara.

My personal distaste for the idea of reincarnation did not stop
with these first objections. There is no question that proof of rebirth
is most difficult to establish, especially if any telepathic or clairvoyant abilities are admitted as ways of securing data supposedly coming from a past life. But why is the evidence for the concept so
violently objectionable to so many people? My own attitude was a
case in point. If the earth is not man's natural habitat, as the Psalm
says—"Know ye that the Lord he is God: it is he that hath made us,
and not we ourselves; we are his people, and the sheep of his pas-
ture (100:3)—then man instinctively and unconsciously would seek
escape from the earth and abhor any idea which would tie him to it.
In my own mind it was hard to accept responsibility for my actions.
It is always more pleasant to try to blame society, one's parents,
neighbors, the Russians, the devil, or even God, than to admit the
possibility that our choices day by day build a more complex pattern than we can or wish to face.

In giving the life readings Edgar Cayce tapped what he called the
"soul memory." He described a recording of thought and action on
"the skein of time-space." This calls to mind William James's "stream
of mind" and Jung's concept of the "collective unconscious." However, there seemed to be an attempt in the readings to give some

detailed and practical information in terms of everyday experience. He seemed to be trying to interpret a universal law in terms of the individual need, pointing to a way out of this dimension of consciousness.

As my father saw it from the unconscious state, the earth is only a tiny point in a vast pattern of what man calls matter. Individual souls in spirit form, through the application of will in the expression of selfish desires, pushed into matter and brought confusion into the earth. Through the guidance of the Christ-Soul the earth has been made a ladder up which souls may return to a consciousness of at-onement with the Creator. Through a series of incarnations in matter in human form the soul can learn to cleanse itself of the selfish desires blocking its more perfect understanding and to apply spiritual law in relation to matter. Urges created in the material plane must be met and overcome, or used, in the material plane.

Rebirth in the earth plane occurs as a result of individual need. It may follow a definite cycle or vary according to the development of the soul in this and intermediary planes. The number of incarnations is not limited. Some souls may exercise choice in the entrance into this plane; others according to their development are drawn through the law of attraction into a particular type of experience. A man who has enjoyed one revolution may show up for another. Sex changes in various incarnations according to development and expression in previous periods. During one lifetime souls are associated with others with whom they have been connected in past lives, or with souls whose development is similar. A man builds his own station in life.

As I understand it, forgiveness of sins in the religious sense is related to the laws of cause and effect. Through a personal application of whatever one accepts as spiritual truths one may move toward universal Christ Consciousness and make of his karma stepping-stones to a greater godlike expression.

A person's will is always a governing factor in his experience and he may choose to use any pattern established in past experiences as a point from which to grow spiritually. The stress placed upon the importance of the will as a factor in the development of an entity and the correlation of environmental influences are outstanding points of emphasis in life readings. Within every being there is a force which seeks constantly to move toward God. This does not mean that man may always overcome and master his surroundings in the sense that he speaks of physical success, but that always there lies within him the ability, the power, to choose the way which will mean a step forward along the path. If a person will make an effort, the next step toward spiritual progress will be opened to him from within. The will must be considered as a faculty of the soul and should be exercised and developed as such. It must not be confused with its expression or activity in the mental and physical worlds where desires become so demanding that it is lost sight of. The loss of will power results in the magnifying of selfish desires to such an extent that the passions of the physical body and conscious mind overshadow the inner desires of the soul. If magnified in the mental and physical life, the search for God may use any condition, any barrier, any problem, as a stepping-stone for further spiritual growth. The fusion of this God-given faculty of every soul with the Divine Will makes possible a perfect attunement with God.

Over and over in the life readings, the statement is repeated, "Mind is the builder." Each life reading contains some admonition and direction for holding the mind to constructive activity through complete and balanced expression in the physical plane. Positive thought and action are stressed as essential for real self-expression.

One of my own experiences, a disturbing one, illustrated to me how inadequate our concept of time is. My life reading from Edgar Cayce, given when I was fifteen years old, contained a description of a previous life during which I was described as taking part in one of the Crusades. The reading suggested that boredom with medieval village life was more the motive for the pilgrimage than the professed desire to free the "Holy City." Apparently I had left a family.

During the Second World War, I was drafted. My abilities in the field of psychic studies were not in great demand. I was finally placed in a Special Service outfit attached to combat troops. The day the war with Germany ended our company was stationed in a little Austrian village in the Bavarian Alps near Berchtesgaden. We had liberated some very fine Austrian beer. I was consuming a canteen cup of this beer while seated in the yard of one of the neat little cottages of the village when my mind began to play tricks on me. The road through the village was crowded. Remnants of the Austrian army, bedraggled, dirty, thin, and exhausted, plodded by. American trucks raced back and forth, picking up airplane engines which were cached at intervals along the edge of the road. The prisoners from a nearby work camp had been released—Poles, Russians, Czechs, and other nationals moved along the edge of the road, looking as if they were about to ask, "Which way is home?" Trucks passed loaded with English airmen who had been shot down in some of the first Romanian oil raids. Imprisoned for years, now free, these men were singing, laughing hysterically, shouting and drinking. They were headed for airfields from which they would be flown directly to England. Excitement, relief, joy, confusion, and fear blended into an emotional wave which seemed almost tangible.

As I sat there looking at this scene, suddenly something clicked in my head, and I saw before me a marching horde of Crusaders. Men in armor on horses, men dressed in leather and walking with spears, servants riding and walking, some with leather coverings on their arms on which perched hooded falcons. Little dwarfs acted as entertainers and were doing handsprings and tumbling feats ahead and to the side of the column. It seemed that I was literally back in the time of the Crusades.

As quickly as the scene had appeared, a curtain was drawn across the mental images. Now came a strange sensation of awareness of the village. I knew where there was the ruin of an old building long ago, torn down as the stones were used for buildings in the village. I knew where there was a stone bridge over a small stream, now filled in. Perception was a mixed, confused pattern combining the so-called past and present. My consciousness was torn between two periods of time.

Then came a peculiar sense of "it's over." A cycle had been completed. I had walked away to fight a war; I had come back to the very spot from which the departure had been made. I thought of my wife and child back home, of my father and mother who had died a few months previously. I wondered if this were the completion of a karmic pattern.

All my attempts to relegate this to imagination and recall of studies of the Crusades, or to blame the beer, have not dimmed the peculiar sensation of getting caught in a timeless world of deep memory.

Yes, the next day without the assistance of the beer, I found what I thought might have been a bridge and the ruins of an old building. This didn't help much; the sensation that something had ended was still with me.

Perhaps all that I can say now about the concepts of rebirth is that for me these ideas have raised many questions about the meaning of life. As the basis for searching inward they become a point of departure. Let us continue the search, withholding final judgment until the light is clearer.

While in the life readings there seemed to be a consideration of what may be called the past, other readings dealt to a limited degree with precognition and prophecy, apparently involving what may be called the future. For convenience, precognition may be said to deal with individual affairs, while prophecy might be designated as concerned with groups or nations and events relating to large numbers of people. Limitations of time and space probably constitute the greatest barriers to expanding perception. It is most difficult to evaluate psychic data involving time.

Precognition might have applied in the case mentioned earlier when Edgar Cayce gave information for a woman who five to seven hours later wrote him a letter asking for the reading. On the other hand, it could be said that she may have been thinking of asking for help before or during the period when he was in the unconscious state in New York City. If this were true, then telepathy should be considered.

The Edgar Cayce records do not embody a great amount of general prophecy. Individual readings do contain data which might be considered precognitive material.

In a few readings given before groups at conferences from 1932 to 1944 there are statements of a prophetic nature. The readings' point of view could be said to be the same as indicated in the Bible story of Jonah. Nineveh, a city whose people had turned from God, was to be destroyed. Jonah was directed in a vision to warn the people of Nineveh. Instead of complying he tried to run away and got into difficulties with the whale. Finally, Jonah returned and preached in Nineveh with the result that the people repented. The city was not destroyed. Jonah was disturbed because God had made a fool of him. In other words, prophecy is possible, say the readings, but it is frequently given in order that changes can be made. This may appear to be an easy "out" for a psychic. One good look at some of the dire prophecies which currently are being circulated would make almost anyone hope that such a theory of possible change is true.

The information in a great many different Edgar Cayce readings describes a world of thought forms, thought patterns, which are built up by individual and mass thought, planning, and purposes held at the mind level. This thought world is a world of matter, but matter in an energy pattern which can be molded by mind. To a sensitive, a prophet, this world may seem as real as the three-dimensional world. This thought world may be the world which is "seen" in precognition and prophecy. The action of will controls which thought pattern or thought form is drawn into three-dimensional expression. Will is free but is also conditioned at any given point of expression in matter at the earth plane level.

The following was an interesting general statement made in a reading on October 7, 1935, on European affairs:

> As to affairs of an international nature, we find a condition of great anxiety on the part of many; not only of individuals but of nations. And activities already begun have now assumed such proportions that groups will attempt to attach penalties and set up groups to carry them out. This will cause a taking of sides, as it were, by various other groups, countries or governments. Such will be manifested by the Austrians and Germans and later on the Japanese joining this influence. Thus an unseen force, gradually growing, must result in an almost direct opposition to the Nazi, or Aryan theme. This will gradually produce a growth of animosities. And unless there is interference by what many call supernatural forces and influences—which are active in the affairs of nations and peoples—the whole world, as it were, will be set on fire by militaristic groups and people who are for power and expansion. 416-7

On the general economic and social conditions in the United States the following is a typical statement from a reading given June 20, 1938:

> Unless dealings one with another are in keeping with His tenets, they must fail; for all power in heaven and in earth hath been given into His hands. In an approach to all phases of human relationships, these ideals must be taken into consideration. *There cannot be one measuring stick for the laborer in*

the field or the man behind the counter, and another for the man behind the money changers! All are equal—not only under the material law, but under the spiritual law. And His laws, His will, will not come to naught! Though periods may come when there will be great stress—as brother rises against brother, as a group or sect or race rises against—yet the leveling must come. *And only those who have set their ideal in Him, and practiced it in their dealings with their fellow man,* may expect to survive the wrath of the Lord. In thy dealings then— whether at home, with the state or national situations or with international affairs—all must come under compliance with that purpose, that desire.

Then there should be—there will be—those rising to power who are able to meet the needs. For none are in power but that they have been given the opportunity by the will of the Father, from whom all power emanates. Hence all will be level in respect to the purpose, "My word shall not fail!" 3976-18

With respect to Russia the following statements are interesting:

(Q) What should be the attitude of so-called capitalist nations toward Russia?
(A) The greater hope of the world will come through Russia's religious development. The one nation or group which is closest in relationship with Russia may fare best during the gradual changes and the final settlement of conditions, as to the rule of the world. (February 8, 1932) 3976-10

(Q) About the Russian situation?
(A) As we have indicated before, a new understanding has come and will come to a troubled people. Here, because of the yoke of oppression, because of self-indulgences, another extreme has arisen. Only when there is freedom of speech, and the right to worship according to the dictates of conscience—until these come about, turmoils will still be within. (June 24, 1938) 3976-19

In a reading given in June, 1939, a question was asked about the Negro in America:

(Q) What should be our attitude toward the Negro, and how may we best work out the karma created in relationships with him?

(A) He is thy brother! Those who caused or brought servitude to him, without thought or purpose, have created that which must be met within their own principles, their own selves. These [Negroes] should be held in an attitude of their own individual fitness—as in every other form of association. For He hath made of one blood the nations of the earth. 3976-24

The following statement was made in June, 1940, in a conference reading before approximately fifty people:

When many of the isles of the sea and many of the lands have come under the subjugation of those who fear neither man nor the devil; who rather join themselves with that force by which they may proclaim might and power as right—as of a superman who is to be an ideal for generations to be established; then shall thy own land see the blood flow, as in those periods when brother fought against brother. 3976-25

The Pearl Harbor attack took place December 7, 1941.

From the unconscious state Edgar Cayce saw what he interpreted as a period from 1958 to 1998 when scientific, economic, political, social, and land changes would be accelerated.

These changes in the earth will come to pass for the time and times and half time [Rev. 12: 14] are at an end, and there begin those periods for the readjustments. For how hath He given? "The righteous shall inherit the earth." Hast thou, my brethren, a heritage in the earth? (June 30, 1936) 294-185

As to the changes physical again: The earth will be broken up in the western portion of America. The greater portion of Japan must go into the sea. The upper portion of Europe will be changed as in the twinkling of an eye. Land will appear off the east coast of America. There will be the upheavals in the Arctic and in the Antarctic that will make for the eruption of volcanoes in the Torrid areas, and there will be the shifting then of the poles—so that where there have been frigid or semitropical lands these will become the more tropical, and moss and fern will grow.

And these changes will begin in those periods in '58 to '98, when these will be proclaimed as the periods when His Light will be seen again in the clouds. As to times, as to seasons, as to places, *alone* it is given to those who have named the Name—and who bear the mark of those of His calling and His election in their bodies. To them it shall be given. (January 19, 1934) 3976-15

(Q) How soon will the changes in the earth's activity begin to be apparent?

(A) When there is the first breaking up of some conditions in the South Seas (that's South Pacific, to be sure) and those conditions as apparent in the sinking or rising of that which is almost opposite to it, or in the Mediterranean, and the Aetna area. Then we may know it has begun. (April 9, 1932) 311-8

If there are the greater activities in Vesuvius or Pelee, then the southern coast of California—and the areas between Salt Lake and the southern portions of Nevada—may expect, within the three months following same, an inundation [caused] by the earthquakes. But these, as we find, are to be more in the southern than in the northern hemisphere. (1936) 270-35

In other readings it was also indicated that land would appear off the east coast of America, specifically in the Bahamas. Expect this, said the readings, in sixty-eight and sixty-nine.

On November 11, 1927, this was given in a reading: the day may yet arrive when one may diagnose the condition of the body through one drop of blood.

On March 20, 1958, newspapers carried the announcements of Dr. Winston Price's work on blood at Johns Hopkins. The article concluded, "His discovery could mean that a medical laboratory can tell what ails you . . . simply by examining a drop of your blood."

Early in the 1930s Edgar Cayce insisted in readings that solar power would ultimately be far more important to man than atomic power.

One final bit of data from the part of the unconscious of Edgar Cayce which seemed to deal with the future. This came through one of Edgar Cayce's dreams and his own interpretation of this through a reading.

To understand the significance of this dream it is necessary to be acquainted with the activities and conditions which led up to it. In November, 1935, the entire Cayce family, including Miss Davis, had been arrested in Detroit for practicing medicine without a license. Court action was postponed until the early part of March, 1936. The family returned to Virginia Beach. January and February of 1936 were low periods in the history of the work. Edgar Cayce was ill. He worried not so much over the outcome of the court action, but because of the persecution which seemed to continue in the face of his attempts to give the readings.

Late in February the family returned to Detroit and on March 3, 1936, court action was over and everyone was free to return to Virginia Beach. While on the train that night Edgar Cayce had the following dream:

He had been born again in A.D. 2100 in Nebraska. The sea apparently covered all of the western part of the country, as the city where he lived was on the coast. The family name was a strange one. At an early age as a child he declared himself to be Edgar Cayce who had lived two hundred years before. Scientists, men with long beards, little hair, and thick glasses, were called in to observe the child. They decided to visit the places where he said he had been born, lived, and worked in Kentucky, Alabama, New York, Michigan, and Virginia. Taking the child with them, the group of scientists visited these places in a long, cigar-shaped, metal flying ship which moved at high speed. Water covered part of Alabama. Norfolk, Virginia, had become an immense seaport. New York had been destroyed either by war or an earthquake and was being rebuilt. Industries were scattered over the countryside. Most of the houses were of glass. Many records of Edgar Cayce's work were discovered and collected. The group returned to Nebraska, taking the records with them for study.

On June 30, 1936, a reading was given in which an interpretation of my father's dream-experience was requested. The answer follows:

The experiences, as has oft been indicated, come to the body in those manners in which there may be help, strength, for periods when doubt or fear may have arisen. As in this experience, there were about the entity those influences which appeared to make for such a period of confusion as to appear to the material or mental-minded as a doubting or fearing of those sources which caused the periods through which the entity was passing in that particular period.

And the vision was that there might be strength, that there might be an understanding, that though the moment may appear dark, though there may be periods of the misinterpreting of purposes, even these will be turned into that which will be the very proof itself in the experiences of the entity and those whom the entity might, whom the entity would, in its experience through the earth plane, help, and those to whom the entity might give hope and understanding.

This then is the interpretation. As has been given, "fear not." Keep the faith; for those that be with thee are greater than those that would hinder. Though the very heavens fall, though the earth shall be changed, though the heavens shall pass, the promises in Him are sure and will stand—as in that day—as the proof of thy activity in the lives and hearts of thy fellow men.

For indeed and in truth ye know, "As ye do it unto thy fellow man, ye do it unto thy God, to thyself." For with self effaced, God may indeed glorify thee and make thee stand as one who is called for a purpose in thy dealings, in thy relationships with thy fellow man. Be not unmindful that He is nigh unto thee in every trial, in every temptation, and hath not willed that thou shouldst perish. Make thy will, then, one with His. Be not afraid. That is the interpretation; that the periods from the material angle, as visioned, are to come to pass, matters not to the soul, but do thy duty TODAY! TOMORROW will care for itself. 294-185

In the foregoing we have examined the power of Edgar Cayce's unconscious mind to exercise dynamic control over his physical body; the photographiclike quality of memory; an apparent "reach" to contact other minds and bring through what seemed to be helpful information on the condition and needs of the physical body; the tapping of what he called the soul memory of past lives; and, finally, the picking up of thought impressions from a world of mental images and from these suggesting future events in our three-dimensional world. Now let us turn to two historic doorways to the unconscious.

2

Two Traditional and Sometimes Professional Doorways to the Unconscious

1

Hypnosis

DURING WORLD WAR II the Germans were reluctant about giving up the forts around Metz, France. For weeks even the movement of our tanks was restricted. Our Special Service Company of approximately a hundred twenty-five men was quartered in a partially destroyed French chateau near Thionville. One of our men was an excellent hypnotist. As a magician, he had used hypnotism for entertainment purposes, but he had never experimented with clairvoyance or telepathy under hypnosis. I encouraged him to pick out the best hypnotic subjects from among the men of our company who would agree to cooperate. Time, one important factor in hypnosis, was at our disposal.

In one of the first evening sessions we opened "a can of peas," so to speak. I haven't yet sorted out all of the implications of the resulting developments. A young man who was selected as a good subject was a quiet person who professed no knowledge of hypnosis or related subjects. He took suggestions to relax and rather quickly began to breathe deeply and rapidly. Instead of obeying the suggestions of my friend, the hypnotist, he began to speak in some unknown language. More accurately we should probably say it sounded like a language. He seemed to be talking with someone we couldn't see. He would pause, apparently listen, then speak again as if he were answering or asking questions. The chateau room was crowded with G.I.'s. Everyone strained to catch the low tones of the apparently unconscious man.

I urged our hypnotist to renew his attempts to regain control and get the young man to respond to his suggestions. His efforts were futile. The boy's one-sided conversation became more animated. He ignored all attempts to interrupt him. It was as if he simply did not hear the voice of the hypnotist. As men in the room realized that we had lost control of the situation, tension mounted. Whispering began in various parts of the room.

Suddenly the young man stopped talking. His face took on an expression of sadness. Tears trickled down his face from his closed eyes. I urged the hypnotist to try his suggestions again. This time the boy responded and in a few minutes returned to consciousness.

Dazed and obviously emotionally disturbed, he left the room without saying a word. I followed, but when I caught up with him he would say only that he would talk to me later. This was the beginning of a series of long conversations, stranger in their way than any in which I have ever taken part. The first one occurred in an odd setting.

That night, I had the guard shift from 2 to 4 A.M. Very soon after I went on duty our hypnotic subject joined me. He explained that as a small boy he had dreamed of his grandfather who came quite often in his dreams to take him on long journeys to strange places. Together they visited Egypt, India, Tibet, and other faraway places. The young man explained that instead of just seeing the places as from an airplane, he and his grandfather actually seemed to go into temples and observe as well as sometimes take part in religious ceremonies. He said that these stories upset his parents so much that they finally took him to a psychiatrist who apparently "suggested" that he stop remembering his dreams, since they seemed to be upsetting him and his family. The dreams stopped.

However, when he went under hypnosis a few hours previously, surrounded by a group of curious G. I.'s, he said that he had instantly gone back to his childhood dreams. Both he and his grandfather had been happy to see each other again. Apparently he had halluci- nated a conversation with this familiar dream image. What amazed him, however, was the fact that he had brought back to conscious- ness with him a memory of his childhood dream experiences in- cluding details of visits to some very strange places. These memories, he explained, were still coming back to him as he talked about the dreams. They continued to flood his mind for days. I listened with amazement to descriptions of priestly rites and ceremonies which could have come, it seemed to me, only from books like the Egyp- tian Book of the Dead or lore of long-dead priests or magicians. That first two hours of conversation in the early morning hours outside that old French chateau seems now like a weird dream of my own.

In the days that followed a wealth of detail poured out in each new conversation. This young man swore to me that he had never read a book on occultism or ancient religions in all of his nineteen years. Later, from his family I confirmed history of the early child- hood dreams of his grandfather and the family concern over them. The point which had upset the family so was the fact that the grand- father could have been only a dream image, they thought, since the little boy had never known his grandfather, who died years before the child was born.

Yes, it seems to me that hypnotism can open doors to some strange and interesting rooms in the unconscious.

My first knowledge of hypnotism began with reading lurid maga- zine articles accompanied by pictures of men with bushy, black eye- brows and fixed stares. As a teenage boy, I witnessed exhibitions of hypnotic powers following magic acts. I always thought they were "fixed." Later I discovered that those who know the most about hyp- notism and use it most extensively admit that no one knows what it really is. One handbook on medical hypnosis in its opening section uses just this phrase: " . . . since nobody really knows what hypnosis is." A Menninger Foundation monograph refers to "the primitive state of our understanding" of hypnotherapy. And a book which describes hypnotism as coming of age contains the following sen- tence: "Even today, although many psychiatrists are busy using it with effective results, there is still disagreement among them as to its fundamental nature and proper function."

In tracing the picture of man's first uses of hypnotism I found it necessary to inquire into the Roman stories of men like Pyrrhus of Epirus, who cured by "touching," and to consider Aristotle's descriptions of the hallucinations which he witnessed in normal people. Some ancient Greek temples contained rooms where sick persons spent the night after the priest had suggested that they "dream" their cures. Egyptian priests used suggestion, and tribal witch doctors the world over have known the power of the rhythmic drumbeat and a bright object to produce a trance state in an unsuspecting subject.

I found that in the fields of medicine and psychology hypnotism had a stormy but continuous development. A Viennese doctor, Franz Anton Mesmer, living at the time of the American Revolution, whose magnetic treatments reputedly cured many neurotically sick people, developed a system of suggestive therapy which was to become known as "mesmerism." At first he created magnetic forces with iron filings and powdered glass in tubs filled with bottles of magnetized water. The magnetic forces were directed to the patients with iron rods. Later Mesmer developed the theory that a universal current flowed through individuals and was passed to a patient by stroking parts of the body, passes of the hands around the body, and fixed stares. He was investigated and denounced by a famous committee which included three well-known persons— Benjamin Franklin; Dr. Guillotine, inventor of the death machine of the same name; and Lavoisier, the great chemist. Today, Mesmer's theories of animal magnetism conveyed with stroking and passes and his concept of a universal magnetic force or fluid are in bad repute. Without doubt, he successfully used suggestion to relieve many of his patients. Hysterical shouting, sobbing, uncontrolled laughter, twitching and jerking characterized the reactions of Mesmer's patients to treatment. The door was opened on an inner world of man filled with strange repressions which could no longer be ignored. Mesmerism was the forerunner of hypnotism.

The Marquis de Puysegur, a student and contemporary of Mesmer, discovered the phenomenon of a deep trance state from which the subject could be awakened without being able to remember what he said or did. This has become known as somnambulism. One of de Puysegur's subjects, Victor, a shepherd boy, is reputed to have given accurate descriptions of other people's physical bodies while he was in trance states.

During the early part of the nineteenth century, John Elliotson, a professor at the University College Hospital, London, experimented with mesmerism in the hospital wards. He finally resigned under severe criticism and started a mesmerism hospital and edited a journal called *Zoist*. This journal reported a variety of cures including surgical operations under mesmerism. Phrenology and clairvoyance were also discussed in *Zoist*. It would have been easier to discount Elliotson had he not also made outstanding contributions to medicine, including discoveries regarding the importance of potassium iodide and the value of prussic acid in treating vomiting.

During this same period James Esdaile, a Scottish doctor working in Calcutta, performed over three hundred major operations and thousands of minor ones under mesmerism. Of special note is the history of the rapid healing of his patients.

James Braid, another Scotsman, began experiments with mesmerism in Manchester, England. He discovered that the phenomena were more directly related to the subject's own mind than had been suspected, rather than being imposed on the subject by the operator. Dr. A.A. Siebault of Nancy, France, began work with hypnosis about the time Braid died. With Professor Bernheim of Strasbourg he founded what was called the Nancy School of Hypnotism. Jean Marie Charcot, the French neurologist, did not accept the Nancy School's ideas that hypnosis was a normal state produced through the subject's mind by suggestion. He considered it similar to hysteria, a kind of mental disorder.

Sigmund Freud, one of the great explorers of the unconscious, investigated and used hypnosis. Later he discarded it as a regular treatment, having found that it was not easy to hypnotize all of his patients and that other methods proved successful.

Pierre Janet, director of pathological psychology at Salpetriere, and later professor of experimental psychology at the College de France, used hypnosis extensively in studying the causes of hysteria.

In the United States between 1840 and 1847 Phineas P. Quimby, whose work was later to arouse controversy in relation to his association with Mary Baker Eddy, the founder of Christian Science, was widely reported to have successfully mesmerized a young man, Lucius Barkman, and produced excellent clairvoyance including medical diagnoses. Later Dr. Boris Sidis, author of *The Psychology of Suggestion* and a number of other books on hypnosis, reported many interesting cases. With one patient, Rev. Thomas Hanna, who suffered complete amnesia after an accident, Sidis was able to prove that the patient had all of his lost memories stored in his unconscious. Hanna had developed two personalities after the accident. Dr. Sidis was able to bring them together and completely cure the minister.

Members of the British Society for Psychical Research, including F. W. H. Myers, author of *Human Personality and Its Survival of Bodily Death,* and Edmund Gurney, one of the authors of *Phantasms of the Living,* experimented with hypnosis and wrote on the theoretical understanding of it.

Following World War I there was a brief growth of interest in hypnosis as a method of treating shell-shocked patients. This interest was revived during World War II. Since 1956 over a thousand physicians have attended symposiums on hypnosis in California. There are an estimated 4,000 dentists trained in its use, with more taking courses each year. More than 6,000 general practitioners and specialists were using hypnosis in the United States in 1959, according to the *Wall Street Journal,* January 11, 1960. This estimate does not include psychologists and psychiatrists. In 1958 the *Reader's Guide to Periodical Literature* listed twenty-three articles on hypnosis. Early in 1959 *Life* magazine carried a graphic article on hypnosis, showing a number of pictures of medical uses for severe burns, children's injuries, childbirth, skull surgery, and relief of pain for a woman suffering from incurable cancer. In 1958, after a two-year committee study, the American Medical Association approved the use of hypnosis as useful in treating some diseases. There seems to be a growing public interest.

In considering various theories about the nature of hypnosis, I think it eventually may be well to reexamine Mesmer's concepts of animal magnetism in the light of modern discoveries of brain waves and body currents. There are two types of information in my father's records which seem to touch on these subjects. We have taken a few faltering steps in experimenting with both concepts.

The first has to do with what are called auras. Sensitive persons, especially children, frequently claim to see around others bands and flashes of color. From the shades and location of these colors around the body some people believe that a great deal of information can be gathered about the physical, emotional, and mental conditions of the person being observed. Under drugs, the perception of color is increased. One is reminded also of many artists' use of the halo. "The Human Atmosphere," by Walter J. Kilner, an English electrician, describes the use of dye-treated screens in observing color around people. It is well known that we do not see all the ranges of the spectrum. A simple prism which breaks sunlight into brilliant bands of blue, purple, yellow, and green makes one acutely aware of sight limitations.

My father claimed to see auras the greater part of his life. In fact this sensitivity was at times the source of much discomfort to him. On one occasion on meeting a close friend for the first time in several days, he remarked, "Your aura is filled with dark red. You have been very angry." The lady in question was somewhat disconcerted, for just a few hours before she had been involved in a violent argument.

On numerous occasions, especially in Virginia Beach during summer conferences of the Association which was studying his work, Edgar Cayce by reading auras would give his impressions of the physical, mental, and emotional states of members of his audience. Among twenty-five or thirty people in one session he was known to have seen colors which he interpreted accurately as indicating scars from an operation, a heart condition, bad digestion, worry over some member of the family who was sick, fear of an animal, indignation over a supposed slight, hate carried for a long time, an interest in music, etc. He would describe a color, its shade, its location in relation to the body, and its meaning for him. These demonstrations were frequently dramatically accurate and most startling for those meeting him for the first time.

New theories of energy and the structure of matter may tend to the development of mechanical instruments for measuring color vibrations about the physical body. It seems reasonable to suggest a possible relation between the auric field and Mesmer's magnetism. The strokes and passes over and around the body used in mesmerism may in some way affect this body-energy field.

In working with hypnosis I have noted many instances when strong feelings of attraction or repulsion are set up between a hypnotist and a subject. Some very good hypnotists can do very little with particular subjects who will respond instantaneously with another operator. Is it possible that a body vibration is involved?

An associate and I once found in trying to duplicate Pierre Janet's experiment of transferring the sensitivity of a hypnotized subject to a glass of water (we used a doll) that distance seemed to make a difference in how well the subject could feel a pin stuck in an arm or leg. We wondered if this was totally telepathic sensitivity or if some extension of body current was involved.

The second type of information to be considered regarding hypnosis is contained in readings originating two types of appliances recommended for treating glandular disturbances, nervousness, and serious illnesses involving nerve impairment. One of these appliances was made up of a metal jacket about the size of a dry cell battery, containing two steel bars surrounded by pieces of carbon and glass set in charcoal in the jacket. Wires attached to the tops of the steel bars led to the wrists and ankles of the patient. The appliance was first placed in a container filled with ice for thirty minutes prior to attaching it to the body. The other appliance was a low-voltage battery. Two rods, one of nickel and the other of copper, extended into a solution of distilled water, zinc particles, sulphuric acid, copper sulphate, and charcoal. The very low current which was set up passed through a wire leading from one rod into a bottle containing a solution which varied according to the ailment being treated. At times a solution of gold chloride was recommended, at other times, silver, iodine, camphor, etc., were used in solution. Another wire led from the other rod to some point on the patient's body. Neither of these appliances involved any accepted medical principles. Both were described in terms of body currents as yet unmeasured. Brain waves, recorded as electroencephalograms, are well known. In England E. A. Eeman's work on body currents in London hospitals has attracted attention. In some ways his theories parallel the data in the Edgar Cayce readings on the appliances.

In terms of the Cayce data, both the idea of auras and body currents are based apparently on the concept that there exists a finer energy pattern in each of us which is the real physical body. The flesh body simply clothes this constantly moving, tenuous self. It seems possible that some types of hypnosis may involve a transference of energy from one body to another affecting these finer emanations. Susceptibility would then depend on mental, physical, and emotional rapport between the subject and the one giving the suggestions. This might account for the strange and almost complete response in some instances, while in others response to hypnotic suggestions is very slow. It is well known that some subjects respond better to one director than to another. It is generally assumed that this response is based on association of ideas; i.e., with a difficult subject, the hypnotist may unconsciously remind the subject of an uncle he disliked. The Edgar Cayce data seem to suggest that physical energy patterns may be involved in hypnosis.

Another method of hypnosis is concerned with the narrowing of attention, a kind of fixing of consciousness at one point until all other perception is excluded. This emphasis does not seem to allow for all the various phenomena possible under hypnosis. Neither do some of the ideas which exclusively relate hypnosis to sleep. Both brain-wave measurement and the basal metabolic rate indicate that hypnosis is more in line with consciousness than with sleep.

Other theories regarding hypnosis deal with reaching different levels of the unconscious. Pierre Janet, as well as F. W. H. Myers, held concepts along these lines.

Certainly it must be recognized that hypnosis begins with the willingness of the conscious mind to take suggestion. To some degree all people are suggestible. This is the basic premise of advertising. When suggestions are made, as in the case of hypnosis, for relaxation and sleep, which are already accepted as agreeable and pleasant experiences, one has a natural tendency to focus attention and follow the suggestion. There is involved also an unmeasured and little understood willingness of a hypnotic subject to obey the suggestions of the hypnotist. This may arise from several factors, such as the need of many people to be directed or led, a desire to get rid of responsibility, or the well-known childhood attitude of appreciating the authority exercised by an older person. Modern psychology has added a great deal to our understanding of the willingness of people to follow suggestion.

At a certain point, when suggestions for relaxation, tiredness, and sleep are continued, the suggestions evidently reach the doorway to the unconscious. An area of the mind accepts suggestion and acts upon it. When such stages are reached, control of the physical body is phenomenal; memory is considerably extended; and hallucinations of the strangest kinds may be induced. Any one or any combination of three of the five senses, seeing, hearing, feeling, can be used as the avenue to the unconscious' doorway. The eyes grow tired by looking at a bright object or a small light. A repetitious sound such as the slow beat of a metronome or the ticking of a clock quiets the conscious mind; or the repetitious stroking of some area of the body may induce hypnosis. Through these means attention is apparently focused, preparing first the conscious, then an unconscious area of the mind, to accept the repeated suggestion.

Hypnosis may be divided into several states, according to the area of the unconscious which is reached: (1) A light hypnosis, wherein the conscious mind is quieted and the body is relaxed and gradually grows tired and sleepy. Consciousness is retained. (2) In a medium stage consciousness remains but it is possible to induce muscular rigidity or a sense of lightness in one of the limbs. Some degree of insensitivity may also be induced. (3) In a deeper stage it is possible to close off conscious memory, induce insensitivity of areas of the body, and produce actual changes in the skin tissue such as red splotches or even, in good subjects, blisters without heat. Also in this stage, unusual hallucinations may be brought about, as well as age regression—the ability to remember details of childhood experiences, consciously forgotten. Suggestions for action or speech to be acted upon after the subject is fully conscious—post suggestions—may also be given during this third stage.

Hallucinations which can be produced under hypnosis vary according to the susceptibility of the subject and the skill of the hypnotist. A reasonably good subject will weep eating an apple if told it is an onion. A more disturbing hallucination can result from suggesting to the hypnotized subject that a certain person is leaving the room. With eyes that do not see, the subject watches the person go to the door, open and close it. He is assured by repeated suggestion that the person is no longer present and will remain out of the room after the subject is awakened. When the subject is brought back to consciousness he actually cannot see the person, and objects he picks up seem to float in the air. The subject may think it is a trick, but nevertheless frequently becomes frightened as the strange movements continue. An incident of this kind took place in France during the series of experiments mentioned earlier, when our hypnotist tried this type of suggestion on our captain. One evening we watched this dignified gentleman crawl under a bed as he became frightened at cigarettes and a football floating up to him.

Some hypnotic subjects who can be regressed can be taken back in time to childhood and give vivid descriptions of seating arrangements in first or second grade or a detailed account of a birthday party at four years of age. When such data can be checked, it is sometimes found that the story has been completely fabricated to "satisfy" the hypnotist, but more often it is found to be accurate to the smallest detail. Some investigators believe that the unconscious memory of the period from conception to birth can be tapped under hypnosis. Obviously such information is difficult to check.

Back of the point of conception lies the unknown. Can hypnosis open the door into this area? Bridey Murphy, the subject of Morey Bernstein's book on a "regression" to a past life under hypnosis, was the subject of a public controversy which spread like a grass fire over England, Ireland, and America. There seemed to have been a great deal of smoke—there was also some fire. If man has stored within him memories of past lives, the key to those memories may be hypnosis.

It is true that several psychologists have found that hypnotic subjects have fabricated so-called past lives from books they have read or from motion pictures or television shows. But can it be said that all of the memories being brought to light in this fashion are fabrications? Much carefully controlled work must be done before all the answers can be given.

Between 1948 and 1954 Linn F. Cooper, M.D., and Milton H. Erickson, M.D., conducted a series of experiments dealing with time distortion under hypnosis. In their conclusions it is stated that a person under hypnosis can be made to experience ten events of a similar nature in five seconds; then in another five-second interval he can be made to experience one thousand similar events. Thought can apparently take place with extreme rapidity under suggestion. Thus therapy which would ordinarily have taken many tedious hours was for an impressive number of patients speeded up.

It should be remembered that subjects differ widely. Hypnotists agree that a large percentage of so-called normal people can be hypnotized. It is an established fact that mental patients are poor hypnotic subjects. Children are generally excellent subjects. There is considerable difference of opinion as to whether one can be hypnotized against his will. Much depends on the ingenuity of the hypnotist and the attitude of the subject. Perhaps the unconscious attitude has more effect than the conscious one. For example, though a person may say that he wants desperately to be hypnotized, he may prove to be a most difficult subject; while one who claims the opposite may subconsciously desire to be the center of attention and prove an excellent subject. Generally speaking, it is not possible to hypnotize someone against his will.

Thoughtful observation and thorough records will convince anyone experimenting with hypnosis that there is an almost tangible link between the mind of the hypnotist and his subject. The subject wishes to do exactly what is asked of him: he can make an arm rigid and hold it in an extended position far beyond conscious endurance; he will put himself in embarrassing situations, bark like a dog or crawl like a snake, ignoring a laughing audience; he will produce so-called facts that are only fabrications, to please the hypnotist. Many of the books on hypnosis discuss the sex factor, since a bridge of affection between hypnotist and subject seems to be built up under repeated experiments. Perhaps this is due to a return to a childish state where authority is needed and desired. The mother or father image may enter the relationship. Or perhaps man is related at the level of the mind in some fashion that we only dimly glimpse. As the area called the collective unconscious is stirred a sense of rapport is created. I believe it is safe to say that these questions raised regarding hypnosis indicate how little we know about the mind of man.

Any good book on medical hypnosis recounts case histories in both number and range which may amaze the average lay person unfamiliar with the widespread use of it. A *Handbook of Medical Hypnosis,* by Gordon Ambrose and George Newbold, mentions such figures as the following:

"In children it should be considered a rule that some form of relaxation, with or without hypnotic suggestion, should be practiced; and the practitioner will often be astounded by the ease of inducing hypnosis in children. Over sixty per cent of them can reach deep hypnosis, and thus analgesia for such simple operations as lumbar puncture, venesection, incisions, etc., can easily and rapidly be obtained."

The same work states that one doctor in dealing with thumb sucking treated twenty children with this method. Eighteen of them ceased the habit with one treatment; the other two required only two treatments. The doctor emphasized the ease in inducing the hypnoidal state and mentioned that every child he treated could be hypnotized.

There are many obvious difficulties in using hypnosis as a doorway into the unconscious. Not all people are good subjects. Furthermore, experiments in hypnosis can become extremely boring and tiring procedures. And not to be ignored are the misgivings the average person may have about hypnosis, conditioned by misunderstanding and misinformation on the subject. In dealing with specific dangers, it seems to me justifiable to raise certain questions:

It seems possible that under hypnosis areas of the subconscious might be opened up, which if brought into consciousness, could become extremely disturbing factors in one's everyday experience. For example, a child who had been frightened by an animal of some kind and who had forgotten the incident might under hypnosis be able to recall the experience and become consciously very disturbed as a result. To handle such cases the hypnotist should be well grounded in techniques for closing off undesirable memories by suggestion. Even more important, he should recognize the existence of "dark" areas of experience in every person.

Another case history from our series of army experiments will illustrate this point. The excellence of the hypnotist, the availability of good subjects, and plenty of time combined to provide some thought-provoking incidents. In this case we tried age regression to a supposed past life. The young man spent considerable time describing details of what he claimed was a life experience in Colonial America. A name, occupation, location, etc., were given. Suddenly the subject became agitated and came back to consciousness before suggestions for erasing the memory could be given. In a very few minutes the group of G.I.'s had what appeared to be a confused, frightened Colonial American in a French chateau in 1941. It appeared that the story of the Connecticut Yankee in King Arthur's court had been reversed. The subject did not appear to know his name except as the Colonial American. He wrote this in what seemed to be a completely different handwriting from that he usually used. As quickly as possible he was put back into a hypnotic trance and awakened in a normal state. A period of emotional disturbance followed this experience. Several years ago I was approached by a group of young men in an Eastern city who were experimenting with hypnosis. They had discovered that both clairvoyance and telepathy seemed to be occurring with some of their hypnotic subjects. I urged them to discontinue further experimentation, however, since the best subject was apparently growing extremely nervous. He was showing signs of quick, unpredictable movements of the hands and feet and slight twitching of the eyes and facial muscles. The hypnotist had kept a very careful journal of the experiments and also a personal diary. Fortunately, his subject, who had begun to demonstrate what seemed to be clairvoyance and telepathy, had also kept a journal.

A comparison of their records, supplemented by private conferences, raised several questions regarding hypnosis which neither study nor experimental work so far has answered for me. For example, in a series of experiments involving deep hypnosis, how much travels from one unconscious mind to the other without conscious knowledge?

Several months after first meeting this group the hypnotist and subject came to me to discuss personal marriage problems. During the period when he worked several times a week with his subject, the hypnotist had begun reading pornographic publications. In questioning those who made up the group, it was discovered that the hypnotist had not mentioned this literature to anyone. He did, however, record this fact in his diary. During the same period his subject began looking for and reading the same kind of filth. His journal noted with surprise these drives and urges which had not previously troubled him. Both men were married and had children. Is it possible that the interest in this subject and the desire to pursue this kind of reading passed from the unconscious of the hypnotist to the unconscious of the hypnotic subject? The effects of such unconscious transference might possibly become more dangerous than the conscious control exercised over a subject. Subsequent to this, both the hypnotist and the subject began beating their wives. How much of the confusion and contention was transferred from the unconscious of the hypnotist to arouse the latent antagonism and rebelliousness within the unconscious of the hypnotic subject? Each case differs according to the suggestibility of the subject, the forcefulness of the hypnotist, and the "condition" of their respective unconsciousness.

Such transference must follow a pattern of attraction. It would be illogical to believe that a completely negative set of urges could be transferred from one unconscious to another unless there existed some attraction—some area of agreement—in the unconscious of the hypnotic subject. It is possible to theorize that the two negative areas stimulated each other until they erupted into consciousness. A hypnotist should be very careful to use all possible techniques of suggestion to release completely and close the door of the unconscious.

Jan Ehrenwald, M.D., in a book previously mentioned, writes, "... it goes without saying that nobody can possibly eliminate in his approach to his fellow man a certain number of unconscious wishes and expectations, unformulated thoughts and ideas that might, under favorable conditions, become telepathically active." The hypnotic state may certainly be considered a "favorable condition."

Some subjects may come out of hypnotic sessions with what appear to be either split personalities or possessing entities speaking through them. This may or may not be a good result, depending on the understanding and perception of the individual involved. If one wished to become a medium, hypnosis might be of help in developing such ability. On the other hand, a person having what appears to be some psychic sensitivity, who did not wish to be mediumistic, might find himself dealing with a problem of considerable proportions. Split personality is the presently accepted psychological term which describes the condition that exists when an area of an individual's unconscious assumes the identity of an authority figure. Sometimes this is a relative who it is hoped continues to live in another world or a romantically mysterious figure like a space man or a priest of some ancient country. The drive for recognition, wish fulfillment, or the desire for control of others can be the motivating urge. If the unconscious claims to be a separate personality, it should be required to establish its identity. The collection of such proofs has been one of the major goals of psychical research. For many the evidence for distinct personalities is conclusive. Others continue the search. It seems that some individuals are more susceptible to psychic experiences than others and that the suppression of consciousness at times allows a break in the unconscious. Whether the theory of discarnates is allowed or the split personality offered as the explanation, hypnosis apparently can produce mediumistic like abilities in some sensitive individuals.

Let me take a few pages from my notebook recounting the development of one of our currently active "psychic readers." Early in the summer of 1945 a twenty-seven-year-old business woman, living in one of our large Midwestern cities, attended a lecture by a metaphysical teacher on the "Power of Mind." Prior to this time she had no interest in spiritualism or related subjects. Following this lecture she began having some strange experiences of seeing lights in darkness and sensing peculiar flickering sensations in conscious perception. She sought help from a close doctor friend of her father.

For almost six months the doctor worked with her once or twice a week, using suggestion. During this period he taught her self-hypnosis, using the ticking of a clock as the repetitious sound on which to focus attention. The doctor read to her long passages from the works of Jacob Boehme. Finally a deep state of sleep was possible. At this point a voice apparently speaking through the young woman indicated that the doctor had completed his work. The voice identified itself as a physician who had been dead for several years and who was to work through the young woman. She was directed to give up her job and begin teaching, allowing him (the control) to speak through her.

The young woman sought help from her friends in evaluating the information which came through her. With their encouragement she gave up her regular job and began giving lectures, classes, and individual readings for people who asked help. From personal counseling and inspirational lectures the work developed into individual karmic readings dealing with descriptions of past lives. Hundreds of persons throughout the country have had such readings. Some say that they have been helped by the advice; others think of the information as being too general to be of value. As with all such data, careful study and documentation are necessary before an evaluation can be made.

When asked how she protects herself, this "sensitive" pointed to the months of preparation and training under the doctor's care. She also spoke of the high purposes and ideals expressed by the controlling voice. She further explained that prior to each session she used the following affirmation: "I am now surrounded by the light of the Christ. Nothing but that which is true and useful can be spoken through me."

She still listens to the ticking of a clock, then touches the center of her forehead three times, once for the body, once for the mind, once for the soul. A shade seems to be drawn aside and she begins to lose consciousness.

I have described this woman's experiences in some detail because they seem to represent a typical use of hypnosis in developing mediumship or what would be called by some a split personality. As I have observed, the individual involved most surely has many physical and emotional problems. At the same time she is certainly in many ways a capable and interesting person.

It would seem wise that people working with hypnosis recognize it as a sharp knife. If used skillfully, under the right circumstances and for the right purpose, it is an excellent therapy and can be a fine avenue for experimentation. It should not be considered a parlor game or a means of entertainment.

Hypnosis was recommended as early as 1911 in the Edgar Cayce readings. In one case it was part of the treatment for a brain lesion, and in another case it was recommended for extreme nervousness which had produced various functional disturbances. In 1922 the treatment recommended for partial throat paralysis included hypnosis. For several cases of mental disturbances involving hallucinations and others of retarded development, hypnotic suggestion was part of the treatment. In none of the nine cases examined was hypnosis the only treatment recommended.

In one instance the following question was asked: "Under hypnosis could I become a reliable vehicle for the transmission of clairvoyant perception?" The answer in the reading was as follows: "Best let hypnosis alone for this body, unless you wish to hypnotize someone else. Practice it within yourself. Let it be self that would be subdued and give the authority to God, not man— through man, but to God." (3343-1)

In another instance in connection with a retarded child he warned, "It [hypnosis] might be used, but be mindful of who would use same." (146-3)

Hypnosis was suggested for a girl nineteen, who suffered from mental difficulties. The connection between spinal pressures and the endocrine glands was indicated. "Physically, there are hindrances in the coccyx and in the lumbar axis, which cause a reaction to the pineal . . . " (1996-1) Sensory and emotional problems were implied.

What conclusions can be reached as to the value of hypnosis as a

safe doorway to the unconscious? Men who developed special techniques and whose personalities fitted the part became tribal witch
doctors in primitive societies, or Franz Mesmers in more advanced
cultures. Alternately, such persons have been worshiped or perse-
cuted, depending on what authorities' toes they treaded upon. In
my opinion hypnosis is a very excellent doorway into the unconscious. In fact it is such an excellent one that it should be used with
greatest care. The rapid developments taking place in psychosomatic medicine, as well as in the field of endocrinology, may reveal
new powers of the unconscious which so far have been only the
subject of speculation. Hypnosis may play a very important part in
the new discoveries. Men fear the use of great atomic forces which
they now have at their disposal. Perhaps they should be in even
greater fear of the tremendous powers of mind which can be awakened. "The secret of the Lord is with them that fear him . . ." (Ps. 25:
14)

2

Mediumship

"GREETINGS, MY FRIENDS! This is Maja speaking to you from the fifth plane. May the peace of the ancients be with you. What is desired of me?" The voice came from an attractive middle-aged woman who sat in a comfortable chair across the small room from me. Her eyes were closed. The deep breathing which had preceded the voice had given way to a more normal rhythm. The sunlight streamed through the venetian blinds forming triangles, squares, and rectangles of light and shadow on the tiletex floor. Mrs. X. was beginning a seance. She was supposed to have lost consciousness. Her guide, a heavenly being who had never been on earth, had taken over the control of her body to use her voice. The time was October, 1958. The place, Virginia Beach.

Maja was known, under another name, to hundreds of persons throughout the country. He would introduce in turns some disincarnates, people who had lived on the earth, "wise ones" like himself who had never incarnated and perhaps one or more space people who claimed to be hovering in their space craft, far above the earth, observing our troubled civilization.

The tape recorder was running now; a friend of the medium sat nearby to regulate the volume control. I would carry on a conversation with "the voices" for approximately an hour. In the short pause after the first remark from the medium my mind flickered to the questions which arose each time I witnessed such seances.

Is this woman consciously faking, weaving together facts and fancy as one would tell a story to children?

Has some part of her unconscious split off from her normal consciousness to create another personality which acts out the parts of the dead, space people, and others? Is she crazy and doesn't know it?

Is it possible that whatever lives on of a dead person can "possess" a body like this and speak through her, pretending to be different beings?

If there are space people, could or would they talk through such a medium?

Whatever one may think, this was an interesting doorway to the labyrinth of the mind.

A distinction between cases of psychosis and individuals who may be classed as mediums should be made. In severe mental disorders a dissociation with rational thought and action occurs. With mediumistic phenomena the person allows and frequently seeks to be a channel for "a force" or "information" which seems to come from outside himself. Such a person might be thought of as being capable of allowing an area of the unconscious to operate which opens on other than our three-dimensional world. The average psychologist or psychiatrist probably would classify a medium as a person who allowed or sought dissociation of personality by attempting to operate from a physically unconscious level.

Training for mediumship frequently takes place through hypnosis and/or under trance (sleep) states which are allowed to rise from the unconscious level to take over consciousness. Untrained spiritualistic mediums have a natural tendency to depreciate the activity of their own unconscious minds and depend on what are believed to be disincarnate entities for telepathic, clairvoyant, or precognitive perception. Such dependence may arise from a desire to place responsibility outside of themselves or a wish to give their information a note of authority. Is the unconscious of the medium always the actor?

The literature of psychical research, especially the Proceedings of the British and American Societies and publications based on studies made in connection with investigations of these societies, provide impressive evidence for the survival hypothesis and communications through mediumistic capacities. The average person is as unfamiliar with this literature as he is with technical papers on relativity. Some of these ideas arouse deep-seated fears of the unknown in people. The result is that they feel and talk negatively about these subjects on which they are inadequately informed.

Unfortunately, too, there has been and still exists a great deal of fraud in the practice of mediumship. The strong compulsions of attracting attention, being considered an authority, or escaping from the monotony of everyday reality are surpassed only by the drive for making money.

Studies on the life and work of many remarkable mediums are readily available. The list is long. The following are only a few whose work has convinced some of the outstanding investigators of psychic phenomena of their times that some aspect of man survives bodily death: Mrs. Lenore C. Piper, well-known Boston medium; Mrs. Gladys Osborne Leonard, English medium and the subject of many studies published in the Proceedings of the British Society for Psychical Research; D. D. Home, an internationally known "physical medium"; Arthur Ford, American psychic, whose autobiography, *Nothing So Strange,* has attracted considerable attention; and Eileen J. Garrett, psychic, author, publisher, and sponsor of scientific investigations of psychic phenomena.

Some type of physical phenomenon, such as the movement of objects or the production of a body secretion called "ectoplasm," is said to take place in the presence of some mediums. Others provide only information through voice or writing which seems evidential in that it is data supposedly known only to a disincarnate relative, or a spirit who acts as a control allowing only certain entities to use the "sensitive." Such persons are known as mental mediums. A brief survey of the work of two mediums, one in each class, will assist in characterizing individuals possessed of such capacities.

Daniel Dunglas Home was an outstanding physical medium. He was born in Scotland in 1833 and reared by an aunt in Connecticut. At seventeen he was forced to leave home because he was thought to be possessed of the devil. Strange movements of objects took place around him. Home was befriended by neighbors and in 1852 was investigated by William Cullen Bryant and Professor David Wells. Reports were favorable to his strange power to move objects without coming in contact with them. A trip to England in 1855 brought him in touch with some of the best-known men and women of his day and led to his appearance in both French and Russian courts.

Sir William Crookes, British physicist famous for his inventions which improved the vacuum tube which was a forerunner of the modern X-ray tube, investigated Home and reported most favorably on his powers to move objects without physical contact. In one such test Home in trance in Crookes's laboratory was able to make a small accordion play inside a wire case. At another session three reputable witnesses testified to seeing Home levitate his own body out one window and back into an adjoining room through another window. Both windows were seventy feet from the ground.

There were periods when Home's powers deserted him, once for as long as a year. When this happened he said so and refused to attempt seances. Though he lectured for money and accepted gifts, he never made a charge for his trance sittings. Home remains the most remarkable of physical mediums on record in the last several centuries.

After reading accounts of the investigations of D. D. Home it seems logical to consider, before going on to mental mediumship, the question which Dr. W. Y. Evans-Wentz puts forward in the introduction to *Tibet's Great Yogi, Milarepa* by Lama Kazi Dawa-Samdup.

"Are there," Dr. Evans-Wentz says he has been asked, "members of the human race who have reached, as Milarepa is believed to have done, the height of such spiritual and physical evolution as this planet admits, and who, being as it were, a species apart from other human beings, are possessed of mastery over natural forces as yet undiscovered, but probably suspected, by Western Science?"

Dr. Evans-Wentz continues, "This, it seems to us, is the most important anthropological question which Milarepa's biography raises."

As author of *The Tibetan Book of the Dead, Tibetan Yoga and Se-*

cret Doctrines, The Tibetan Book of the Great Liberation, and other scholarly works on early religious beliefs, Dr. Evans-Wentz has an interesting background from which to raise such a question.

The introduction from *The Tibetan* by Rechung, disciple of Milarepa, claims for his master, powers which are reminiscent of Elisha or Elijah of Old Testament fame, for whom axes floated and fire came down from heaven. Among a long list of spiritual attainments, Rechung states that Milarepa could talk to dumb beasts; overcome all dangers from the elements and direct them to his own profit and use; fly through the sky; walk, rest, or sleep in the air; produce springs of water or fire from his own body; project his subtle body, supposedly an energy pattern less dense than the flesh body, to shrines and temples; and cure chronic diseases.

The time of Milarepa's birth (probably around A.D. 1052) and the place, Tibet, were a long way from Home's birth in 1833, in Scotland. Milarepa's different kind of search for enlightenment brought occult powers which were only "by-products," natural results of the growth of spiritual awareness. Yet, they were very similar in some respects to those claimed for Home in the nineteenth century.

Mental mediumship was ably demonstrated by Mrs. Lenore Piper of Boston during the latter part of the nineteenth century and the early part of the twentieth. During the beginning years much of Mrs. Piper's information was supposedly given by "Phenuit," a French doctor who lived about 1790. William James, the outstanding American psychologist, investigated Mrs. Piper. His reports on her work were most favorable. In 1887 Richard Hodgson, an Australian, who had just completed a rather discrediting investigation of Mme. Blavatsky, one of the founders of Theosophy, began a study of the Piper phenomenon. An interesting series of communications were given through Mrs. Piper, supposedly from a friend of Hodgson who before his death had promised to communicate with him. In trance she was able to identify many friends of the dead man whom she had never seen and supply data about them of the most evidential nature. Mrs. Piper was invited to England and was there tested by the British Society's Research Council. Her work brought favorable comments from many of the founders of both the British and American Societies for Psychical Research. She raised questions which have never been answered about evidence for survival of personality after bodily death.

I would like to make several comments, in considering the data from the Edgar Cayce records dealing with mediumistic-type communication. In the usual sense Edgar Cayce was not a medium. His voice was always his own. No guides or controls came forward to identify themselves and take over his physical body. In communicating with the minds of people either living or dead, the flow of information seemed to come through his own unconscious. Even when in a few instances specific entities were mentioned as the source of the data, there seemed to be an attunement of Edgar Cayce's unconscious mind with theirs. His voice and body were not affected. The physical body may be only a small part of the real self, the total "entity" or soul. It seems that in certain degrees of unconsciousness there are areas which may be doorways to coexistent dimensions of mental activity. When movement in consciousness, sometimes called loss of physical consciousness, takes place, the more extended self is able to "see," "feel," "hear"—know—beyond what we now sense of time space. Certainly Edgar Cayce's experiences describe this type of movement in consciousness and perception in other dimensions. Mediumship may, it seems to me, be extended by definition to include the mental bridges between coexisting states of mental activity in time-space, as well as those between the so-called dead and the living.

Approximately thirty-seven times Edgar Cayce began speaking after the conclusion of statements constituting the reading. In all of these instances it seemed that he had moved in consciousness to another position. He was no longer seeing or "in touch with" the person for whom information was given. In some of these instances he described a scene in what he called time-space; in others he gave information on other people, and in some cases he stopped to talk with people who were dead.

The following was given January 24, 1925, at the end of a reading interpreting a dream:

> Have some terribly hard times in China today. In the Manchurian region, a flood and fire both. Many peoples are passing into the borderland, their entities taking their position as has been manifest through their environment in the earth plane at present time. There are those conditions arising from this great boredom in the consciousness of many that will

bring the revolution in the minds of many peoples ... 3976-3

The reading goes on to suggest that China will be the birthplace of the next great revival of Christianity. In the light of the theory of reincarnation, perhaps the years of missionary work have not been lost, as those who were trained in Christian teachings are reborn.

On June 14, 1932, one of the most unusual bits of voluntary information ever given by Edgar Cayce followed a physical reading which described normal body ailments. The complete suggestion to awaken him had been given three times.

Here with the Master. See what they have for supper—boiled fish, rice with leeks, wine and loaf. One of the pitchers in which it is served is broken. The handle is broken as is the lip to same. The Master's hair is most red, inclined to be curly in portions. Yet he is not feminine nor weak but strong—with heavy piercing eyes that are blue or steel-gray. His weight would be at least a hundred and seventy pounds. He has long tapering fingers. The nails are well kept with a long nail, though, on the left little finger. He is merry even in the hour of trial. He jokes even in the moment of betrayal. The whole robe of the Master is not white but pearl gray—all combined in one, the gift of Nicodemus to the Lord.

The better looking of the twelve is, of course, Judas; while the younger is John with oval face, dark hair, smooth face—the only one with short hair. Peter, the rough and ready, has a very short beard—rough and not altogether clean. Andrew's is just the opposite—very sparse but inclined to be long more on the side and under the chin, long on the upper lip. Andrew's robe was always near gray or black while his clouts or breeches were striped. Those of Philip and Bartholomew were red and brown.

The sack is empty. Judas departs. The last is given of the wine and loaf. The Master lays aside his robe which is all of one piece. He girds the towel about his waist which is dressed with linen that is blue and white. He rolls back the folds and kneels first before John, then James—then to Peter, who refuses. Now comes the dissertation as to "He that would be greatest among you should be the servant of all." The basin

used is without handle and is made of wood. The water is from
the gherkins that are in the wide-mouth shibboleths that
stand in the house of John's father, Zebedee.

And now comes, "I have finished . . . " They sing the ninety-
first Psalm: "He that dwelleth in the secret place of the Most
High shall abide under the shadow of the Almighty. I will say
of the Lord He is my refuge and my fortress; my God; in Him
will I trust." He is the musician as well for He uses the harp.

They leave for the garden. 5749-1

Some few of the unrequested readings contain what seem to be
evidential bits of communication. In volume this is not impressive.
However, others give interesting descriptions of the conditions in
this "unknown country" which we enter at death. As has already
been pointed out, there are too few travelers who can describe their
experiences. In this light, the following may be considered:

While living in Selma, Alabama (1912-1923), Edgar and Gertrude
Cayce became well acquainted with a Dr. S. Gay. As the family physician, he operated on Edgar Cayce for appendicitis and delivered
the child Edgar Evans, born to Gertrude Cayce while in Selma. Dr.
Gay died while the Cayces were still in Selma.

On May 6, 1929, in Virginia Beach, following a reading for two
men who were in distant cities, and after Gertrude Cayce had given
the suggestion for Edgar Cayce to wake up, the following was given
voluntarily in Edgar Cayce's normal speaking voice:

Here, Sister, before you change this, let me give you a little
piece of advice concerning what you are working with. There
are many questions often asked you, and you often feel others
are not considerate of the position you occupy, with the forces
as are manifested through Cayce. These are the things that will
possibly aid you in understanding just what takes place, and
as to how you—personally —may assist or may aid the individual seeking to know that as may be helpful, beneficial to
themselves or their loved ones; or, where others seek to gain
for themselves that same experience of the position you, yourself, now occupy in obtaining for others or for self such information.

This is the condition that is ever present when such information is obtained: When the consciousness is laid aside, there is that as takes place much in the same manner as the spring to an automatic curtain roller. This then is able to be pulled down or raised up with the release of the spring. Some call this going into the unknown. Some call this spiritual, or spirit communication. Some call it the ability to gain the force of the activities of the fourth dimension—which is nearer correct than any explanation that may be given—the plane that is of the inter-between, or that of the borderland. All individuals occupy this plane through that period of the gaining of the consciousness of that sphere they themselves occupy, until such a period or such a time that there is that joining together of such forces as may again bring that individual entity into the realm of physical experience or being. Now each individual seeks experiences, see? Each individual must experience conditions in order to make them a portion of the total record of himself as an entity functioning in many planes of consciousness. Then, know whenever there is the whole-hearted desire of all [those on the earth and the plane of communication] there may be the perfect action of the roller or spring, or there may be the perfect application of the information that may be gained. But Sister, know this, whenever you, yourself, are in the position of the questioner, or the one seeking to gain for another such information, call on me. I will answer. This is Gay. We are through. 538-28

This appears to be a direct telepathic type of communication. In this one the personality of Edgar Cayce does not seem to be talking with another personality (Gay). The thoughts apparently are acting directly through the subconscious. Is it possible that Edgar Cayce moved to Gay's plane of consciousness and there was in direct contact—rather than Gay's moving to the level of physical consciousness? Gay's explanation of the phenomena of the readings as "activities of the fourth dimension" fits this idea of movement in consciousness.

Notice that he mentions rebirth. Gay was not known to have accepted the idea of reincarnation. This subject was not a part of Edgar Cayce's physical consciousness until life readings began in Dayton years after Gay died. There is nothing conclusive about this either way—for or against the idea of rebirth. It is simply an interesting note on communication dealing with ideas which were not part of the doctor's thought process at death.

Gay seems aware of at least some of Gertrude Cayce's attitudes and thought patterns. This could have come from Edgar Cayce's subconscious, masquerading as Gay, of course. In this light, however, it is curious that Gay phrases his last suggestion as he did. Gertrude Cayce conducted practically all the readings when this communication came through. When Gay knew Cayce on the earth plane, various people acted as conductors. Time seems out of focus.

The following is a different type of communication which came after two check physical readings on April 10, 1929. This unsolicited information begins:

Now there are many here that would speak concerning the various things as have been given regarding the educational end of the institutional work. Three would speak concerning the varied approach, of the way as given by each.

As we find, Robertson would say—In the presentation of the pamphlets as lessons, the spectacular of each individual experience is an approach.

While we find Funk would say—The reason and the self-application would be the better approach.

While we find as is presented by Hudson—That the way of individual approach is the manner that should be presented in any information as is given to the public, knowing that—as has so often been said—this is first to the individual, then to the classes, then to the masses.

Classes being the classification under the three heads as may be presented under the teaching or the influence of each of these who were teachers in their physical experience. One the wanderer, the other the student, the other the reasoner— or the exhorter. In each field there is a class. While individuals differ, let the first principle be the starting point. ALL is One! We are through for the present. 5756-7

The Robertson referred to here may be Morgan Robertson, the American author whose sea stories reflect his years of experience as a sailor and an interest in the supernatural. Funk is possibly I. K.

Funk, world traveler, co-founder of Funk and Wagnalls of dictionary fame, and a man known for his scientific interest in psychical research. Hudson could be Thomson Jay Hudson, author of *The Law of Psychic Phenomena* and other books in this same field.

Here the communication is one of ideas rather than of description, but it also contains a definite reference to personalities existing in some level or plane of consciousness. It is possible that in movement through various levels Edgar Cayce became aware of these thought forms as attitudes held by these men. However, the reference which relates their ideas to activities in the present experience cannot be ignored as a possible type of communication.

There is another interesting kind of communication described in the readings which involves the theory of guardian angels. In one person's reading devoted to general questions, a guardian angel was described as an entity in another level of consciousness who was a brother in a prior incarnation in the earth. The ties are in the mental realm and have to do with ideas, ideals, purposes, etc. This would indicate that in the realm of the mind we are related to other souls much more closely than we are consciously aware. This relationship exists with entities both in and out of physical bodies. Angel is used here to describe a protective soul, not a celestial being.

On July 9, 1934, Gertrude Cayce, Gladys Davis, Mildred Davis, and L. B. Cayce were present to hear a check physical reading on the regular appointment schedule. After the reading was completed and the suggestion had been given for Edgar Cayce to wake up, he began speaking:

There are some here that would speak with those that are present, if they desire to so communicate with them.

Mrs. Cayce: We desire to have at this time that which would be given.

Mr. Cayce, after a long pause: Don't all speak at once. [pause] Yes, I knew you would be waiting . . . Yes? Haven't found him before? All together now, huh? Uncle Porter, too? He was able to ease it right away, huh? Who? Dr. House. No. Oh, no—no, she is all right. Yes, lots better. Isn't giving any trouble now . . . Haven't seen her? Why, where have you been? Oh. She is in another change? How long will they stay there? Oh, they don't count time like that . . . Oh, you do have 'em. Well, those must be pretty now, if they are all growing like that. Yes? Yes, I'll tell her about 'em. Tell Gertrude you are all together now, huh? Uncle Porter, Dr. House, your mother? And Grandma. Oh. Grandpa is still building? Oh, he made the house ... yeah? Tell Tommy what? Yes! Lynn? Yes, he's at home ... Oh, you knew that! Huh ... Ain't any difference? ... Well how about the weather? ... Oh, the weather doesn't affect you now—doesn't change ... Oh, you have what you want ... depends on where you go ... Sure, then you are subject to that anyway ... Little baby, too! How big is it? Oh, he is grown now, huh? Yes. Coming back! When? Oh! Uh-huh. All right ... Why? ... Oh yes, they hear you ... I'm sure they do. I hear you! ... For Gertrude? Yes, she is here ... she hears you. Oh, yes.

Mrs. C.: I don't hear. May I have the message?

Mr. C. [Continuing]: Sure, she hears you; don't you hear her talking? No, I don't know what she says.

Mrs. C.: I don't hear. Will you repeat the message for me?

Mr. C.: Mama and Dr. House and Uncle Porter and the baby ... we are all here. Grandpa has built the home here, and it's NICE! And we are all waiting until you come, and we will all be here ready ... we are getting along FINE, doing well, yes! No. No more troubles now, for spring borders all along the way [?]. For we have reached, together, that place where we see the light and know the pathway to the Savior is along the narrow way that leads to His throne. We are on that plane where you have heard it said that the body and the mind are one with those things we have built. Yes, I still play baseball, and Charlie has recently joined my club, and I am still captain to many of 'em. Well, we will be waiting for you! 5756-13

Through this we get a sense of movement on the part of some phase of Edgar Cayce's mind ... "I knew you would be waiting," and "... all along the way," etc. Evidently he stopped on the way back from the level of attunement from which the reading was given. He recognized several people who wished to communicate and began a conversation with them. Those present in the room when the reading was being given at first could hear only one side of the conversation. Then he repeated a specific message as given to him. This is similar to the communication from Dr. Gay.

A young man, evidently in his mind, continued the kind of physical activity ("I still play baseball") which he had enjoyed on earth. He died of tuberculosis and had been forced to give up the game during the last years of his life. The brother also speaks of a home being finished by the grandfather. This home had become a symbol of family stability and was "a point of return" when in trouble, for various members of a large family. The grandfather was building it when he died and it was added to during the young man's lifetime. The brother seems to have begun to recognize this home as a place on a path rather than as a "heaven" or stopping point.

Notice the references to the weather and a different measure of time. The persons mentioned all died at different times. The baby referred to may have been Gertrude and Edgar Cayce's child who had died while an infant. In this boy's mind, at least, growth had continued. Does the coming back refer to reincarnation? He did not believe in rebirth when he died.

On July 17, 1934, a reading was given by Edgar Cayce to explain the communications in the above reading given on July 9. The suggestion used and the major portion of the reading follow:

Suggestion: You will have before you the body and inquiring mind of Edgar Cayce and all present in this room, in regard to the experience following the reading Monday afternoon, July 9, 1934, explaining to us what happened ... and why at that particular time, answering the questions that may be asked.

Answer: Yes, we have the body, and the inquiring mind, Edgar Cayce, and those present in the room July 9, 1934.

In giving that which may be helpful, for the moment turn to that known as the body of self and by those present in the room respecting what is ordinarily termed spirit communication or ... should be (and that which has caused much of the dissension) ... soul communication. For the soul lives on and is released from a house of clay. The activities in the world of matter are only changed in their *relationships* to that which produces them and that which the physical body sees in material or three-dimensional form.

There were those that were in attune ... through the vibrations from that sounded in the room at that particular period ... and these sought (many—even many that spoke not) to communicate that there might be known not only their continued existence in a world of matter but of finer matter. They sought, through those channels through which the soul-force of the body was passing at the particular time, to produce that which would make their presence known.

Although the various communications given at the time were from those thought to be dead (from the physical viewpoint) or in other realms, yet their souls, their personalities, their individualities live on. The personalities are lost gradually . . . [as growth continues].

(Q) Why did we hear only one side of the conversation?

(A) Denseness of matter to the spirit realm. All who attuned themselves felt the presence of those influences. The Master said, "They that have ears to hear, let them hear." There be none so deaf as those who do not *want* to hear. All could hear if they would attune themselves to the realm of the activity during such an experience. The conversation dealt with matters that were to them, are to them, very vital in their experiences in the present plane.

How (some would ask) did the body, Edgar Cayce, or soul, attune self at that particular period and yet not remember in the physical consciousness? This is because *the soul passes from the body* into those realms where information may be obtained. Help was sought on the 9th of July for the physical condition of a body. This realm from which such information is obtainable is either from those that have passed into the realm of subconscious activity or from the subconscious and superconscious activity of the one through whom information is being sought. This particular body, Edgar Cayce, was able to attune self to the varied realms of activity by laying aside the physical consciousness. If the body, from its material and mental development, were to be wholly conscious of that through which it passes in its soul's activity in such realms, the strain would be too great. Material activity could be unbalanced and the body become demented. And he is thought crazy enough anyway! 5756-14

Following approximately seventeen life readings, Edgar Cayce remembered a dreamlike experience of passing through many different levels where activities are taking place. These may be thought of as planes, or states of consciousness, or dimensions. Apparently, he stopped at various levels when the previous communications were given. He described this as follows:

I see myself as a tiny dot out of my physical body, which lies inert before me. I find myself oppressed by darkness and there is a feeling of terrific loneliness. Suddenly, I am conscious of a beam of white light. As this tiny dot, I move upward in the light, knowing that I must follow it or be lost.

As I move along this path of light, I gradually become conscious of various levels upon which there is movement. Upon the first levels there are vague, horrible shapes, grotesque forms such as one sees in nightmares. Passing on, there begin to appear on either side misshapen forms of human beings with some part of the body magnified. Again there is change and I become conscious of gray-hooded forms moving downward. Gradually, these become lighter in color. Then the direction changes and these forms move upward and the color of the robes grows rapidly lighter. Next, there begin to appear on either side vague outlines of houses, walls, trees, etc., but everything is motionless. As I pass on, there is more light and movement in what appear to be normal cities and towns. With the growth of movement I become conscious of sounds, at first indistinct rumblings, then music, laughter, and singing of birds. There is more and more light, the colors become very beautiful, and there is only a blending of sound and color. Quite suddenly, I come upon a hall of records. It is a hall without walls, without a ceiling, but I am conscious of seeing an old man who hands me a large book, a record of the individual for whom I seek information.

In other accounts of similar experiences Edgar Cayce described what seemed to be classes where teachers were directing and training souls preparing to return to earth. Beyond the hall of records there were areas of color and music for which he could give no adequate word pictures.

In seeking information on communication through Edgar Cayce's readings by direct questions the following is a sample of ex-

planations obtained. Evidently entities occupy different positions
on these planes according to their development. A mental attunement could be set up with any of those within the range of, what
Edgar Cayce called, a sphere of communication. This is explained
in the following:

*(Q) Is it possible for this body, Edgar Cayce, in this state, to
communicate with anyone who has passed into the spirit
world?*
(A) The spirit of all who have passed from the physical
plane remains about the plane until its development either
carries it onward or returns it here. When it is in the plane of
communication, or within this sphere, it may be communicated with. There are thousands about us here at present.
*(Q) To what place or state does the subconscious pass to re-
ceive this information it gives?*
(A) Just here in the same sphere as when the spirit and soul
are driven or removed from the body or the person. 3744-2

*(Q) What is meant by "souls within this sphere may be com-
municated with by Edgar Cayce in the psychic state"?*
(A) Each and every soul entity, or earthly entity passing
through the earth's plane, leaves in that plane those conditions that are impressions from the soul or spiritual entity of
the individual. This then becomes the fact, the real fact, in the
material world.
The body, Edgar Cayce, in the psychic or subconscious
condition, is able to reach all subconscious minds, when directed to such by suggestion—whether in the material world
or in the spiritual world, provided the spiritual entity has not
passed entirely into another level. Then we reach only those
radiations left in the earth's plane. These are taken on again
when re-entering the earth's plane, whether the entity is conscious of the same or not. *The consciousness of this movement
and development must (eventually) be reached by all.* 900-22

... the physical world, and the cosmic world, or the astral
world, are one—for the consciousness, the sensuous consciousness, is as the growth from the subconsciousness into

the material world. The growth in the astral world is the digesting and the building of that same oneness in the spirit, the conscious, the subconscious, the cosmic. We find, from one to another, individuals are retained in that oneness, until each is made one in the Great Whole—the Creative Energy of the Universal Forces as are ever manifest in the material plane. 5756-4

To summarize: It is indicated that death does not necessarily bring immediate spiritual enlightenment. Communication is controlled by attunement established on both planes There must be a mutual desire. Much communication may take place with thought impressions. Stress is placed on the physical plane as just one level of consciousness, part of a whole, like a room in a house.

Sometimes places or houses act as mediums, it would seem. My notebook contains several accounts of purported haunted houses. Here is one which raises a number of questions in my mind.

By coincidence the phone rang one evening just as I had turned on the television to catch the late news after coming in from a meeting. As the scene filled in on the screen I was face to face with a very lively television ghost who was materializing in front of three frightened people. The phone rang again and I answered.

The voice at the other end of the wire sounded strained and hesitant: "Your name was given me by friends who said you might be able to help us." The man introduced himself as Captain _____ from a suburb of Norfolk. I asked what sort of problem was involved and again there was hesitation. Then Captain _____ continued, "I don't want you to think we are crazy but we seem to have a ghost in our house."

At this point I thought one of my teenage friends was playing a joke on me. I even thought of an old friend who calls up now and then and impersonates a variety of people. Once he was the American Express agent trying to deliver a crate of mosquitoes of Wisconsin variety. Then as the captain became a bit hysterical I realized that this might well be a genuine problem. I invited him to bring his family to see me the next morning. At ten o'clock Captain _____ with his wife, a baby in arms, and a small daughter of six were in my office. They told a strange story.

The family had moved to the Norfolk area less than a year before.

Houses were scarce at the time, so they rented an old house which had apparently been empty for some time. They made no demands through the agent who indicated that the owner would take a moderate rent if no requests for repairs or redecoration were made. Both Captain_____ and his wife insisted that they did not talk with anyone but the agent. It wasn't for several weeks, in fact not until they began to be disturbed by "the presence" in the house, that they asked neighbors about the history of the house.

Within the first week both the man and his wife claimed to have felt depressed and disturbed. They began to hear independently and while together peculiar noises, especially from one upstairs bedroom. The six-year-old daughter began asking her mother and father about the noises. She refused to go into the room.

One evening while sitting in the downstairs living room all three of the family heard a distinct noise in the bedroom. The captain described it as the sound of a seaman's bag being dragged across the floor. This was followed by the clacking of the latch, the type which is pressed down with the thumb to release the catch, on the door to the hall. After this evening the noises in the house increased and finally were heard in the hall and living room when the family was in the kitchen. The family dog became a coward and refused to leave Mrs._____ except to go outside. The sense of the presence of someone or something in the house grew so oppressive that the family had moved into one of the three upstairs bedrooms. The master bedroom where the noises were heard was deserted. Finally, the captain said the noises grew so bad they began to inquire of neighbors about the house and they were told a rather gruesome story.

The couple who had previously lived in the house had quarreled bitterly over the husband's heavy drinking. After a series of scenes which were described in detail by the neighbors, the woman left the man in a drunken state. As the house was closed the neighbors assumed both man and wife had left, so almost a week passed before the wife returned to find the husband dead in the upstairs master bedroom. Apparently in a state of depression he had shot himself. Then, suffering and bleeding profusely, he had tried to get to the bedroom door. There he had collapsed and died.

After hearing the story, as might be expected, the noises had seemed to the captain and his wife to grow much worse. When questioned closely, the couple described soft tappings on various pieces of furniture; a sound of dragging of a heavy, soft object; the clack of the door latch, though no movement was ever seen; the clatter and movement of pieces of a fireplace set; thumping in the upstairs hall; the sense of a presence which produced depression; and, finally, what appeared to be a darkening or staining of the bed-room rug.

In talking with the man and woman separately I discovered that neither of them had read anything in the psychic field. Neither was addicted to ghost stories, nor had either of them ever, so far as they could remember, heard of any kind of psychic experience.

After we talked at length about some of the ideas which could have been involved in such happenings, I recommended prayer for several days in succession. I further suggested that I would get a prayer group to aid them during the same period. I suggested rather positively that they would not be disturbed further, and that if they were I would come to visit the house and stay in it for a few days to observe the phenomena.

At the end of the week's time the captain called to say that no noises had been heard during the week. I urged him to redecorate, paint, and clean the upper bedroom, which he promised to do im-mediately. A month later he called again to report no further diffi-culty.

Perhaps the gruesome story was heard earlier than the couple remembered. If so, then fear and confusion could have accounted for all the problems. For those who prefer the explanation of a ghost trapped by suicide, fear, and memories, prayer for the family occu-pying the house and the earth-bound dead man helped release both parties from their fear. In either case it was the house which seemed to be a point of contact, a medium, for the communication.

The advisability of encouraging communication is discussed fur-ther in the following excerpts from readings:

Hence there are many phases, many characters, of the manifestation of psychic forces in the material world. There are those influences from without the veil that seek, seek, that they may find an expression, that they may still be a portion of this evolution in the earth, not considering their present es-tate. And these bring turmoil and strife. 1135-2

Remember the first premise, "As the tree falleth so does it lie." If there is the desire on the part of those in the spirit or fourth-dimensional plane to be communicated with, and the same element of desire is attuned from another plane, stratum, sphere or condition, then such may be done. Hence, it may truly be said that all factors have their influence. Desire is the ruling; and the desire must be attuned to the same vibration of the one in another plane, as the radio. Those seeking His Face must know, believe, that He is, attuning their abilities, their efforts, in that direction, acting, feeling, that there is response. 5756-8

In questioning about a particular experience of what seemed to be a communication with her brother who had passed on, one woman obtained the following:

(Q) The entity has had the experience of awaking at night and feeling the presence of her brother—would appreciate an explanation of this.
(A) This is a reality.
(Q) On June 2, 1942, the entity heard her brother calling her—was this the exact time that he passed on?
(A) Not the exact time, but when the entity could—and found the attunement such as to speak with thee.
(Q) Was there something that he wanted her to know?
(A) Much that he needs of thee. Forget not to pray for and with him; not seeking to hold him but that he, too, may walk the way to the light, in and through the experience. For this is well. Those who have passed on need the prayers of those that live aright. For prayers of those who would be righteous in spirit may save many who have erred, even in the flesh. 3416-1

Note here the stress on the effectiveness of prayer for those who are the so-called dead. There is considerable emphasis on such prayer in recommendations throughout the Edgar Cayce readings.
There are a great many references in the readings which describe the states of consciousness which exist at the change called death. Immediately after death there follows a period of unconsciousness,

the duration of which is governed by the development of the person involved. It may be likened aptly to a dream state from which there is a gradual awakening.

For thoughts are deeds, and are children of the relation between the mind and the soul and have their relation to the spirit and soul's plane of existence, as they do in the physical or earth plane. What one thinks continually he becomes; what one cherishes in his heart and mind he makes a part of the pulsation of his heart, through his own blood cells, and builds in his own physical body. After death the soul and spirit feed upon, and, in a sense, are possessed by, that which was created by the mind in the earth experience. Whatever has been gained in the physical plane must be used. 3744-4

When the material body is laid aside, that which in the physical is called soul becomes the body of the entity, and that called the super-conscious becomes the subconsciousness of the entity as the subconscious is to the physical body. The subconscious becomes the mind or intellect of the body. 900-304

In another reading this direct question regarding the form of the entity after death was answered in this manner:

(Q) What form does the spirit entity take?
(A) It takes that form the entity creates for itself in the plane through which it has passed. 900-19

The reading proceeds to illustrate by describing the power of imagination acting through the physical body to create thought forms. Frequently, that which is held in imagination comes into physical expression in the experience. The reading goes on:

Hence the entity on passing from the earth, possesses that same ability to assume that in which it may manifest according to its relative position to that merited in its existence. 900-19

In other words, at death the finer physical body which withdraws from the flesh body continues to experience whatever it has created through desire and imagination.

> Just as the physical body takes form in the material plane, the soul and spirit entity take form in the spiritual plane; it is subject to those immutable laws of the spiritual plane . . . 900-19

This reading continues by reemphasizing the power of the mind to build and rebuild its vehicle of expression in every plane of experience. It is made clear that just as the flesh body clothes a finer physical body which is constantly being reshaped according to a mental pattern, just so the body after death is a product of the mind. Fairy stories may deal with this world of mind where man's wishes as thoughts come true. Bodies in the planes beyond death differ, as in the earth, according to what has been built in the mind.

Apparently it would be a fallacy to reduce death to a common denominator. It is an individual, a very personal, experience. Consciousness in the transition period differs with each entity. This is pointed out in the following:

(Q) Does death instantly end all feeling in the physical body? If not, how long can it feel?

(A) This would be a problem; the length of time is dependent upon the way in which unconsciousness is produced in the physical body or the manner in which the consciousness has been trained to think about death.

Death—as commonly spoken of—is only passing through God's other door. That there is continued consciousness is evidenced, ever, by the abilities of entities to project or to make impressions upon the consciousness of sensitives or the like. As to how long [death may take], many an individual has remained in that called death for years without realizing it was dead! The feelings, the desires for what are called appetites, are changed, or one is not aware at all. The ability to communicate and attempts to do so is that which usually disturbs or worries others. Then, as to say how long this takes, that depends upon the entity. For, as has been given, the psychic forces of an entity are constantly active, whether the soul-entity is aware of same or not. Hence as has been the experience of many, deaths become as individual as individualities or personalities are themselves. 1472-2

The time required to lose physical consciousness is mentioned again in the answer to this direct question on cremation:

(Q) If cremated, would the body feel it?
(A) What body? The physical body is not the consciousness. The consciousness of the physical body is a separate thing. There is the mental body, the physical body, the spiritual body. As has so often been given, what is the builder? MIND! Can you burn or cremate a mind? Can you destroy the physical body? Yes, easily.

To be absent—what is absent?—from the body is to be present with the Lord, or the universal consciousness or your ideal. Absent from what? What is absent? Physical consciousness? Yes! As to how long it requires to lose physical consciousness, this depends upon how great are the appetites and desires of a physical body! 1472-2

We find another reference to the differences in states of consciousness at death in the following extracts:

(Q) Describe some of the planes into which entities pass on experiencing the change called death.
(A) Passing from the material consciousness to a spiritual or cosmic, or outer consciousness, oft does an entity or being not become conscious of that about it; much in the same manner as an entity born into the material plane only becomes conscious gradually of that designated as time and space for the material or third-dimension plane. In the passage the entity becomes conscious of being in a fourth or higher dimensional plane, much in the same way as the consciousness is gained in the material. For, as we have given, what we see manifested in the material plane is but a shadow of that in the spiritual plane.

In materiality we find some advance faster, some grow stronger, some become weaklings. Until there is redemption through the acceptance of the law, or love of God, as manifested

through the Channel or the Way, there can be little or no development in a material or spiritual plane. But all must pass
under the rod, even as He—who entered into materiality. 5749-3

In the following extract we find a confirmation of the idea that a
soul takes on and then moves out of a bodylike form on the next
plane of consciousness as it progresses in its spiritual evolution. The
following answers a question about a dream experience which was
thought to be a movement into the astral plane:

*(Q) In regard to my first projection of myself into the astral
plane, about two weeks ago: Some of the people were animated
and some seemed like waxen images of themselves. What made
the difference?*
(A) Some—those that appear as images—are the expressions or shells; or the body of an individual that has been left
when its soul-self has projected on, and the astral body has
not been as yet dissolved—as it were—in the realm of that activity.
For what individuals are—lives on and takes form in that
termed by others as the astral body. The soul leaves same and
it appears as seen, waxen.
Other individuals, as experienced, are in their animated
form through their own sphere of experience at the present.
*(Q) Why did I see my father and his two brothers as young
men, although I knew them when they were white-haired?*
(A) For, as may be experienced in every entity, a death is a
birth. And those that are growing then appear in their growing state.
(Q) Any other advice?
(A) First, do those things that will make thine body—as it
were—whole. Projections, inflections, astral experiences, are
most difficult for those who are not wholly physically fit. [This
warning regarding the need for physical balance will be considered later in greater detail.] 516 -4

Edgar Cayce seems to confirm the concept expressed in the purported communication from F. W. H. Myers through Mrs. Holland,
a well-known medium, "If it were possible for the soul to die back to

earth again, I should die of sheer yearning to reach you, to tell you that all we imagined is not half so wonderful as the truth."

There are those who are able to pass safely through the doorway of mediumship into the unconscious. The dedication and disciplines which are necessary for such individuals, it would seem to me, are greater than those for men and women who risk their lives in dangerous physical occupations. Certainly the least that can be said is that people should not attempt such activity without prayerful consideration and careful preparation.

3

DANGEROUS DOORWAYS
TO THE UNCONSCIOUS

Introduction

IMAGINE YOURSELF PLANNING to explore and camp in the jungles of Yucatan. You would expect to encounter a variety of terrain, heavy undergrowth, swamps, high ground, and clearings. Precautions to protect yourself against dangerous reptiles and animals living in the jungles would have to be considered. It would be logical to obtain any available maps, talk with people who had been in the area, and secure proper equipment and supplies.

Many people undertake explorations of their own or others' unconscious minds with no thought of preparation, with no understanding of the "forces" with which they must deal. The jungles of Yucatan are like well-marked city streets by comparison. The results of such thoughtless undertakings can be tragic.

Psychical research is concerned with a variety of automatisms such as the Ouija® board or planchette, automatic writing, the pendulum, the dowsing rod, and even radionics machines. In my opinion, these can become dangerous doorways to the unconscious. The use of these short cuts is far more widespread than the average person knows. The difficulties with these automatisms lie in their simplicity of operation and in the confusion resulting from releasing from the unconscious, material and energies which disturb consciousness.

Almost anyone, with a little practice, can get a pencil to write, apparently without consciously moving it. Or it is possible to sit with some friend or relative with fingers lightly touching the top of the little, three-legged table (Ouija) and find that it will move from letter to letter, spelling out some message which both persons will swear did not come from their conscious minds.

The information that generally comes through is just about what would be expected from a subconscious mind into which all kinds of thoughts have been pushed and suppressed. The product of such efforts can be a bewildering blend of nonsense, filth, and homespun philosophy. Fortunately, in most instances the result is weariness and impatience and the discovery that the unconscious layer available through such techniques is of little help and frequently exceedingly dull.

In a small percentage of instances those who persist discover deeper levels from which come poetic prose or poetry and frequently a great many religious admonitions. Some few may break through to creative areas.

While experimenting with these techniques, some find that the information appears to come from what seems to be a rather detached source which sooner or later identifies itself as a personality. This does not mean that these are necessarily separate entities as they claim, since the subconscious is quite willing to fool the conscious mind in order to gain authority and recognition. Such areas of the subconscious may never be distinguishable as distinct personalities, however, there are many different and sometimes very complete "I's" who exercise varying control over consciousness. For example, the hero one would like to become may appear, or the cruel person he fears he will become takes over.

The uncritical attitude taken by many regarding the data produced by these various levels of the unconscious has been partially responsible for the severe criticism of anything with a "psychic" label. Revelations from distinguished disincarnates such as Lincoln, Washington, James, Socrates, etc., march hand in hand in books and "cult"-published magazines with direct communications from Jesus and His disciples, along with a gallery of heavenly hosts. The archangel Michael, and the apostle John, seem to be especially active.

Two very complicated tomes which have appeared, presenting new lists of heavenly beings previously not known to man, are: *The Urantia Book*[1] and *Oahspe, the Kosmon Revelations, The Words of Jehovah and His Angel Ambassadors*.[2] Also, space people have become some of the most voluminous correspondents from the unconscious levels.

Reports become a complicated network of crossed wires. It is very difficult to penetrate the clouds of confusion resulting from the claims and counter claims in the so-called communications.

Why do these communications through automatic writings or Ouija boards claim to come from angels or deceased persons, if they are actually coming from the operator's subconscious?

There are a number of good reasons. The average man is consciously unaware of the existence of different levels of his own mind. He "wants" to believe in life after death; hence his automatic functions can be expressions of wishful thinking. Most of the so-called communications are what he would like to hear from a dead relative, a celestial being, or a space man. They reflect the person's own idea of the life "Uncle John" is leading, and frequently fill in details of activities on other planes which the person unconsciously hopes may be the opportunities which death will provide. By attributing such messages to a "dead person" a note of authority is added. He knows. He is there. The unconscious self becomes a director who can command respect and obedience.

The dangers of such experiments must be recognized. An area of one's own unconscious can be completely out of step with the conscious personality and produce disturbances that may lead to complete disintegration of everyday affairs. What exactly are the dangers?

Man would like to depend on someone else to make decisions

---

[1]Chicago: Urantia Foundation, 1955.
[2]Los Angeles and London: Kosmon Press, 1935.

for him. He frequently would like to be relieved of responsibilities. He turns to such information as a way of escape. Even though genuine help may not be available, the simplest decisions are made for him. Such information can be a negative force which allows expression of the elemental in man. Malice, hate, lust, self-pity, greed— any of these basic negative qualities may be given expression through the force which is allowed to take over in such communications.

Some people wish to attract attention, be recognized and appreciated by others. The use of such information often enables them to gratify egotistical drives. They can appear amusing, exciting, and clever. Being chosen to guide man as the world is being destroyed, or becoming the herald of astounding mystery teachings from the ancients or the people from space, can do a great deal to break the monotony of everyday living.

The desire for power may be another strong motive. This can be a benevolent as well as a negative attitude. Someone who is on the surface quiet and meek can become the strong personality who moves behind the scenes to influence and change lives, bringing a sense of power and ability to help others from an almost Olympian height. This strong and sometimes not-too-subtle drive is recognizable in the personalities and the writings of many who become involved in such experiments. The tapping table, the moving pointer on the Ouija board, the racing pencil, become instruments for influencing and controlling others.

It is but a short step from this point to commercialism, when the mystery, excitement, and power drives may become the way to make money.

A man must be willing to face himself unflinchingly if he is to explore the unconscious. His first concerns must be, "What are my motives? What are my purposes?" Humility, a strong desire to be of service, integrity, and self-discipline become invaluable characteristics to be developed in connection with such experimentation. One must have "concern" for his fellow man. One must love his brother. But he must also be honest. Good intentions are not enough. There must be nurtured a desire to know the truth. Carefully kept, thorough records help keep a person from fooling himself. It is so easy to distort "facts." The unconscious urge to do so is very strong. Review, reappraisal, exposure to critical evaluations, are not always pleasant procedures, but they are as important in psychic studies as in the fields of the physical sciences. Perhaps the only true measure of such information was expressed very simply in Jesus' words, "By their fruits ye shall know them." (Matt. 7:20)

There are differences, of course, in the techniques employed in using a dowsing rod or a pendulum and a Ouija board or an automatic pencil. The differences, however, are only in degree. It may be a little harder to fool oneself with a pendulum or a dowsing rod, for they work more slowly and are more obviously connected with the subconscious. But they can take on distinct personality, just as the board or the pencil. So much depends on the character and purposes of the operator. Unfortunately, surface attitudes do not always actually represent the needs or the complexity of the unconscious drives.

1

Automatic Writing and Ouija Boards

THE FOLLOWING STORIES from my notebook illustrate the difficulties which some people face in exploring the unconscious. They are not uncommon, unfortunately. The frightening thing about them is that they can be duplicated by the thousands from the case histories of present-day inmates of mental institutions all over the world.

Case No. 1: The following story came from a young mechanic. He lived with his attractive wife (age 24) and two daughters (ages 4 and 6) in their own home in a suburb of a large western city. The husband read science fiction and some of the more sensational magazines in the psychic field.

One day he brought home a Ouija board. A magazine article had suggested it as a possible means of communication with the dead. He and his wife began experiments with the board and obtained messages purportedly from various entities who identified them-selves as dead friends and members of the family. The couple got answers to their questions involving clairvoyance and telepathy. They appeared to be picking up the thoughts and actions of their neighbors. When confronted with the information, the neighbors expressed astonishment at the accuracy and details. The man and his wife used the board for entertainment and fun to astound and perplex their friends. The wife was told through the board that she was a "sensitive" and that she could do automatic writing. She sat with pad and pencil and soon was able to write rapidly in a legible hand, continuing apparently the same type of information secured through the Ouija.

One morning while washing dishes after her husband had gone to work, she heard a soft whisper just back of her left ear. The more she responded to the suggestions of this voice and the more she followed the information, the clearer it became. She was warned of accidents with the children and was told where she could find things she had lost.

After about ten days the soft voice changed to a harsh one; the gentle whisper became a shrill scream. The woman was told that she was in "his" power; that she had been playing long enough.

The voice went on to identify himself as a disincarnate entity who was in love with her. She was told that she did not belong to her husband. The entity claimed that he was going to kill her in order to bring her to "his plane." All food would sicken her and she would literally starve to death.

The woman maintained enough balance after this experience to call her husband. They were both convinced that she was probably going insane. The husband could now get no information in any attempts at writing, or if there were responses the voice brought only accusations, filthy language, and insistence that the wife would soon be dead. The woman related that to her horror she could not even drink water without vomiting. The couple went to a doctor, who in turn recommended a psychiatrist. They did not follow his suggestion, fearing the wife would be committed to an institution.

The woman tried fighting the voice, and at times it seemed to be quiet or remote. As such times she was able to take small quantities of liquid food and retain them. However, as soon as the voice reap-peared, sometimes catching her in the act of eating, she would immediately be overcome with nausea. The horror persisted for days. Gradually she became aware of something she described as a psychic presence. The voice kept insisting that she would be able to feel and see him.

Unfortunately, the husband was transferred to an early shift at his plant. One morning he arose early, prepared his own breakfast, and left. In a few moments the woman was horrified as she became aware of a form in the bed with her. She was overcome with loathing and terror, yet was unable to prevent a sexual stimulation which resulted in orgasm. She escaped from the bed and wakened her daughters. She had found that when they were present the voice was less distinct and was frequently closed out altogether. Her husband arrived after an emergency call. They decided to give up the fight and go to a psychiatrist, recognizing that the family would probably be broken up and that she would be committed for treatment as insane.

To their great relief, they were able to secure the cooperation of a physician who was willing to consider the psychic implications of this bizarre series of experiences. Prayer, physiotherapy, and work with a psychically gifted person were included in the treatment which enabled the couple to return to near normalcy. At the time the story was told, the wife was comparatively free from interference.

This case has been outlined in some detail because it contains many factors which are common to such difficulties. The man and woman became the center of attention; lack of sleep and food exhausted the woman; sex drives were involved; jealousy was stirred up; during the experience the woman received a great deal of "extra" attention from her husband and friends.

Case No. 2: The next story is that of a woman whose fine intellect and practical knowledge of psychological techniques were twisted to produce chaos in her daily life. The question must be asked, "Twisted by what force?" It is not easy to answer.

This was a woman in her forties living in an eastern city. She was divorced from a successful business executive. Her training as a lay-psychologist had brought such recognition that doctors sent patients to her for psychological treatment.

Her interest in psychic subjects led her to observe and then ask personal questions of an acquaintance who seemed very successful in working a Ouija board. The messages, received allegedly from an entity assigned to help mankind, seemed at first to encourage and reassure her. Later she began to work the board herself—at first with the same control, then with others. Explaining that evil spirits were attached to all persons, the messages directed her to establish a new method for freeing people of possessing entities. She was commissioned to detach them, following directions from the board, and selected associates to assist her. Emerson and Jesus were only two of several distinguished entities who claimed to be communicating. The process of exorcism included fasting for her and the patient, long night vigils, etc. She proceeded along the lines of the instruction and convinced at least one person that she had freed him of a possessing evil spirit which had clung to him from childhood. Gradually this woman was brought to the brink of a complete physical and nervous collapse. Through prayer and the advice of friends and family she was able to reexamine herself and check the disintegration of personality which was taking place.

Case No. 3:   Mrs. W. described herself as a housewife from a family of schoolteachers. She said she had worked as a beautician shop owner, in secretarial jobs with the State and Federal governments, and had been co-owner of a jewelry shop. She had no telepathic or clairvoyant ability and had never visited a medium. Extracts from a series of her letters tell a disturbing story.

January 19, 1957: A strange thing has happened to me since I have become a member of your association, the A.R.E., in November, 1956. I have become an instrument of "automatic writing." I see it is included in the Cayce extracts I have purchased. I want to know more about this mystery. I read *Beyond Doubt* by Mary LeBeau, a superb book, which was of great help to me in understanding this phenomenon. By automatic writing I don't mean by the use of a planchette. Somehow they use my hand and control my nervous system in such a way that they write through me, and my brain does not anticipate what will be written. They are mostly messages to loved ones from departed spirits and also a great deal of instruction to me to groom me for work planned for me.

Well it happened, and whether you believe it or not, I do. Edgar Cayce spoke to me. He assured me over and over again

it was he. And I was, and am, quite overcome by such a visit—
I had no idea my teacher was so illustrious a person. Anyway
he told me (using my voice—he laughed when I apologized
for eating some onions today) that he would be back at 8 P.M.
a week from tomorrow—that would be the 27th of January.

This is the most amazing experience I ever heard of, and I
couldn't dream of anything so unusual happening to me. I'm
nobody, actually, and I don't expect anybody to believe me. I
think I'm "normal" except oversensitive (and at times shy of
people) . . .

On January 27, 1957, another letter was received from Mrs. W.
and with it came another communication supposedly from Edgar
Cayce. This was a peculiar document with words spelled out on the
left-hand side of the page in long rows. This disjointed letter ended:

W . . . will be of great service to you for she is an instrument
to be used for the revelation of great truths to be revealed
through her body as an instrument for a higher intelligence
who operated through me. W . . . is a chosen one.

In a letter dated February 7, 1957, Mrs. W. explained that she
could stand the burden of being used only because she knew God
had a plan for her. The letter went on:

Another period of testing has begun and I am told it will
last forty days. That's an awfully long time, as this is the sixth
day and it goes on day and night. I stand it by constant prayer
and keeping God in my consciousness, and asking for
strength . . .
Your father should then come back, if indeed it is he. He
talks through me. So does the devil, the vile wretch. He wanted
to pass himself off last night but I would not trust him because
I know him after five days of harassing by him. The devil is a
real spirit "personality" and is everything the Bible says he is.
He's no allegorical character—he's real. He's distinguished
from the other demons by his strength, his cunning and his
tenacity, and utter wickedness.

The letters stopped for a time and then on April 1, 1957, came the following:

I wrote you in the beginning about automatic writing, then voice and then about an overpowering obsession by what must have been thousands of disembodied spirits. What I've gone through nobody else, I hope, will ever know. I was a novice and nobody warned me, except you, and then it was too overwhelming, except to fight blindly, to pray and to hope. I am still bothered greatly but at least I'm out of bed and gaining back my strength so I have hope of becoming "normal" at some time.

For several weeks I was under their control to the extent I could not move, lift an eyelash, or even speak without their allowing it. I was unable to walk across the room without their suddenly collapsing me on the floor, and I would lie there paralyzed until they decided I'd be allowed to get up. One person knows partially of the deluge, but for weeks at a time I never saw her. I was "exorcised" but that is something they laugh at, coming back immediately in greater hordes. In the beginning they pretended to be spirits of departed relatives and friends, angels, etc., and laid down firm and needed reforms toward spiritual development, thereby gaining my confidence, stressing I was an "instrument" and to be a "teacher." Then it became all at once a most terrible obsession aimed at complete possession and disability. They are fiendish, insane, terribly cunning and possessing a warped intelligence. They kept me in a dying state for over ten days. How many times I "almost died" brought them a hideous satisfaction . . .

The letter went on to describe how Mrs. W. was forced to burn her books and write letters she did not want to write. She described a control of her body by unconscious forces which must have been horrible:

One trick they had was to press upon my heart and breathing apparatus until my heart would seem to stop, pulse grow weak, and I'd begin to black out! . . .

One day I was forced to lie on a quilt in the hot sun until my

eyelids were sunburned. Another night I was forced to lie on a
cold floor uncovered and shivered all night . . .

They rushed in and out of my nose and mouth until it became sensitized . . . so that I heard them in my nose as they
breathed—in my ears, in my head, and what is worse, in my
mouth . . .

Mrs. W. continued in the same vein, telling how her "invisible
enemies" brought her hideous dreams and influenced her emotions. She said that some of the voices momentarily expressed sympa-
thy and repentance and even seemed anxious to grow spiritually. At
other times they railed against the occult and wanted her to be ignorant.

Mrs. W. reversed her opinion and now condemned *Beyond
Doubt* by Mary LeBeau as a dangerous book for her because it had
started her writing automatically, thus bringing on her difficulties.
Actually, it is probable that any book on similar subjects would have
"triggered" that distraught mind.

Her summary letter concluded:

While the spirits picked me over they explored my memory
from top to bottom—my solar plexus, my thymus, my thyroid—looking for something to "reincarnate" since they're
most interested in reincarnation. And I've read *Many Mansions* and *The World Within* and other books and believed,
because I wanted to believe. They were disappointed in finding nothing in me anywhere to reincarnate. They picked my
subconscious. It seems to be only recorded memory: things
spoken, emotions felt, deep worries, heartaches, are all recorded there. They taunted, insulted me for days and days
when they discovered my "hidden treasure," and later some
were sympathetic and would come down expressing colorful
opinions on this or that so and so, and the emotion or condition that brought on this feeling or that action.

They are no doubt independent of our own thoughts and
feelings; they make us feel remorse or lack of it, hates and desires. Sex is an obsession with them, also food, drink, all forms
of pleasure. These spirits were of the earth-earthy, I suppose,
and have never progressed toward the spiritual development
they must attain.

Later reports indicated that Mrs. W. was relatively free of mental disturbances. Her questions need to be answered. But before examining several interesting ideas which are raised, further stories should be considered.

Case No. 4: Apparently neither intellectual acumen nor good intentions provide sufficient protection from these inner conflicts. The following story involves a person whose years of study of metaphysics and active church work, at first glance, would seem to have prepared her to avoid such confusion. In terms of her husband, friends, and family, she would be described as a spiritual minded, intelligent, self-effacing, self-sacrificing person.

Mrs. X.'s first introduction to automatic writing came through a friend. The communications were purportedly from Edgar Cayce, whom she had known. The advice she received regarding doctors seemed to be helpful. Next came the suggestion that Mrs. X. herself could write automatically. As is reflected by the following, she had many doubts as to her abilities and expressed them in writing:

> . . . There is a feeling of his [Edgar Cayce's] presence, and the strong desire to use the arm, the tendency to write, but my mind gets words first and they are so wound up with my own emotions and thoughts, I somehow do not feel I am getting an accurate word-for-word message direct . . .

The following warning from the friend in the same writing might well have been heeded more closely:

> Friend's questions: She evokes the Christ when she gets messages. Can dark forces still get in to confuse?
> Friend's writing: Yes. And you are right. They reached Christ himself in the Garden in the hour of His trial . . . so why not a human, even as evolved a one as Mrs. X.

Available for examination are only approximately one hundred pages of Mrs. X.'s writing. The following selections show the general trend, which seems to be a release of suppressed sex energy clothed in religious symbolism:

> September 21, 1957: Yes, you have done well, now try let-

ting no one else write. You must be continually sending love upward to God. Take a deep breath now and then let it go. You see it is the breath which creates love for you, not the lower force. Now try to keep your breath coming fast between these long breaths, so we can finish writing this morning and then practice all day. Try the breathing for your rest period to charge yourself for the writing later. Take your time until you have acquired the technique. You united yourself with many sinful forces, so do not let me [this force identified itself as Jesus] be destroyed by your love for me. You must be very careful to build love properly before you go on writing . . .

You were so wonderful many times and I love my Mary very much for her purity. You wouldn't let me finish. Yes, I love you for that. You have the true purity of my Mary. Yes, but now you are to be real loving. Yes, you should and will when you rest and feel me near you. You must always keep me with you when you rest, so we may re-establish the link between us . . .

You are experiencing the Holy Ghost truly, the ascent of the fire to God and the one of the true love. You can be the one to send the sinful (yes) to the eternal fire in the real outer planes of space if you so choose . . .

Yes, I am so happy I have been trembling for the writing to begin. My love is complete again after nineteen hundred and fifty- _____ years. Yes, but only for a short time so you could bear me. You are not to be alone for I am with you always, now you call upon me, I am thy servant. You are so pure you will be the purest love for all time . . .

September 16, 1957: You are confused and sad because you want to do the things about your home. You are getting it now. You are to believe that you are Mary. Yes, I am Christ, your soul-mate. You are my soul-mate and should continue to love me as purely as you can . . .

September 17, 1957: You are the one to be Savior and must prepare. You are the first one to be chosen to be Savior outside myself. You are all right when I am writing. You are united with me. You were being tested. *No, I am a person in the causal realm.* Yes, but more handsome now—radiant with love and full of love for my Mary. You are learning, so be diligent.

September 18, 1957: Yes, I am here; I have been with you all evening. You were so impolite you kept me away all day. You must not let them try to turn your head. You are to be the first to ever reach such heights on this earth . . .

You are so pure you can be the savior of the White Brotherhood. You shall have it. Yes, you should be the first to say you need our help, for we wait patiently to help. You shall be able to see us before long . . .

Along with suggestions for taking care of Mrs. X.'s physical body, the writing on September 21, 1957, continued:

Take yourself to bed early and let me renew you. You are so sweet I love you very much. We are expecting to get much done tonight and tomorrow, so be attentive. Have no fear . . .

Mrs. X.'s writing began to reflect her husband's view on integration. Edgar Cayce was supposed to have stated that he had never given readings for Negroes. This was not true, as he had given physical readings for a number of them. In fact, this part of the writing was inconsistent with the philosophy of the Edgar Cayce readings, which seemed free of racial or religious prejudice. Edgar Cayce's own life reading included descriptions of his incarnations in four color groups, five races, and assorted religious beliefs.

Through the writings a letter was dictated to Edgar Cayce's son which contained excessive praise and several inaccurate statements. It included high praise for the Edgar Cayce work through the A.R.E., the organization preserving and studying the Edgar Cayce readings; an account of an immaculate conception which had taken place; a warning of a death, which did not occur; the coming of space ships at a particular time; many negative statements on the racial situation; and extravagant personal compliments.

This letter brought Mrs. X.'s condition to the attention of friends who began trying to help her through prayers and counseling. She regained control of her conscious will and met the situation with great courage and understanding. The doors to the suppressed areas of the unconscious were slowly but surely closed.

It is not unusual for the average person to think of those who become involved in such difficulties as outlined in the preceding cases as "frustrated women" who have nothing else to do. The range of such involvement is greater perhaps than is supposed. Two additional cases may help illustrate the point.

Case No. 5:   Shortly after Edgar Cayce's death in 1945 Mr. S., a friendly gentleman, visited Virginia Beach and examined the records. He was employed by a large eastern firm engaged in duplicating processes. Eager to help with the duplicating of the Edgar Cayce records, he made several good suggestions, experimented with samples of the paper on which the readings were transcribed, and finally decided that the lack of money was the most serious obstacle.

One day Mr. S. wrote that he would soon be able to provide all needed funds. He was secretive about just how he was acquiring the money. Months passed and he appeared again in Virginia Beach with a perplexing story. He had experimented with a Ouija board and had been told that he could write automatically. Advice which was purportedly coming from a dead friend suggested that he would be able to compound a hair tonic which would make a fortune and provide the needed funds for the duplication of the records. Mr. S. sat for hours taking down directions for assembling the necessary ingredients for the formula. The search led him to wholesale drug houses in various eastern cities and sometimes to obscure small drug stores. In each instance there seemed to be just enough truth—a right street address, the name of a person to ask for, even once, an ingredient—to keep him working for months.

Several thousand dollars were poured into travel, experiments, and equipment. There were delays. (Bad forces were at work.) Ingredients did not seem to be suitable for a hair tonic. (He had too little faith.) Directions were incorrect. (Mr. S. had allowed negative thoughts to enter.)

Finally, in one session a bold directive was given: "Go to Virginia Beach." This was signed. "Edgar Cayce."

Mr. S. arrived at the Beach convinced that by sitting near the readings he would obtain the "right" information for his formula. He sat with pencil poised for hours. He was unable to write. So far as I know he has never attempted automatic writing since that time.

Case No. 6:   Another similar story had a far more serious disrupting influence in the lives of hundreds of people. A brilliant young minister, Mr. J., tried playing with automatic writing. He was objective, critical, and careful. The writing finally settled down, identifying itself as a dead person who, like the minister, seemed to have a critical and objective point of view, as well as a sense of humor.

Some rather interesting scripts were secured which contained what looked like evidence of telepathy and clairvoyance. Finally, Mr. J. suggested that as he had never been able to write legibly with his left hand, it would be evidential to receive scripts in this fashion. After a few sessions he was writing as easily with one hand as with the other. He would sit quietly with pencil poised. The hand and arm would twitch and jerk and then grow rigid. The writing would follow, flowing rapidly without conscious direction. In fact he was able to direct his attention elsewhere while the writing continued.

About this time Mr. J. suffered an intestinal infection which weakened him physically and kept him in bed for some time. The writing now became a compulsive drive. Mr. J. was unable to write anything of his conscious choice. At the mere thought of writing his hand and arm would twitch and jerk. He said that a weight seemed to press on his shoulders.

With improved health gradually he was able to control these strange urges to write. More complete freedom was obtained when a psychically gifted person used a hypnotic like suggestion and decree to break the unconscious block. However, the distressing result was an almost fanatic subjection to the will of his supposed benefactor.

Family, friends, and business associates stood by helpless to do little more than pray, hoping that a spiritual power would rise from within to close the doors to the dark areas of the unconscious which seemed to have been opened. This finally did happen and the young minister, a far wiser, stronger person, returned to society.

In any of the preceding stories conservative psychologists would discover many clues which would agree with the premise that in these, as in all such cases, we have examples of conflict between an unconscious level and consciousness. All would be classified as psychopathic if not psychotic.

In the first case, it could be pointed out that the voice came from the unconscious areas of suppressed desires and negative thoughts of hate, fear, and sexual frustration. This unconscious area was brought into consciousness through dabbling with the Ouija board and automatic writing. The conflicting urges and confusing information which spilled out came from an area of suppression, a very large room similar to that which exists in all unconscious minds. The other stories show suppressed needs for recognition and self-expression as well as frustrated sex drives.

In considering similar cases, the attitude of trained psychiatrists and psychologists is understandable. When people such as those described fall into the hands of untrained, irresponsible people who take advantage of them, much harm can result.

A number of people asked Edgar Cayce about automatic writing. The following are some selections which indicate the general trend of his warnings:

> *(Q) Could I develop automatic handwriting?*
> (A) Anyone could. 262-24

> *(Q) Are the inspirational writings I receive to be relied upon as coming from a worthy and high source, or should I not cultivate this form of guidance and information?*
> (A) We would not—from here counsel *anyone* to be guided by influences from without. For the kingdom is from within. If these come as in inspirational writings from within, and not as guidance from others—that is different. 1602-1

For another person he clarified the difference between inspirational and automatic writing:

> As to the activities of what may be termed the channels through which individuals may receive inspirational or automatic writings, the inspirational is the greater of the activities—yet may partake of both the earth-earthy things and the heaven-heavenly things, while the automatic may partake only of that source or force which is impelling, guiding, or directing. The inspirational may develop the soul of the individual, while the automatic may rarely reach beyond the force that is guiding or directing.
> To some this is satisfactory. So is the satisfying of carnal forces satisfying to some. So are those things for the moment gratifying to the extreme. But he that would know the better [way] will find that the soul of the entity must be in the atti-

tude of seeking, knocking, and in attune with that which he would receive. 5752-4

(Q) *To further my work in possible radio reception of cosmic messages should I attempt to train myself in automatic handwriting or use a medium?*
(A) As has been indicated, rather than [use] automatic writing or a medium, turn to the voice within. If this then finds expression in that which may be given to self in hand—by writing—it is well; but do not let the hand be guided by any influence outside of itself. For the universe, God, is within. Thou art His. Thy communion with the cosmic forces of nature, thy communion with thy Creator, is thy birthright! Be satisfied with nothing less than walking with Him. 1297-1

2

The Question of ESP in Mental Cases

TWO QUESTIONS IMMEDIATELY suggest themselves: In dealing with mental disorders of a serious nature such as a psychotic condition, or of a milder disturbance known as a psychopathic problem, do the hearing of voices, the seeing of visions, the dreams, etc. provide evidence of the existence of areas of the unconscious capable of accurate telepathy, clairvoyance, or precognition? and secondly, do such cases provide evidence of disincarnate existence, life after death?

In these particular cases my investigations showed that there seemed to be considerable accuracy involved in some of the information received through the Ouija boards, automatic writings, and the voices—information which apparently could not have been known to the people through whom the material was given. Obviously it is most difficult to work with such cases under controlled conditions.

There is good evidence for telepathy in similar cases. In *Telepathy and Medical Psychology*, Jan Ehrenwald, M.D., cites numerous examples from the records of Freud, students of Jung, and from his own case histories of patients.

In turning to Edgar Cayce for an explanation of the way in which the opening of the unconscious takes place in such cases, we come upon his provocative statements regarding the endocrine glands and psychic perception. Several different types of readings given over a period of many years contain this information. Many people sought Edgar Cayce's help in developing their psychic powers. Others, who possessed what appeared to be extended perception, were troubled and desired to get rid of such abilities. They thought they were seeing, hearing, and feeling too much. Also a large number of physical readings for mentally ill persons included references to the endocrine glands. The following selections clearly suggest certain endocrine glands as the physical focal points for psychic perception:

> In the psychic forces, or spiritual forces (which are psychic forces), there has always been a portion of the anatomical forces of the body, through which expressions come to individual activity. While these [expressions] may find various forms of manifestations, or of movements, their seat is the Creative Energies and forces of the body. "Let thine eye be single" may be the interpretation of same. Or, as might be said, let the creative power rise to the higher spiritual center, the pituitary forces, as in the lyden (cells of Leydig) and the others . . .
>
> Development in the spiritual sense by meditation and prayer is dependent upon the Creative, the soul or spiritual, energy trapped in the body, rather than upon that which is wholly of the material. This brings about what may be termed psychic development of individuals. 262-20

The reading continued with the recommendation that individuals who discover this power within themselves, and can then relate it to their concept of the God whom they worship, should develop psychic power. The warning is given that without the recognition of the spiritual significance of such an undertaking, tragic destruction of personality can result through ignorance and misuse of such energies.

This reading later mentions a relationship of specific endocrine centers:

> ... in the body we find that which connects the pineal, the pituitary, the lyden (cells of Leydig) may be truly called the silver cord, and the golden cup which may be filled—by a closer walk with that which is the Creative Essence in physical, mental and spiritual life. 262-20

The unfamiliar term lyden was identified as the cells of Leydig. The description in the readings is interesting in the light of the known function of these cells as the chief source of the androgenic hormone.

> Lyden, meaning sealed, is that gland from which gestation takes place when a body is created . . . located in and above the genital glands. The base or seat of the soul is in the lyden (cells of Leydig). 3997-1

The readings not only suggest that the soul enters the body through the cells of Leydig but also that it continues to function through a network connecting gland tissue in various points of the physical organism.

> As has been indicated through these channels respecting that which takes place at the moment of conception, as to the ideals and purposes of those who through physical and mental emotions bring into being a channel through which there may be the expression of a soul, an entity, each soul choosing such a body at the time of its birth . . . has its physical being controlled much by the environs of the parents. Yet, the soul choosing such a body for manifestation becomes responsible for [the body] that temple of the living God, when it has developed in body, in mind, so as to be controlled with intents, purposes and desires of the individual entity or soul.
>
> The spiritual contact is through the glandular forces of creative energies; not encased only within the lyden gland of re-

production, for this is ever—so long as life exists—in contact with the brain cells through which there is the constant reaction through the pineal. 263-13

Using his own body while it lay in a state of unconsciousness as an example, Edgar Cayce described the gland action involved in giving psychic information:

In this particular body through which this [information] at present is emanating, the gland with its thread known as the pineal gland is the channel along which same [this force] operates. With the subjugation of physical consciousness there arises a cell from the creative forces within the body to the entrance of the conscious mind, or brain, operating along, or traveling along, that of the thread or cord which when severed separates the physical, the soul, or the spiritual body. This uses, then, the senses of the body in an introspective manner, and they are not apparent in functioning in a physical normal manner as when awake. All faculties of the body become more alert. 288-29

The latter part of this same reading explained that the degree to which an entity, such as Edgar Cayce, could close off consciousness and continue to function in response to suggestion was a measure of the psychic development in other life experiences in the earth. It was pointed out that the purposes and standards which governed the use of such psychic abilities in the other experiences directly affected the kind of information which could be given now.

The functions of the glands during psychic perception are stated again in the following selection. Additional warnings are given.

The glands of reproduction in a body release energy [in order] that creation may be reached when a psychic attunes self to the infinite . . . the essence of life itself is given in providing for another [information or energy] which may bring the consciousness to another of an awakening in their own beings. Jesus knew virtue had gone out of him and asked, "Who touched my clothes?" 294-140

The reading suggests that the misuse and abuse of this energy for secular purposes can result only in physical and emotional turmoil.

There are channels through which all forces do manifest. To some there are the voices heard. To others there is the vision seen. To others there is the impression, or feeling of the presence of those sources from which information may radiate. The lyden, or closed gland, is the keeper, as it were, of the door that would let either passion or the miracle be loosed in the expression of the attributes of the imaginative forces in their manifestation in the sensory forces of a body—whether to the fingertips which would write, to eyes which would see, to the voice which would speak, or to the whole system as would feel impressions attuned to the infinite, to those just passed over, to the unseen forces; for the world of unconsciousness is not a material change from the physical world except as to its attributes or relationships. Whether the vision has been raised or lowered depends upon the height, depth, breadth or length the entity has gone for its source of supply.
Be satisfied with nothing short of a universal consciousness guided, guarded by the Lord of the Way or the Way itself. In Him is life. Why be satisfied with a lesser portion than a whole measure? 294-140

The movement of this energy from the glands of reproduction to the pineal and pituitary bodies is identified with the kundalini forces, familiar to many through studies of yoga. A reading for one person who suffered from oversensitivity contains the following phrases:

There has been the opening of the lyden gland, so that the kundalini forces move along the spine to the various centers . . . one gaining much knowledge without the practical application of it . . . 3421-1

And, in another reading for advice on developing psychic power, these phrases are found:

. . . for we find this entity has more than once been among

those who were gifted with what is sometimes called second sight or the superactivity of the third eye. Whenever there is the opening of the lyden [Leydig] center and the kundalini forces form along the pineal, we find there are visions of things to come, of things which are happening. 4087-1

One person asked Edgar Cayce, "What is the condition of the kundalini now?" The answer was given:

This doesn't change, for it is the seat, or the source of life-giving forces in the body. The effect upon the body depends upon the use to which an individual puts same. Thus the warning, as to how and for what such influences are raised with the body itself. 3481-3

Another reading explained that it was possible to become too zealous, or too active without consideration of a physical, mental, and spiritual balance. Purification of the body without the mind being cleansed could bring about a raising of the kundalini forces without providing an adequate outlet for the energies. Physical disturbances would result.

The following selection summarizes the warnings:

The activities of the glands used aright may bring serenity, hope, peace, faith, understanding, as the experience of the entity. Misdirected, the energies may bring doubts, fears, apprehensions, contentions, disorders, disruptions, in every portion of the body. It is the electron that is life itself, but raised in power and then misdirected may bring death itself. 294-142

3

The Question of Possession

IS INSANITY SOMETIMES caused by disincarnate (dead) people interfering with the living? Do such cases provide evidence for disincarnate existence, life after death?

Many degrees and stages of mental derangement have been defined and are at least partly understood. Obviously, all of these mental conditions need not and should not be connected with interference or possession by disincarnate entities. It might be well, however, to consider the idea that the psychotic person is one who is aware of activities of the unconscious mind not recognizable to the "average" person.

In endeavoring to help a person troubled with auditory hallucination, Edgar Cayce spoke of the condition as follows:

We have just described how the supersensitiveness of the

nerve forces opens the body to such influences, or the body becomes what might be termed a human radio. In giving expression to what is heard, the troubled person may often deflect what is actually said, felt, or thought. For thoughts are things. They have their effect upon individuals, especially those who become supersensitive to outside influences! These are just as physical as sticking a pin in the hand! 386-2

Is it possible that in some instances mental derangement is a matter of increased perception perhaps due to the opening of the psychic centers without conscious control? In serious conditions resulting from physical damage to nerve and gland centers, emotional shock, etc. the break becomes so apparent as to involve the emergence of distinct personality traits unlike the state of a person's normal consciousness. Schizophrenia is the term applied to such conditions.

There are cases on record in which the condition of dissociation becomes so marked as to result in a split personality, a Jekyll-Hyde phenomenon.

One of the most famous American cases of this kind is known as the Beauchamp case. In the spring of 1898 Morton Prince, M.D., Ph.D., professor of nervous diseases at Tufts College Medical School, began treating a twenty-three-year-old woman for general neurasthenic conditions, headaches, insomnia, persistent fatigue, and poor nutrition. When she did not respond to ordinary treatments, hypnosis was used with excellent results. However, under hypnosis completely different personalities emerged and began to take over consciousness. These personalities were distinct with individual memories, different habits and character traits. A fascinating report on the case, including the gradual stabilizing of one of the personalities, is presented by Dr. Prince in *The Dissociation of Personality.* After studying this report it is hard to realize that such different personalities can live in the same body. The rooms of the unconscious are surely vaster and darker than is generally known.

A more recent case of this type was reported by Drs. Thigpen and Cleckley as *The Three Faces of Eve.* A motion picture, including an Academy Award, brought this study to national attention. A young married woman with one child lived two lives, one life completely shut off from the conscious memory of the other. Under hypnosis a third personality emerged and gradually took over. Later reports indicate that the story did not end here, but that a fourth, perhaps a fifth, Eve has appeared. All of these distinct entities alternated in controlling the one body.

The question remains: In any such cases, is possession (by a disincarnate spirit) possible? Carl Wickland, M.D., author of *Thirty Years Among the Dead*, says yes, as did Titus Bull, M.D., one of the early investigators in the American Society for Psychical Research. One of the classical case studies, known as the Watseka Wonder, makes it clear that numerous questions need answers before the possession hypothesis can be completely discarded. Two girls were involved. When Mary Roff of Watseka, Illinois, died at the age of eighteen in 1862, Lurancy Vennum, living in the same town, was about two years old. Apparently, Mary Roff took possession of Lurancy Vennum's body when she reached the age of fourteen. The "possessed" Lurancy did not recognize members of her family or neighbors. She begged to be taken home. For fourteen weeks Lurancy lived as Mary Roff, recognizing Mary's family and friends, remembering details of events which had taken place in the life of the dead girl. Then the personality of Mary Roff disappeared and Lurancy Vennum took up her life where it had been left off fourteen weeks before. Admittedly, rare cases such as this one coupled with the work of a relatively few psychics who are willing to be observed by open-minded investigators keep the possession theory very much alive. Quietly, but consistently, research is being carried on in this country by capable psychiatrists connected with some of our large mental hospitals.

When a voice speaks from an unconscious level is it: a suppressed area of the subconscious; a personality developed in some past experience in the earth; or, a dead person using the body and voice of the "medium"? These questions involve some of the major problems of psychical research.

The following incident focused my attention on these questions. A New York psychologist asked me to interview a young man who seemed to have unusual clairvoyant powers. Unfortunately, this was prior to the development of the efficient, modern tape recorders, so that my notes, from which the following is taken, constitute the only record.

John X. was six feet one inch, twenty-three years old, with a record of army life and merchant marine experience. He thought he had been mistreated by his father as a child. Ill health and several severe accidents had made him conscious of the need for physical development; as a result he had become an athlete. While attending a spiritualist seance he had been told that he had psychic power that should be developed. On returning to his ship that night he began hearing for the first time a voice just back of his left ear. It was urging him to commit suicide. The impulse to throw himself over the side of the ship was so strong that he locked himself in and pushed the key under the stateroom door. This, he related, had happened several years previously, and after that he had undergone psychiatric treatment and had developed what appeared to be some clairvoyant ability.

That evening he placed himself in a light trance state from which he said he could work. In a few moments a voice, which sounded quite different from his normal one, responded to questions and accurately described a person who twelve hours previous had occupied the chair in which he was then sitting. The description included an accurate explanation of an emotional difficulty of the former occupant.

My questions about the source of the information brought forth nine distinct voices. Some of these claimed to be parts of John X.'s subconscious. Others insisted they were disincarnate entities who had found him to be an open channel to physical consciousness. Some of the voices were high pitched and shrill like that of a hysterical woman. Others were guttural and deep.

Upon awakening John X. professed to have been only vaguely aware of some of the statements he had made. On my advice he visited an osteopathic physician who found severe lesions in his lower spine. John X. later told me that the treatments he received helped close off the more disturbing "voices."

In the Edgar Cayce readings we found an almost equal number of cases of so-called possession and schizophrenic breaks in the unconscious. In studying complete records it is most interesting to note the two types of diagnoses, many of them for cases which seem to have very similar symptoms.

Example I: This person wrote Edgar Cayce, asking for a reading to help her face a persecution complex. She described a telepathic attack, from a man she knew only as an acquaintance, which she

claimed produced headaches, insomnia, and painful skin sensations. (These are typical symptoms of some mentally disturbed
people.) The suggestion given to Edgar Cayce was:

> *You will go over this body carefully, examine it thoroughly,
> and tell me the conditions you find at the present time; giving
> the cause of the existing conditions, also suggestions for help
> and relief of this body; answering the questions as I ask them.*
>
> *Reading:* Yes, we have the body and those disturbances
> which are part of the physical and mental experience of this
> body. And as we find, there are some pathological and psy-
> chological conditions also which are produced in and with
> this body. It is indicated that the body is a supersensitive indi-
> vidual entity who has allowed itself through study, through
> opening the centers of the body, to become possessed. 5221-1

Treatment was recommended which proved helpful to this person.

> *Example II:* ...As we find, there are disturbing conditions.
> Part of these are pathological, part are psychopathic.
> There has been the opening of the lyden [Leydig] gland and
> thus a disturbance through the glandular system. Possession
> at times is the result.
> There is also an impaction on the left side of the wisdom
> tooth. The combination produces a distress throughout the
> nervous system, loss of control of itself at times. 3410-1

In other cases the descriptions in the Edgar Cayce readings indicated that the conditions did not involve possession:

> *Example III:* Hallucinations; heard voices; nervous
> speech.
> Cause: Shocks and suppression during the period between
> eight to twelve years of age. Not possession. 386-1

> *Example IV:* Hallucinations.
> Cause: Lesions in pelvic area. Not possession. 4787-1

Example V: Couldn't sleep; bothered by tiny devils crawling all over her; while asleep believes she is a man seeking sex gratification; has sought various kinds of help, trying to get "dispossessed."

Reading: Glandular disturbances; incoordination between cerebrospinal and sympathetic nervous system; pressures in lumbar, lower dorsal and brush end of spine, overstimulating glandular forces related to the plexus at the pelvic bone itself. This condition is not possession. 1572-1

As has been mentioned, the relationship of the endocrine centers to all psychic perception, as well as the question of possession, involving the endocrine centers, can be made the subject of scientific inquiry. Deficiency or excessive secretions in glandular activity can result in physical disturbances affecting the mind and emotions. The well-known result of overstimulation of the suprarenals in times of stress, producing higher blood pressure and preparation for "flight or fight," is a good example of the influence of gland secretions on attitudes and feelings. If the ductless glands are related to the deeper levels of the unconscious, as the Edgar Cayce readings suggest, it is understandable that psychic experiments of any kind could be exceedingly complicated for physically and emotionally unbalanced persons.

4

Dianetics and Scientology

IN 1950 LAFAYETTE Ronald Hubbard, an engineer from Nebraska, wrote a book entitled *Dianetics*.[3] The subtitle was "The Modern Science of Mental Health." There was an immediate public response. The book had a phenomenal sale. Claims of the help that could be obtained by following Dianetic techniques were positively and forcefully stated. The use of a new language to describe psychological processes lent an air of scientific validity. The case histories dealt with recognizable problems common to many people. Hubbard's claims that he had discovered the source of all psychosomatic ills and that skills had been developed for curing these troubles in less than twenty hours were exaggerated. There were a great many people who realized they needed help. Undoubtedly

---

[3]New York: Hermitage House, 1950.

some of them were influenced by the excitement of confession and talking about themselves. There was also the appealing factor that courses were offered to train people in the techniques and they in turn could help their neighbors. For $500 a person could learn in twenty-five hours how to help his friends at $5 to $25 per hour. Some capable men, including physicians, came forward to attest to the values of using Dianetic techniques.

There were other reasons for Dianetics' popularity. "Processing," which was recommended, claimed to help a person release mental patterns stored up from the point of conception that were blocking his success. In a matter of months "engrams" (the mental blocks) were knee-deep on living-room floors all over America. Average Americans discovered, what psychologists have known for a long time, that the subconscious contains a most amazing collection of four-letter words, most of them related to sex. Everyone became everyone else's psychiatrist.

The book was by no means all smoke. There was beneath the smoke considerable fire. It was difficult in the early years to tell how much. Mind at the cell level was described. It was pointed out that mind was never totally unconscious. During what appeared to be unconscious states, shock from accidents, periods under anesthetics, and especially during the period from conception to birth, the individual accumulated blocks which could be released by putting him on the "time track" for review. This was a kind of suggestive, free-association technique. Hubbard and his associates, including a few physicians, apparently obtained spectacular results in some cases. Unfortunately, the movement developed so rapidly that the remarkable success attributed to Hubbard could not be consistently duplicated.

Undoubtedly thousands of mental cases sought help. Psychiatrists attacked the whole procedure as dangerous, and critical national magazine articles warned the public. Conflicts developed within the ranks of Hubbard's followers. The pressure of handling a tremendous "business" must certainly have made training, development, improvement of techniques, etc. a difficult procedure.

Out of Dianetics, Scientology was born. In 1955 one of Hubbard's students wrote that the investigation of the human spirit, or Thetan, was the third echelon of Dianetics and that Hubbard called this third echelon, Scientology. This same student pointed out that in

1950 Hubbard gave the impression that Dianetics was a psycho-therapy and that he (Hubbard) changed his mind, as did many who worked with him. J.F. Horner, writing in *Summary of Scientology*, published in England in 1956, explains it as follows: "However, the techniques of Dianetics required too much skill and knowledge for adequate application by most individuals, so Hubbard turned back to Scientology to develop a further understanding of life itself and create better techniques which could be easily taught and uni-formly applied with predictable results." The spiritual turn was em-phasized a bit later when Horner continues in the same pamphlet: "It has been established through observation and experience that man is, as himself and not as his body, an immortal being; that he does not possess a soul—he is a soul."

The first extravagant statements have been qualified; there is no longer so much emphasis on the declaration that the source of *all* trouble is what has been done *to* an individual. At present there are a number of Scientology Centers, many groups, and the Hubbard Guidance Center in Washington, D.C., as well as one in London. Af-ter talking with some of those who have been processed at the Washington headquarters and others who have talken the course for auditors, I would say that the following seems to be a fair ap-praisal. The books and other literature on Scientology contain some thought-provoking ideas which are not new but do involve tech-niques for helping people in disturbed emotional states. Scientol-ogy is attempting to help many persons such as chronic alcoholics, drug addicts, and the mentally retarded, who are not being ad-equately reached through existing church or psychological chan-nels. The movement attracts people with a mechanistic philosophy and seems to help some of them toward a better adjustment to life. Difficulties apparently arise most often in connection with men and women who undertake to process others without adequate train-ing.

The growth of Dianetics into Scientology is of considerable in-terest in the light of our concern over the doorways to the uncon-scious. As wholesale processing got under way a great many "auditors" (those who processed others) began to discover levels of the mind hitherto unsuspected. This included regression to what appeared to be past lives and an extension of consciousness to in-clude clairvoyance, telepathy, and other psychic abilities.

It is undoubtedly true that many people who claimed to have been helped returned to their old patterns after processing. Certainly, too, a great many people, especially mentally and emotionally unstable persons, were perhaps hurt through the "good intentions" of untrained and inexperienced "do-gooders."

This has a parallel (as odious as it may be to Scientologists) in the history of hypnosis which has been damned by authorities in many different times and places. Judgment should be based on more than prejudice. Is this another sign of the overflowing of the unconscious of man? It will not help to look the other way while the muddy water gets deeper. It seems encouraging to note the more spiritual concern of Scientology and its search for what may be higher spiritual levels of the unconscious.

The work of this group has been described in some detail because it seems to illustrate the tremendous public interest and need for better understanding of the activity of the unconscious mind. Especially during the early years of this group's experimentation heavy doses of vitamin compounds were administered before each regression session. This may have accounted for some glandular stimulation. In my interviews with twenty-three "auditors" all reported that "past lives" were described by about two thirds of the persons processed in reverie, and further that clairvoyant and telepathic abilities were observed in approximately a third of their subjects.

5

Peyote, Mushrooms, and LSD

THE USE OF drugs as a doorway into the unconscious is a complicated subject. Within the past few years both private and institutional experimentation have proceeded at a very rapid pace. It is difficult to keep informed of the published reports of work being done in the field, much less keep abreast of studies and personal experiences which never are printed. Since my own experience with this approach has been limited to study of reports, observation, and a great deal of listening, my presentation here will be brief. I will describe a primitive approach and outline some of the serious studies being undertaken in our own country, touching only in an illustrative way on experimentation, which in some respects is both the most dangerous and interesting.

Spineless cacti, moist, greenish mushrooms, and a drug from a rye fungus open doors into the unconscious for the Indians of our

Southwest and southern Mexico as well as for investigators from our modern colleges and hospitals. In his book, *The Doors of Perception,* Aldous Huxley outlined some of the medical research being conducted several years ago with the drug mescalin—a derivative of peyote—the spineless cacti. He mentioned the adrenal stimulation and described his own sensations of seeing unusual colors after taking mescalin. In the November, 1955, issue of a now defunct publication called *Frauds and Rackets,* Huxley was accused of starting a widespread use of peyote. This article quoted Dr. Clarence G. Salsbury, then Arizona State Commissioner of Health, as saying that experiences with the peyote cactus buttons could be likened to experiences from taking a combination of marijuana, cocaine, heroin, and wood alcohol. The author of this article went on to condemn the use of peyote as habit-forming and suggested that its use was spreading. (The fact that he gave an address where peyote could be ordered probably helped increase distribution.) Aldous Huxley certainly did not consider peyote to be habit-forming. Neither do many physicians who have taken it and reported their experiences.

Recently a little book entitled *Beyond the Light,* by Fay M. Clark, described a near-death, out-of-the-body experience which caused him to begin a search for a way to withdraw from consciousness. He tried experiments with mescalin. Clark outlines his experiences of taking from fifty to four hundred seventy-five milligrams of mescalin in a series of tests. Much of the book consists of his answers to questions asked him while under the influence of the drug. He certainly does not classify the drug as habit-forming. On the other hand, he strongly recommends medical supervision in taking mescalin, and more than idle curiosity as a basis for experiments. Clark was a serious-minded, sincere person when he began his experiments. He now seems to be a more spiritually minded one.

The use of peyote as one of the most widespread religious practices of many Indians of the Southwest is an interesting study in itself. The fresh peyote plant or the dried tops (buttons) are eaten, or a water infusion of the dried buttons is taken as a tea. The Indians believe that God gives His power to them through peyote. It is taken for minor ailments, or in serious illness quantities of it are consumed both by the ill person and relatives and friends who pray for him. Dried buttons are carried on the person as a charm. In special religious ceremonies which last for hours, prayer, singing, eating of the peyote, and contemplation are parts of a formal ritual. Five individuals conduct the ceremonies. There is the Roadman (the leader on the way); the Drum Chief; the Cedar Chief, who is in charge of the incense; the Fire Chief, who is also a sergeant-at-arms; and a close female relative, who has special prayers to perform.

Peyote is taken for healing, for cleansing, in order to have visions and to have mystical experiences. The Indians believe that peyote has healing and cleansing properties. They also use it to increase the power to heal when prayer is directed to others. The peyote visions include communication with the dead, sensitivity to others (including telepathy), speaking in tongues, powers of introspection for correcting faults, and guidance in making decisions of all kinds. The more complex mystical experience is uncommon, being confined to advanced practitioners of peyote rites.

To the Indian the preparations for taking peyote and the ritualistic practices connected with the ceremony are very important. The body is bathed; the mind must be freed of all evil thought, and an attitude of humbleness is essential. It has been suggested that the taking of peyote may be compared with the use of the sacraments of the bread and wine of the Christian communion. The Indian uses peyote to have a direct and personal experience comparable to the coming of the Holy Spirit in Christian tradition. A Comanche Indian is reported to have said, "By using peyote we talk to Jesus, not about Him as the Christian does."

Equally as curious as peyote are the sacred mushrooms which produce visions, as reported by R. Gordon Wasson and his wife. Mr. Wasson, a vice-president of J. P. Morgan and Company, and his late wife, Valentina P. Wasson, M.D., had been studying mushrooms for more than thirty years. In 1955 in a Mexican Indian village Mr. Wasson and a friend took part in a religious ceremony which involved eating "sacred mushrooms." Later his wife and daughter also ate similar mushrooms. All of them experienced unusual visions. Mr. Wasson described his experiences of vivid harmonious colors, and then scenes more vivid than anything ever seen with his own eyes. The daughter reviewed her childhood in detail. Mrs. Wasson visited the court of Louis XV and identified herself and her sister with a tiny pair of elegant miniature china figures who were dancing to Mozart's music. Later a tribal shaman, or medicine man, after eating mushrooms described what the Wassons confirmed to be an accurate clairvoyant vision of their son's actions in New York City.

Mr. Wasson reports that mushrooms have a strange history which is entwined with legend and the supernatural. The Dyaks of Borneo, the natives of New Guinea, the peoples of China and India, as well as the Indians of Mexico and Central America used mushrooms in religious ceremonies. As Wasson puts it, "In man's evolutionary past, there must have come a moment in time when he discovered the secret of hallucinatory mushrooms. Their effect on him, as I see it, could only have been profound, a detonator to new ideas. For mushrooms revealed to him worlds beyond the horizons known to him in space and time, even worlds on a different plane of being, a heaven and perhaps a hell."

More details on the mushroom as a stimulant to psychic sensitivity are presented in a book by Andrija Puharich, M.D., *The Sacred Mushroom*. Dr. Puharich, noted investigator of psychic phenomena, reports on his work with a young sensitive, Harry Stone, who while in infrequent trance states wrote Egyptian hieroglyphics describing a mushroom cult in ancient Egypt. The *amanita muscaria*, the species of mushroom used in Egypt, was found in Maine near Dr. Puharich's laboratory. He gave the mushroom to another sensitive, Peter Hurkos, the Dutch psychic. The results are described in Peter's own words: "Andrija, I have seen things which I don't believe I could ever describe to you in a million years. I was not here in this room. I don't know where I was, but I was in some far-off place of indescribable beauty. The colors, the forms are beyond description." Peter added that he didn't want to take the mushroom very often for he might not want to come back.

Fortunately, Dr. Puharich's medical knowledge of the drugs contained in the mushroom enabled him to supervise the experiments without serious danger to the participants. An overdose of the *amanita muscaria* might make it impossible for a person to return to consciousness.

One of the most powerful and widely used of the hallucinogenic drugs is LSD. It was discovered in 1943 by Dr. A. Hoffman in a Swiss laboratory. Hundreds of scientific papers have been written on experiments with it, some dealing with hospital treatment of insanity, others with the treatment of alcoholism, and still others with depth psychotherapy. Effort has been made to keep the distribution of

LSD under medical supervision. In 1962 experiments to measure the depth of religious experience under the drug were made the basis for a Ph.D. thesis at Harvard.

Robert S. Davidson, Ph.D., a clinical psychologist who wrote the introduction and appendix to *Exploring Inner Space* by Jane Dunlap, says of LSD, "The drug does have the power to expand consciousness and to make one aware of a fundamental unity of all life processes."

In a report issued from the International Foundation for Advanced Study, Menlo Park, California, by J. N. Sherwood, M.D., M. J. Stolaroff, and W. W. Harman, Ph.D., the following comment on the use of heavy doses of LSD suggests the existence of healing powers of inner areas of the mind so far only imagined to exist: "Many of the beneficial effects of LSD-induced experiences have been reported elsewhere. These include the abreaction of pent-up emotions, and increased psychological understanding. However, there is an additional aspect of the large-dose technique which seems to play a most significant role in producing personality transformation: the discovery by the subject of the vast extent of his own being, having understanding and abilities far greater than previously imagined." The report mentions also the work of another investigator who speaks of "peak experiences, mystic or oceanic experiences so profound as to remove neurotic symptoms forever after."

One can only urge the searcher to consider that he is likely to discover the bad as well as the good within himself. Guidance from understanding and medically trained persons is most desirable. High purposes and goals for the searching within are essential to safe passage.

6

Experiences of Fatigue

WHEN MAN GROWS weary or bored the doors of the unconscious sometimes automatically swing open to a world of visions and hallucinations as strange as those induced through drugs. These experiences are just enough like the reports which come from other sources to make it apparent that we really know very little of what goes on beyond the limited range of consciousness.

Dr. John C. Lilly, formerly of the United States National Institute of Mental Health, suggests two general types of hallucinations, one associated with surplus energy and the other a fatigue type. Reports from those taking long sea voyages alone fall under the latter type. One man reported getting sick and passing out on the cabin floor. When he came to, he saw a tall man at the helm of his sloop, who announced that he was a pilot who had come to aid him. "Lie still Senor," he said, "and I will guide your ship tonight." Another lonely sea voyager reports, "... then the sun went down and the stars came out and I dissociated myself from the raft and all the realities and went off into space on my nightly travels." Fred Rebell in his *Escape to the Sea* reports similar experiences: "One night I was floating in the air—roughly a hundred miles to the N.N.E. of my boat's position." Rebell located a vessel by "hallucination" many miles away. Later he verified this. Charles Lindbergh reported many strange sights and sounds as he grew more and more weary on his first flight across the ocean. As experiments with space locks and suits continue with men preparing for travel beyond the earth's atmosphere, hallucinations perhaps will reveal new levels of the unconscious.

All the various doorways to the unconscious seem to indicate the existence of areas and powers of the mind we do not yet understand. Fortunately, for the average person, movement through some of these doorways is difficult; thus dangers associated with them are reduced. Ouija boards and moving pencils are tedious and dull. Mescalin is expensive and frequently makes one sick. Mushrooms are hard to secure. There are still too many questions to be answered about LSD for it to be widely used. For the average person perhaps there are better, safer avenues to the inner world.

4

SAFER DOORWAYS TO THE UNCONSCIOUS

1

Personal Psychic Experiences

SHOULD THE AVERAGE person attempt to explore the unconscious—experiment with telepathy, clairvoyance, precognition, or communication? Many persons will take the position that such explorations should be left to the experts. Let us return to the analogy of the discovery of a new continent. Adventurers and explorers may blaze the trails, discover the mountain ranges and the largest rivers, but the work of settling and developing the land must be done by the people. It is possible that mankind has reached a point in space-time when the unconscious must be explored and understood. To turn back without further examination, in my opinion, would be as foolish as giving up after brief attempts at establishing colonial settlements in the New World. There seems reason to believe that understanding of the unconscious can bring man valuable knowledge—of his own real nature, of his true relationship with his fellow man, of his kinship with what he calls the Creative Force. His heritage, in a historical, evolutionary, and spiritual sense, may be locked within this unconscious. This vast and seemingly mysterious area lies at least partially within man himself. It would seem that physical consciousness may be merely an extension of this hidden self into what we call our three-dimensional world.

Considering experimentation with psychic phenomena as ventures into the unconscious, the following questions still must be asked: *Is experimentation with psychic phenomena dangerous? Is the average person capable of being a good investigator? What can be gained by such investigations?*

It must be recognized that both scientific and public opinion frequently label psychic experiences as signs of abnormality. In spite of the work of many courageous champions, most of whom have been the objects of criticism and scoffing, psychical research struggles to maintain respectability. There are more scientifically trained persons interested and concerned in careful investigation in these areas than is publicly known. Some of the problems which hamper these persons are: the close relations which seem to exist between the experiences of psychotic personalities and sensitives (psychics); the uncritical attitude of the average person; fraud and commercialism. Intelligent public interest will do much to meet all of these difficulties and will help insure trained leadership for better research at the laboratory level.

As the "man on the street" has a psychic experience he becomes a laboratory within himself. As he observes such experiences in those around him, he becomes to a small degree an investigator. Right attitudes and elementary technical knowledge can be helpful. Now to the questions.

Is experimentation with psychic phenomena dangerous? To answer this question an individual must take a good look at himself. Superstition, gullibility, emotionalism, neurotic tendencies, a body which is physically sick—all of these are characteristics that should be warning lights. Careful, personal controls that apply in other fields of investigation must be observed: honesty with oneself and others, open-mindedness, persistence, etc. The real dangers of investigation in psychic areas exist in the very nature of the person himself: the wish to be the center of attention, desire for power over others, greed, hate, anger, self-pity, or fear. If one has stored within his own subconscious a great deal of any of these negative emotions or attitudes, such influences will pour out as he opens a door into psychic realms. More than this, the relationship with other minds, such as the possibility of the existence of a collective unconscious, or perhaps the operation of telepathy, must be considered. Psychiatrists and psychologists would be the first to point out that fears, guilt, and other conflicts are suppressed or repressed in the subconscious, and that to open doors that would release these urges without proper guidance might bring disturbing results.

For many the doors are already open. Would it not be best for such individuals to understand a little more about their own unconscious and be better prepared to deal with such experiences? Definitely, for some people, there is danger in the investigation of psychic phenomena, but there may be even greater danger in not being prepared to cope with the experiences which are called psychic.

Is the average person a good investigator? The answer to this question must be no. Relatively few people are aware of the complex operations of the human mind. Spiritual powers that may function in and through the mind are either not recognized as existing or are confused with superstitions and beliefs that have no foundation in actual experience. It would seem wise, therefore, for anyone who undertakes even a cursory examination of some of his own or others' psychic experiences to prepare himself to use sound methods of observation and study. In learning to fly an airplane one would not only study the manuals showing its operation but would also work with someone who has had experience and could demonstrate a good flying technique. There are many good books in the field of psychical research. For many years there have been both British and American Societies for Psychical Research, established and operated by individuals with both scientific and scholarly aptitudes. The wheat can be separated from the chaff in the writings dealing with psychic studies. Once the search has been begun, one will be led, as in any other field of study, from one helpful book to another. Better and better minds are being drawn into parapsychology. There seems to have been a healthy growth of interest among college groups during the past several years, as seen by the development of undergraduate parapsychology societies and the number of colleges and universities giving courses related to psychical research. Thus, the person who seeks to prepare himself for investigation in these directions will find not only good books which may be used for guidance but also many alert minds traveling the same path.

What can be gained by such investigations?   Through attempts to understand his own psychic experiences and those of people close to him, a person may profit a great deal by becoming better acquainted with new dimensions of himself. One may improve his method for observation and self-discipline in other areas of life. The use of common sense is a good point at which to begin. It will be found that one may increase his control of negative attitudes and emotions as he improves his habits of observation and self-analysis. Such investigations may well lead one to a new philosophy of life, a way of turning from materialism to an examination of the possibility that mind and spirit actually are creating and then working in and through matter, instead of evolving from and depending upon it.

There is of course a growing number of people, which is larger than is suspected, who must face and try to understand experiences that are beyond conscious comprehension. Reference is made here not to the insane or borderline cases of insanity, but to an increasing number of persons who are having psychic experiences that apparently cannot be measured by material standards. The conflicts arising sometimes make them question their own sanity. For such persons, carefully planned study and examination of psychic experiences may prove to be a very real and practical kind of help. Moreover, a person may open doors to resources within himself that will enable him to perform greater services for his fellow man. He may gradually become conscious of a spiritual energy which flows in and through him and is ever available. Can this be the doorway referred to in, "Seek, and ye shall find; knock, and it shall be opened unto you" (Matt. 7:7)? The kingdom of God may lie as much inside as outside of man. One personal experience seemingly bridging the chasms between body, mind, and spirit will bring more meaning to life than listening to many lectures or sermons or the reading of a dozen books. One step along the way which leads to inner searching may enable one to reappraise his whole set of standards and values. With more and more opportunity for free, open discussion of the questions and problems raised in this field of research, more critical methods will be evolved.

The following suggestions have been selected primarily from the Edgar Cayce records. In recommending them I do not suggest they are important simply because they are contained in these records. In working with people who were curious about psychic phenomena, and especially in dealing with those who were having difficulty in controlling psychic sensitivity, these ideas have assisted greatly. People have been helped to recognize and correct physical disabilities that were causing oversensitivity. Others have been led to reappraise so-called "psychic data" and avoid becoming the victims of their own or someone else's unconscious domination. On the other hand there are those who have found new insights and guidance especially through the suggestion for dream study, prayer, and meditation.

There is a need for information as to what has been accomplished in the field of psychical research, but far more important is the necessity for developing techniques for inward steps that can be used successfully in our culture. If these ideas seem too simple or "down to earth," keep in mind that what is being suggested is not an escape from reality or just an adventure but a search for insight which will have direct bearing on mental and spiritual goals in everyday living.

2

Balance

IN GUIDING OR observing others as well as undertaking any personal exploration of psychic experiences, one of the most important considerations is the matter of an even distribution of energy in physical, mental, and spiritual activities. This may be called balance. This idea may appear to be in contradiction to the experiences of many sensitive people. Psychic phenomena seem to occur more often when the body or mind is tired or exhausted, or when overstimulated. The suggestions that follow are in line, however, with the concept that psychic experiences may be the activities of the real self and are not by nature confined to the realm of abnormality. Certainly one will find it much easier to measure and understand such experiences if they can be observed through the clarity of a state of physical, mental, and spiritual balance. Diet is an extremely important factor in such balance.

Environment and work habits must be considered, but for most people foods generally are too heavy—meats, starches, sweets, condiments, etc. Synthetic foods are frequently lacking in necessary vitamins and minerals. One should begin by *obeying* the laws of balanced eating *which he recognizes.* A deliberate choice of food that is known to be harmful, or the refusal to choose food believed to be good, builds blocks at the subconscious level, preventing a person from recognizing the guidance which is continually available to him. It will be argued that an ignorant or misinformed person can simply go on gradually killing himself with bad dietary habits. Admittedly, different persons have different needs. But the real guidance for choices can come from the unconscious *as an individual takes a step along the path he believes to be right.* The process of bringing oneself to these small first steps in self-discipline is far more important than blind choice of some new diet fad.

In organizing thinking toward the practical application of a balanced diet, the following excerpts from the Edgar Cayce readings may help. Some of these suggestions were given for people attempting to appraise their personal psychic experiences.

> Study those charts pertaining to keeping well balanced in the chemical forces of the body. Not in such a way as to become a human pillbox, but rather to know the law and to keep it. 2981-3

> Never when under strain, very tired, very excited, or very mad should the body take foods into the system, and never take any food that the body finds is not agreeing with same. 137-30

> Do include often in the diet raw vegetables, prepared in various ways, not merely as a salad, but scraped or grated and combined with gelatin. 3445-1

> Eat more vegetables! The leafy variety would be preferable to those of the pod nature such as dried beans or peas, or the like. 1657-2

Suggestions for eating more vegetables and salads appear frequently in the readings. The following outlines for meals suggest helpful combinations and warn of others:

Mornings: Whole grain cereals or citrus fruit juices, though not at the same meal. When using orange juice, combine lime with it. When using grapefruit, combine lemon with it, just a little. Egg, preferably only the yolk, rice, buckwheat cakes, or toast, just any one of these, would be well of mornings.

Noons: A raw salad, including tomatoes, radishes, carrots, celery, lettuce, watercress—any or all of these, with soup or vegetable broth, or seafoods, or the like.

Evenings: Fruits, such as cooked apples, potatoes, tomatoes; fish fowl, lamb, and occasionally beef, but not too often. Keep these as the main part of a well-balanced diet. 1523-17

Mornings: Citrus fruit juices or cereals, but not both at the same meal. At other meals there may be taken or included with the others—other cereals—at times dried fruits or figs combined with dates and raisins—these chopped very well together. And, for this body, a mixture of dates and figs that are dried, cooked with a little corn meal—a very little sprinkled in—then this taken with milk, should be almost a spiritual food for this body. Whether it's taken one, two, three, or four meals a day. But this is to be left to the body itself to decide.

Noons: Foods such as vegetable juices, or these combined with a little meat juices and a combination of raw vegetables; but not vinegar or the like with same, but oils, if they are olive oil or vegetable oils, may be used with same.

Evenings: Vegetables that are of the leafy nature; fish, fowl, or lamb, preferably, as the meats—or their combinations. These of course are not to be all the foods, but this is the general outline for the three meals for the body.

But remember for this particular body equal portions of black figs or Assyrian figs and Assyrian dates—these ground together or cut very fine—and to a pint of such a combination put half a handful of corn meal, or crushed wheat. These cooked together—well, it's food for such a spiritually developed body as this. 275-45

It was pointed out that as physical exercise or manual activity decreased, the amounts of alkaline-reacting foods should be increased. Foods combining fats and sugars and starches were labeled acid producing. One reading summarizes this point of view as follows:

> Have 80 percent alkaline-producing to 20 percent acid-producing foods in the diet. It is well, however, that the body not become as one who can't ever do this, that or the other—or at a slave to an idea of a set diet. But do not take citrus fruit juices and cereals at the same meal. Do not take milk or cream in coffee or tea. Do not eat fried foods of any kind. Do not combine white bread, potatoes, spaghetti, or any two foods of such natures, in the same meal. 1568-2

The advisability of choosing foods grown in the area where the person lives is stressed in a number of readings:

> Do not have large quantities of fruits, vegetables, meats, that are not grown in or that do not come from the area where the body is—at the time it partakes of such foods. This will be found to be a good rule to be followed by all. This prepares the system to acclimate itself to any given territory. 3542-I

> Have vegetables that are fresh especially those grown in the vicinity where the body resides. Shipped vegetables are never very good. 2-14

No less important than the consideration of diet is the matter of exercise in keeping physically fit:

> We find that these conditions arose as a result of what might be called occupational disturbances: not enough in the sun, nor enough hard work . . . the body is supposed to coordinate the spiritual, mental and physical. He who does not give recreation a place in his life—and the proper tone to each phase–fools himself.
> There must be a certain amount of sleep. Didn't God make man to sleep at least a third of his life? Then consider! These

are physical, mental and spiritual necessities. This is what the Master meant when He said, "Consider the lilies of the field, how they grow." Do they grow all the while, bloom all the while—or look mighty messy and dirty at times? It is well for people, individuals, as this entity, to get their hands dirty in the dirt at times, and not be the white-collared man all the time! . . . From whence was man made? Don't be afraid to get a little dirt on you once in a while . . . And take time to play a while with others. There are children growing. Have you added anything constructive to any child's life? 3352-1

Stretching was frequently recommended as an excellent exercise. Walking was highly endorsed in many readings, as in the following:

Walking is the best exercise, but don't do it spasmodically. Have a regular time and do it rain or shine. 1968-9

The following extracts from Edgar Cayce readings dealing with balanced mental activity were interesting to me:

Do not allow any of the elements that would cause distress to the mental forces—through anger toward any individual or groups—to find lodgment in the mental and soul develop-ments of the body. For it is the *application* of the knowledge of these laws that keeps you whole—that keeps you on the even keel of development, whether of the physical, mental, soul or spiritual. 140-2

For know, ever, that in the correct development in every entity, the mental forces must be the directing forces, partak-ing of many elements. For all elements have their relationship one to another in each soul. On the mental the soul feeds. The body must be *well-rounded* in physical and mental attributes, so that the soul may develop, and the spiritual will remain . . . as the guiding force in the correct and upright channels. 900-8

In relating balance to the spiritual aspect of life, again it would have to be defined as an individual thing. For some it would be a matter of regular church attendance, or daily prayer, or for others it might be the reading of sacred or inspirational literature on a daily schedule. Or perhaps living according to the precepts of some religious teacher might for some constitute a spiritual life. Whatever the concept one has of his spiritual life, it is important, it seems to me, to bring the thinking into focus so there can be a schedule of daily attention directed toward spiritual things.

The following seems to me a good summary from the Edgar Cayce readings concerning balance in all activities mental, spiritual, and physical:

> Take time to be holy, but take time to play also. Take time to rest, time to recuperate; for thy Master, even in the pattern in the earth, took time to rest, took time to be apart from others, took time to attend a wedding, to give time to attend a funeral; took time to attend those awakenings from death and took time to minister to all.
>
> So in learning thy experiences in the earth, not as routine but at regular periods have thy rest, have thy labors, do feed the mind; do feed the soul, just as it is necessary to feed the physical man. These will declare just as much dividend as does that necessity of feeding the body. Without mastication there is indigestion and suffering. So with the foods of the mind and soul, it must be masticated and put to use, and these will bring much more harmonious experience. 5246-1

> Realize that all power (gas, drug, mineral, vegetable) receives its spiritual essence from an all-wise Providence that has left such manifestations in a material.
>
> Be thou wise: not in thine own conceit but in the wisdom of the Lord, and subdue the earth; making these coordinant, as it were, with that which is in thine own body, mind and soul. For when the earth was brought into existence or into time and space, all the elements that are outside man may be found in the living human body. Hence these in coordination, as we see them in nature—air—fire—earth—make the soul, body and mind one coordinating factor with the universal creative energy we call God. Then coordinate thyself with God—with nature, with the environ thou art in—through thine inner self. 557-3

3

Observation

CONSIDER THAT THE study of personal psychic experiences is like setting up an experiment in a laboratory. Daily activities constitute the laboratory situation. To get the best possible results one must become a good observer, as free as possible from tensions brought about by any unbalanced physical, mental, or spiritual activity.

The powers of observation can be so improved that increased awareness will become a natural result. There are five obvious windows through which man looks out on the world in which he live– the eyes, the taste buds, the ears, the nose, and the skin. What are their functions and the states of awareness which they create?

A man sees a small oak tree on the roadside. The leaves still cling to it, though they have turned a brownish red with the coming of winter. This tree is silhouetted against the sky. Its trunk is about eight inches in diameter. The branches reach out about fifteen feet on each side. Perhaps he has passed it many times. It is just an oak tree.

He now approaches the tree with the idea of examining it more carefully with each of the five senses. He moves closer and looks at the trunk. Two columns of ants are moving up and down on it. He notices the rough texture of the bark. He chews a bit of it. Bitterness. One of the four types of taste buds has been stimulated. He smells the leaf. Then smells the bark. Vivid pictures float up from childhood memories of happy hours in the woods. Now he breaks a branch and notes how different the smell of the inner fiber is from either the bark or the leaf. The man is quiet now. He listens to the movement of the tree as the wind rushes the leaves. He places his ear close to the trunk and hears the stretch and strain of the wood as it bends and gives and returns to position. He breaks another limb and hears the crack as the wood is splintered. His fingers move over the bark and then over the smooth spot of an ax scar. He feels the smoothness of the leaf. The man has come to know this tree on a different level of awareness.

Beyond this new awareness of the tree, much is going on which the man knows exists but which he cannot comprehend with his senses—the movement of the sap, the growth of both the roots and the limbs, the magic absorption of sunlight, and the change of carbon dioxide to oxygen. In fact, there is a whole world of the tree's activity beyond this perception.

In every one of the senses there are ranges beyond man's normal perception: the brilliant-colored spectrum of the prism; the fingers of the blind racing swiftly over Braille letters; a dog, nose to the ground, following unerringly the twisting trail of a rabbit; sounds beyond the range of the human ear, heard clearly by an animal.

For many persons deeper understanding and appreciation of life can result from extending and enriching perception through these senses. Psychic perception, to some extent at least, might be thought of as following sense perceptions to the borderline, where almost within the range of man's eyes and ears and touch, matter becomes energy, mind, and spirit. Man begins to sense the oneness of all the universe.

Consciousness varies for each individual and, in fact, is different from moment to moment. People seldom stop to recognize or consider the degrees of consciousness. One could test the truth of this assertion, in his own case, by stopping at any given moment and recalling the extent of his awareness during the preceding few minutes. What sounds were heard? Did an automobile pass or a plane fly over? Was the clock heard ticking? What odors were sensed? Were any pressures on the body noticeable? Were there any sensations in the internal parts of the body? Was the right hand warmer than the right foot? Besides those things on which attention was focused, did other objects stimulate the consciousness? Did anyone enter the room? If so, what color dress or suit did the person wear?

Consciousness would be considerably changed after a period of such questioning. Almost everyone is familiar with the fact that sometimes he is more alert than at other times. Perceptions are keener at certain intervals during the day, according to physical conditions. An individual can expect an expansion of consciousness as he becomes aware of its various levels and practices simple experiments to extend its range.

Actually, a majority of people spend their lives in a very limited state of awareness. They are very much like men standing in the center of a large warehouse: the five senses deliver all sorts of packages, bales, and boxes. These are stacked up around them, gradually shutting off perception of the world beyond the confines of the warehouse itself! The packages, bales, and boxes are representations of the so-called realities of the outside world. Consciousness becomes more and more limited as the senses are curtailed and dulled. It becomes necessary to depend on previous states of awareness, and then memory of them begins to fade. Day by day man limits himself, until he is disturbed and frightened by the taste of strange foods, by an unfamiliar odor, the sight of different colored skins, the touch of unfamiliar objects, or the sound of more complicated music than he is accustomed to hearing. Conscious attempts to increase sense perception will not only bring a richer experience at a mental and physical level but will also help increase psychic sensitivity. Be prepared to see more, hear more, smell more.

One of the favorite themes of fairy tales is the fuller awareness of the animal world which opens to some fortunate seeker. "The White Snake"[1] is a typical example. A servant knows that his king regularly

---

[1] *Grimm's* Fairy Tales, trans. Luca, Crane, and Edwards (New York: Grosset and Dunlap, Inc., 1945).

eats a small piece of a white snake. He tries this and is then able to communicate with a fish which finds a lost ring for him, and an army of ants who help him perform the humanly impossible task of collecting ten sacks of millet seeds. He continues with the assistance of his new friends of the animal and insect world to achieve "happiness" by marrying the princess (spirit) and becoming king. Students of metaphysics find childhood fairy tales a considerable source of inspiration and help. They are a rich storehouse of mystical and occult lore—"for those who have eyes to see and ears to hear."

4

Self-Appraisal in Discussing the Psychic

EXPLORATIONS INTO THE realms of the psychic should begin with as thorough a self-examination as is possible. In this matter one cannot afford to be careless. One word of caution before considering a few suggestions about techniques for self-observation. This should not be a process of self-condemnation. When one catches himself in an obvious falsehood, he must not try to explain it away, but on the other hand, neither should he allow depression over the discovery of such a weakness. One might try some of the following exercises and then devise other tests for himself.

The way psychic data are discussed with others should be examined critically. One may take his best psychic story and review it step by step in his mind. Has anything been added to the original story? Have the adjectives grown more colorful with each telling? Has the truth been shaded to any degree? Now trim this story, prune it of all bits of exaggeration, and then make a point of retelling it in its new and purer form.

Here is another approach. Select a story from a good book on psychic experiences. Get the facts clearly in mind. Now examine the story for all its weak points. Prepare to tell this story but also by question and comment to point out the weaknesses in it. At the first opportunity tell this story to a group of people and carefully observe their reactions to the questions and doubts which are raised. Through this process one may become more aware and more critical in his observations of his own and others' experiences. It should be remembered that this is a process of appraisal, not condemnation.

One should take time to read a book or two which critically appraise the whole field of psychic research. William S. Sadler, M.D., *The Mind at Mischief,*[1] Joseph Jastrow, *Wish and Wisdom,*[2] or a more modern one, Martin Gardner, *In the Name of Science*[3] are typical.

When it is convenient one should discuss with a psychologist or psychiatrist his appraisal and explanation of a favorite psychic story. The following points may be kept in mind. Stories of a psychic nature are frequently distorted, either because people relate other people's experiences as if they were their own or because it is difficult to overcome a natural desire to exaggerate for the sake of attracting attention and make one's point so irrefutable as to confound the listeners. After a story has been told several times, one comes actually to believe it as told. Only very careful self-analysis will reveal the basic fallacy. We have a strong tendency to hear only what we want to hear. Facts and items in connection with psychic experiences which are in opposition to our established beliefs are frequently discarded. This, of course, is as true of the negative approach to the examination of psychic experiences as to the positive side of this question. The unusual, the exciting, in the form of a psychic experience or psychic story is a great relief. There is much of the child in all men, in creating a world of make-believe, where wishes and hopes take the place of actuality.

---

[1] New York: Funk & Wagnalls Co., 1929.
[2] New York: D. Appleton & Co., 1935.
[3] New York: G. P. Putnum's Sons, 1952.

5

Ways of Experimenting with Telepathy

EXPERIMENTATION WITH MIND-to-mind communication can be exciting and helpful. Even if it is considered to be a game, it must be remembered that the best games have rules which must be obeyed if there is to be real enjoyment.

I have tried the following group experiments with good results. It was explained that an experiment in telepathy and clairvoyance was to be conducted in an attempt to discover who could be a good "sender" by visualizing clearly. Everyone was directed to close his eyes and imagine a white motion-picture screen. They were told to see a tree on this screen and instructed to fill in the branches and the leaves and see the color. They were to keep looking until they saw this tree very vividly on the white screen. Several minutes elapsed. Then one by one each person was asked to describe what he saw. The three persons who saw the tree in the clearest detail were asked to go into another room. After being separated from the group, it was explained to them that they were to discuss and decide on a scene involving action and all three were to concentrate on it as it was sketched. Each of the persons in the adjoining room was given a pencil and paper. It was explained that the "senders" would endeavor, at a given signal, to project a scene to them. No clue as to the type of scene was given. Those remaining in the room were asked to visualize again the white screen and at a given signal to draw whatever they saw appear on it. The correspondence between what was sent and received surprised everyone.

Another experiment which may well provide an interesting evening's entertainment, as well as bring some insight into the operation of telepathy and clairvoyance would be to use a pack of twenty-five cards containing symbols five duplications of five different symbol–making twenty-five in all. Rather than use Dr. J. B. Rhine's ESP cards, which are marked with crosses, wavy lines, squares, etc., a set of symbols which might have special interest and significance to the audience may be devised. This idea has been used effectively by a Virginia advertising concern which published a little booklet, *You and PSI*.[1] Their deck of twenty-five cards, which was included with the booklet, bore business symbols—%, @, / and ¢—all familiar to the average person in business. If a session with neighborhood wives was planned, a light bulb, a fork, a broom, etc. might be the symbols. They should be well known and easily recognizable.

It might be helpful if the group are directed to use the white screen on which to visualize the symbol appearing in black. Or, if they prefer, they may visualize a black screen on which the symbols appear in white. One of the group is asked to sit across the room from the others and slowly go through the deck of twenty-five cards which has been shuffled, looking for a few seconds at each card, and then visualizing it on the screen. The receivers in turn visualize the symbols as they are sent to the screen, writing them down opposite numbers from one to twenty-five. The procedure should be repeated three times with the deck before the scores are tabulated. Once the group have gotten familiar with the procedure, they may shuffle the deck and place it face down on a table. Each one present

---

[1]Richmond: Cargill & Wilson, 1956.

then attempts to go down through the deck, writing opposite the number the twenty-five symbols as they believe they appear. Consistent scoring averaging more than five symbols out of twenty-five may be considered significant.

An even simpler approach to experiments with telepathy and clairvoyance can be handled by making an agreement with a friend or relative to think about him at a certain time during the day. At the fixed time visualize the white screen and think about the person. Jot down impressions, words, or descriptions of scenes which come to mind. The results may prove startling. This experiment requires patience and persistence. Remember, if one were attempting to communicate with another person in a new language which the two were practicing together, it would be necessary not only to study the language but also to become familiar with the same vocabulary and practice it regularly with one's colleague. To begin to communicate telepathically or clairvoyantly, one must persist in his experiments. Any impressions that one received, regardless of how abstract or unrelated they may seem to be, should be recorded. A great many people have found that they are able to communicate in this fashion with particular individuals.[2]

For several months in 1934 I met weekly with a group of eight young people in Norfolk, Virginia, to discuss psychical research and conduct experiments in telepathy and clairvoyance. We worked with cards and drawing experiments. Between meetings members in the group paired off and tried to transmit impressions at specific times. Some interesting results were obtained.

One of the members made a trip to Washington, D.C. When it was learned that he was to be away over the period of the weekly meeting, it was agreed that at the time for the regular meeting he would perform a particular act unknown to the group. The members of the group would attempt to draw an impression of his act. At the appointed time members of our group took paper and pencil and moved to various places in the home so no two were near each other. Two members of the group drew a rose in a small vase; another one wrote white rose, and a fourth wrote smell. Two days later

---

[2]Upton Sinclair, *Mental Ratio* (Springfield, Ill.: C. C. Thomas, rev. ed. 1962); Wilkins and Sherman, *Thoughts Through Space* (New York: Creative Age Press, 1942).

a card arrived from the group member in Washington bearing the following: "8 P.M. Tuesday [date], walked into lobby Annapolis Hotel. Took white rose from vase on table. Smelled it and put it back." Signed, "M.A." The group members were startled, to say the least, and decided to rethink their ideas on telepathy.

These suggestions have been given as illustrations of what is possible in the way of devising simple, yet effective experiments. These are not laboratory procedures, but they can be interesting and personally most convincing. The following steps may be checked: (1) Write everything out at the time of the experiment, putting in both time and date. (2) Where possible, mail data on cards, that will bear proper post marks for future reference. (3) Take care that individuals in a group are separated so that no visual or sound communication is possible. (4) Have all witnesses sign data giving full names and addresses.

It can be of great help in the field of psychical research to recognize the need for open-minded, yet critical appraisal of evidence for psychic perception. The simplest procedure frequently produces the best evidence. Carefully recorded, spontaneous examples of psychic perception sometimes provide the most arresting evidence for its existence.

6

Using Your Dreams

ON THE MORNING of March 29, 1929, Raymond Reeves awoke and immediately reached for the pencil and pad on his bedside table. He wrote the following dream: "Got the impression regarding the market that we ought to sell everything, including our box stock. A bull seemed to be following my wife who had on a red dress."

On April 6, 1929, Reeves dreamed of a gang of men who were responsible for the death of another man. One of the men had a hypodermic needle which had been used on the dead man. He turned and tried to stick the needle into Reeves.

Reeves was a member of the New York Stock Exchange. The dreams were submitted to Edgar Cayce for interpretation through his psychic readings.

The interpretation of the first dream stated that this was an impression of conditions which were to come about. A downward movement of long duration was about to take place. Even the stocks thought to be the safest, such as a box stock of which Reeves thought highly, were to drop in price.

In interpreting the second dream on April 6, 1929, the same day Reeves had the dream, the following statement was made in the Edgar Cayce reading:

> The injection indicates the attempts to bolster the market. There must surely come a break where there will be panic in the money centers, not only of Wall Street's activity but a closing of the boards in many other centers and readjustment of the actual specie—higher and lower quotations to continue for several moons while adjustments are being made—then break. 137-117

For Reeves the bull was surely a symbol of the market at the time of his dream. His wife sought a divorce shortly after the dream. The bull was following her. The red dress could have been a danger signal.

On October 29, 1929, several moons after the April 6 dream, sixteen million shares of stock changed hands, including unrestricted short selling. By the end of 1929 the estimated decline in the values of stocks had reached the staggering total of fifteen billion dollars. One of the worst depressions in American history began.

Were these precognitive dreams or just good subconscious reasoning of a stockbroker? From his unconscious state Edgar Cayce confirmed and amplified the warnings, thus confirming the statements he had made many times regarding the value and importance of dreams as a doorway into the unconscious.

In fact the Edgar Cayce readings on dreams, of which there are more than six hundred, go much further in emphasizing the importance of dreams when they say that nothing of importance ever happens to a man which is not first previewed in a dream.

Dreams are the language of the unconscious. For approximately one-third of his life, in sleep, man is in a mental and physical state in which this language comes through, first fragmentarily and then, as attention is focused on it, in more complete patterns. Modern psychologists and psychiatrists recognize their importance as a means of understanding and helping patients. Freud called dreams the "via regia," the royal road, to the unconscious. His studies proved that they were closely related to his patients' innermost thoughts and feelings. Emil Gutheil, M.D., author of *The Handbook of Dream Analysis,*[1] says that no dream is unimportant: " . . . each dream carries a significant emotional and intellectual cargo." Carl Jung, recognized by many as one of the most resourceful explorers of the unconscious, stated that dreams are specifically the utterances of the unconscious. He stressed that they were almost exclusively about and out of oneself and give a truer picture of the subjective state than is possible to ascertain through conscious thought.

Dreams have played a strange part in the history of man. The Old and New Testaments contain stories of dreams which changed the lives of the dreamers and those who depended on them. For example, Joseph, a son of Jacob, who became adviser to an Egyptian Pharaoh, was a successful interpreter of dreams; as was a later Joseph whose dreams saved the life of his Son, Jesus.

One of the best-known dreams, dealing with a scientific discovery of importance, was that of the German scientist, Kekule. From a dream he was able to draw the structure of a benzine molecule seventy years before it could be seen with an electronic microscope.

While working on a sonata, Tarlini, the Italian violinist, dreamed that he saw and heard the devil playing his composition. From this he was able to reproduce what he had heard in his dream. This became one of his best-known works, "Sonata with the Devil's Trill."

Apart from the creative type of dream there are those which relate to various kinds of psychic perception of which precognition is one of the most interesting. Abraham Lincoln's dream of his own death is designated as one of the precognitive type. Another unusually impressive dream of this character is reported by J. W. Dunne, an engineer who recorded a long study of his own and other people's dreams in his book, *An Experiment with Time.*[2] He also presents his findings and theories on time. In the spring of 1902, while with the British army in South Africa, he dreamed of seeing an island about to be destroyed by a volcano. In his dream he tried to warn the four thousand inhabitants and rushed from one official to another. They refused to listen to him. The next delivery of newspa-

---

[1] New York: Liveright Publishing Corp., 1951.
[2] London: Faber & Faber, Ltd., 3rd ed., 1934.

pers brought accounts of the volcano disaster in Martinique. He misread the papers and thought that the forty thousand people reported to have been lost read four thousand. The true figure of the loss of life was neither four nor forty thousand, but the peculiar mistake in the dream was taken by Dunne to have been related to the newspaper account.

Dreams are excellent source material for the study of all kinds of psychic experiences, including what appears to be telepathy, clairvoyance, precognition, communication with the dead, memory of past lives, astral projection, etc. Is it possible that many more psychic experiences appear in dreams than we are able to recognize, when we record them in a fragmentary manner or ignore them completely? The Mohammedans say that our dreams are like unopened letters.

The following which I have collected from neighbors and friends may be said to be typical examples of each of the above categories.

Telepathy? A young man working in an insurance office in Hartford, Connecticut, dreamed of the wedding of a young woman in his office. He saw the date, June, 1937, six months prior to his dream, the place, the people who were present and a description of the small plain wedding ring of white gold. The next day when he laughingly told the girl about his dream she was shocked. The marriage had taken place just as he described it. She had kept it a secret. No one in the officc knew of the event. Notices had not appeared in the local papers.

Clairvoyance? In the spring of 1908, William C. and his brother, Roger, were living in Los Angeles, California. One day they received a letter from a friend, a Mr. Rudolph, living in New Jersey, informing them that friends of his, Mr. and Mrs. Harry Campbell, were taking a pleasure trip and expected to be in Los Angeles. The letter explained that Rudolph did not know what hotel the Campbells intended using but he felt sure that William and his brother could locate them within a few days at one of the better hotels. He had forgotten to mention the brothers to the Campbells. For several days the young men made the rounds of a number of hotels without success. Finally when call after call at various hotels produced no results, they decided that the Campbells were not visiting Los Angeles. On Monday morning William awakened, realizing that he had dreamed something about the Campbells, but he could not remember his dream. At the breakfast table the dream came back to him and he told his brother, Roger, the following:

"In my dream I heard a voice saying, 'Are you looking for the Campbells?' I answered, 'Yes,' and the voice continued, 'You will find them at the Van Nuys Hotel.' In reply I asked, 'Which Van Nuys?' The voice answered, 'The Main Street Van Nuys.'" There were two Van Nuys Hotels.

Roger laughed at his brother and kidded him about the dream. To prove there was nothing to it he insisted that they stop by the Van Nuys and ask for the Campbells. This they did and were surprised to find that the Campbells had registered there sometime on Saturday. Their search had stopped on Friday. The dream took place on Sunday night.

Precognition? Mrs. A.'s husband was a switchman on a train pulling coal from the mines in Henryetta, Oklahoma. During the night of October 4, 1934, she dreamed that he came home with blood streaming down his cheek. Mrs. A. was frightened because the dream was so real. She told her husband about it when he came home at 4 A.M. He laughed at her. The following morning at 2 A.M. he awakened his wife. When she opened the door she was horrified to see him standing before her with blood streaming down his face just as she had seen him in her dream the night before.

Communication? Horace H. dreamed of waiting in a large hotel. A train arrived and his mother and father (who had died several years previously) got off. Both parents seemed well and happy. Horace embraced them. The physical sensation was quite real. All three then entered the dining room of the hotel and talked for what seemed a long time. Horace could not remember the conversation but realized it was on a cheerful note. His parents showed him tickets which were different colored from his own. The train arrived and they departed. Horace waited for a train going in the opposite direction. He awoke feeling as if he had talked with his parents.

Memory of Past Life? In the following dream the person stressed the vividness of the experience. The costumes were what one would expect in the period, and the physical sensations of heat were very real. John Lane dreamed that he saw himself with Lot, his wife and daughters as they fled from Sodom. Lot's wife was killed by falling lava. Lane escaped.

The cataloguing and classification of psychic experiences in one's dreams might be reason enough for the careful daily recording of them, but a great deal more is to be gained through this doorway into the unconscious. The Edgar Cayce readings pointed out the importance of dreams as a source of guidance for physical, mental, and spiritual problems. The following are extracts which stress their value:

Consciousness is sought by man for his own diversion. In sleep the soul seeks the real diversion or the real activity of self. Those who are nearer the spiritual realm more often retain their visions and dreams on awakening. Self rarely desires to condemn self except when self wars with self. 5754-3

The study of the subconscious, subliminal, psychic, soul forces, is and should be the great study for the human family; for through self man will understand his Maker when he understands his relation to his Maker . . . In this age there is not sufficient credence given dreams; for the best development of the human family, knowledge of the unconscious, soul or spirit world should be increased. 3744-5

The great truth that must become apparent is the ease with which the individual may apply what may be obtained from his own subconscious self—the cosmic forces or universal consciousness . . . This truth must be made known to the layman, the individual, the scientist, the mathematician, the historian. Any individual seeking information through these sources finds it to be true . . . This has been true in every age. 254-46

Hence, as has been given, pay more attention to the dreams of each and every one, if the physical forces, the mental elements, the body-mind, the mental attributes, the spiritual development, would be such as to make advancement in a material world. 294-34

The following are typical examples of the introductions in readings dealing with interpretations of dreams:

These are phenomena or experiences for the body to use
and to apply in its everyday walks of life . . . The body must
approach [the interpretations] with the correct purpose . . .
Although the dreams may be explained for the entity, the
whole reaction must be solely within self—if the body is to be
able to apply that gained through the experience. For remember, these are only illustrations, and not the means of escape,
but given so that one may have an understanding of how to
apply within self, first in the spiritual sense and then in the
material sense, as an outgrowth of doing that known. (March
24, 1928) 4167-1

. . . to every normal body with a developing mind, conditions are often presented through the subconscious forces
during the sleeping state, wherein truths are given; visions are
seen of things to be warned or taken advantage of; conditions shown in which would be brought advantages to the
body—physically, mentally, morally, spiritually and finan-
cially.   294-34

The dreams when correlated with those symbols relating
to the various phases of the individual, give that individual a
better understanding of self, if correctly interpreted. 3744-5

On the morning of March 31, 1926, Edgar Cayce dreamed of
scalding to death in the bathtub. The impression was a vivid one. As
a whole series of dream interpretations was being undertaken during the period, this dream was included. It should be noted that
during the time he suffered from neuritis. As in many cases details
of the dream were recalled through the reading. This was the comment on the dream:

There was seen and felt within the entity the necessity of
overcoming physical pain by immersing the body in warm or
hot water. When the body is reclining in same, it is overcome
by the heat, from the effect of too much relaxation for the high
blood pressure in the heart's action. Death ensues. Someone
approaches and attempts to gain entrance. The various activities that follow are seen: the preparation, the notification of those

who are to be advised concerning the demise of the entity; the preparation and journey to the place of interment; the feeling of the change at a given place when the body is brought; and the actions concerning conditions as ensue when the changes that become necessary in the family affairs of the individual take place; and the following (death) of the individual held so dear in the physical mind.

In this then we find there are many various conditions that are presented to the entity for study. Many lessons may be gained from the full concept of this as is viewed. First and foremost—the physical defects in the body need attention, else death might occur. Also, this lesson should again be considered: even though the physical body may be laid aside, the operation of "the work," as is seen and carried on in this state, will be going just the same. The impression, the lessons, the guiding forces, the directing, and the help and assistance to many will continue, especially to those with whom the entity feels, in the physical, the close endearment, the close connections.

This lesson should be gained: Life is action of the mind. While mind is divided into different phases, their active forces are one and the same. The physical body proves to be a hindrance to the active force of mind rather than a help, save as the mind may be applied in the physical plane to the assistance and aid of other individuals. 294-70

I mention the following points not as evidence for prophecy but simply as interesting coincidences. The cause of Edgar Cayce's death, as diagnosed by the physician, was pulmonary edema, water on the lungs. As noted in the comment on the dream, death of a person held "dear in the physical mind" followed his own death. Gertrude Cayce, my mother, died within three months of my father. He had this dream and the interpretation in 1926.

More specific dream interpretations from the readings may be helpful at this point. It should be remembered that these are individual, not general, readings. Each person's "language of the unconscious," though it may contain some universal symbology, is a private language, a set of personal symbols. The following are briefs of dreams and the suggested interpretation from the Edgar Cayce readings.

Dream—A. bought a pair of riding pants. They seemed very good until on close examination it was revealed that they were too large and rather worn.

Int.—Plans for horseback-riding, which was contemplated as a health measure, would prove good if enjoyed in moderation.

D.—Combing hair with kinks in it.

Int.—Advised to reconsider decisions made that day—kinks would be discovered in reasoning.

D.—A mother saw son, who spoke of his uncle's illness, standing by fire escape.

Int.—Precognition of uncle's illness. Mother urged to use son's advice (fire escape) to help her brother.

D.—Wife dreamed of riding a horse which reared up with her. Husband caught and quieted animal.

Int.—Urged to follow husband's advice.

D.—Saw wild man running loose in streets, storm in house, curtains at window blowing.

Int.—Wild man was self's temper which was upsetting home conditions.

The following list of symbols and their meanings was worked out from a series of readings received by a man seventeen years old.

Dog—trust.
Fire—disturbance.
Fence—closing self in.
Speech-making—what is being presented to others.
Fish, caught—achievements.
Pool—pool of life.
Slimy creatures, hornets—obstacles.
Dirigible—high ideals.
Tools—preparation for lifework.
Water—spirit.
Part of body removed—giving up part of lifework.
High hill—spiritual attainment, view.
Smooth road—physical ease.
Elephant—power of mind, memory, cunning.
Turtle being fed—strength, new life.

During sleep we take stock of what has been done during the waking state. The range, complexity, and value of the experiences during sleep can become apparent only as the language is understood. An adequate vocabulary can be built up only from a collection of dreams.

For the past several years groups of young people have come to Virginia Beach during the summer months to take part in group projects which I have organized and designed to test ideas in the Edgar Cayce readings. Many of these projects have been focused on recording and group discussion of daily dreams. Members of the group have been encouraged to continue their work of dream recording and self-analysis. Several months after taking part in a project, one young man from Columbus, Ohio, reported the following dream and his analysis of it:

I saw myself standing on the beach fishing. By me was a small self, the size of a boy but a replica of myself, who was crying for the fish the larger self was attempting to catch. Finally I caught a large flounder and handed it to the smaller self. As he began to eat the fish it flopped out of his hands and fell behind a small bush on the beach. When I stooped to pick up the fish I found a beaver and white rabbit eating on the fish. The beaver ran away and did not return. The rabbit jumped into the water but finally returned wet and bedraggled.

The young man worked out what proved to be a very helpful explanation by asking himself over and over what each symbol in the dream meant to him. Then by comparing it with preview dream symbols he put together a fairly coherent interpretation. The water was spirit, the fish was spiritual food. The smaller self was at first thought to be the childhood during which spiritual guidance had been denied. After reexamination the smaller self was considered to be the real or higher self *which was crying for spiritual food.* The beaver and the rabbit were symbols of activities which were interfering with spiritual life, were "eating it up." The beaver was the daily work or job. The white rabbit was associated in the young man's mind with sex activity. As a child he remembered the deep impressions of the sex activity of his pet white rabbits. In reviewing the influence of his job, the young man recognized the disturbance he felt over being involved in the manufacture of war materials. Associates at work had been responsible for drinking habits which led to family difficulties. Coupled with the drinking, sex problems had resulted in separation from his wife and children. To this young man his dream was of considerable help in analyzing his difficulties and facing himself.

There are times when the language of the unconscious is so clear and concise that it is impossible to mistake its meaning. The following seems to have been a very helpful dream at a very practical level. A woman wrote from Canada:

> . . . After listening to your tape on dreams from the Phoenix Conference we decided to try remembering our dreams and feel that we received one message of real benefit to a member of our group. This fellow, Mr. X., had an asthmatic condition and would have such severe coughing spells that he would black out at times. The doctors seemed to be puzzled, said it was an unusual condition and couldn't help him much . . .

> At our next meeting, a week after hearing the tape, Mrs. X. recalled a brief but vivid dream she had had. It didn't mean anything to her but she related it anyway as follows: She could see a hand come out and pour two ounces of lemon juice into a glass, then come back and add an ice cube. Just the hand. That's all there was to it yet it was very vivid in her memory. As we had been remembering Mr. X. in our meditation period, we felt that it was a message, so suggested that Mrs. X. give her husband two ounces of lemon juice each day and just try it. It couldn't do any harm, anyway.

> The results are that after two week's time, his cough was so much better that he hasn't blacked out since (four months) and his cough or asthmatic condition is completely cleared up. The odd part of it was the fact that he enjoyed the lemon and could take it straight with just the ice in it. His system must have needed it.

> We thought you might be interested to know that your talk on dreams has certainly done a lot of good for this man.

The Edgar Cayce readings outline three general types of dreams:

those resulting from physical stimuli, i.e., the hard place in the bed, the cold breeze from an open window, indigestion, etc.; those from the unconscious, wherein the activities and thoughts of the day are measured by the unconscious desires, attitudes, and purposes; and those that offer guidance from the higher or superconscious mind. This is generally symbolic, but sometimes takes on the atmosphere of the "vision."

When suggestions are made to record and study dreams, people immediately begin forming objections, making excuses, and finding ways to avoid the hard work necessary in becoming acquainted with the unconscious through this doorway. They point out that people cannot understand their own dreams. Help in the form of therapy is necessary. They remember some of their crazy-mixed-up, frequently uncomprehendable dreams. These apparently made no sense at all and others were too grotesque, sometimes too revealing to consider. How, they ask, can we be expected to ferret out anything from such a hodge-podge?

Such persons might recall their first experience in studying a foreign language. Each day they were given a few new words to learn—gradually building a vocabulary in the new language. They learned something about verb conjugations, sentence structure, etc. Almost immediately they were able to read simple sentences and paragraphs. They were not expected to take one word, one phrase, or one sentence and from it know how to read the language. In like manner, it is not possible to take one dream and from it understand the symbology, the language, of the unconscious. Each one must write a book—his own book. This is hard work but it is a sure, sound, and safe way to examine the mysterious region called the unconscious mind.

To begin writing this dream book, one should place a notebook or a pad and a couple of sharpened pencils where they can be reached easily upon awakening. As the person goes to sleep he should say to himself several times, "I will remember my dreams." If he is willing to devote just a little time and effort he can become acquainted with one of the most exciting and interesting dimensions of the real self.

As the dream book is written the individual can become the best interpreter of his own dreams. There are a few very specific and very simple suggestions which may be of help: the barrier to remembering dreams must be broken by convincing the subconscious that there is a conscious desire and need to remember them. This can be done, as indicated, by giving oneself a specific suggestion just before going to sleep: "I will remember my dreams." The action of placing near at hand the pad and pencil will be an additional positive suggestion. When one awakens, without asking himself whether or not he had a dream, he should automatically pick up the pencil and pad. The dream, fragmentary though it may be in the beginning, will be ready for the writing. It will be found that by jotting down words, phrases, or brief sketches of some peculiar scene sequence, it will later be possible to recall many more details. When a dream appears in a complete form it can sometimes be outlined and filled in later. Dreams that appear in color should be marked, as well as those which apparently have deep emotional content. Some dreams appear as scenes where the dreamer is detached from the action. Other dreams will involve the dreamer as a participant. Gradually, it will be realized that practically all, perhaps all, dreams in some way involve the dreamer, though he may appear in many strange disguises. Dreams should be dated. The sequence can be most important when used at some later date. What are considered important dreams may be recorded in detail, but at least snatches and phrases from all of them should be kept.

Essential to understanding and clarifying dreams is a daily period of "meditation" to be discussed later. Consciousness flows like a small brook in a nightly dream sequence. When a brook is stirred up, muddy water results; trash floats by. The regular daily meditation period is the quieting and waiting period which is necessary to allow the stream to clear. Slowly, but surely, it will clear. Just so, the dream flow from the unconscious will clear gradually, revealing more and more of the aspirations, purposes, and ideals of the inner self. Thus it is possible to gain the guidance, understanding, and strength needed for a more balanced life.

7

Meditation

THE TECHNIQUE FOR meditation which is outlined in this
brief introduction is recommended for personal testing. Results will
follow patient and persistent daily practice. Perhaps this can best
be accomplished in small groups of people who come together for
this specific purpose.

For a number of years since Edgar Cayce's death in 1945 people
have come from many parts of the country to Virginia Beach to examine and try suggestions found in the readings. Every Association
conference includes small group discussions and experiments
dealing with meditation. The following has been compiled from my
notes on such discussions.

Meditation, as recommended here, is not suggested as a substi-
tute for prayer. Indeed prayer, as will be seen, can sometimes make
meditation possible. What then is the difference between prayer and

meditation? Many forms of prayer are familiar to the average person, such as petition, praise, thanksgiving, worship, and confession. Prayer is related to the action and the attitude of the individual. In prayer man may be said to seek a relationship with God. He talks to God.

Meditation can be described as a process of being still. It is characterized by focus of attention and release of tension, followed by relaxation, receptivity, discovery. The Edgar Cayce readings say that meditation is the

> . . . attuning of the mental body and the physical body to their source. For you must learn to meditate, just as you learned to walk, to talk, to develop any of the physical attributes of your mind as compared to the relationships with facts, the attitudes, the conditions, the environs of your daily surroundings. 281-41

Meditation is a process of stilling and focusing consciousness so that higher areas of the unconscious are unlocked. A man must dare to think of himself as related to God. He must dream of himself as something more than a product of his own material experiences in the earth. To achieve such a high purpose, this time for stillness must become a daily discipline for body and mind.

The first view which man takes of himself from the vantage point of reflection is not pleasant. As the readings put it:

> Ye find yourselves confused at times respecting from whence ye came and whither ye goeth. Ye find yourselves with bodies, with minds, not all beautiful, not all clean, not all pure in thine own sight or in thy neighbor's. And there are many who care more for outer appearances than that which prompts the heart in its activity or in its seeking. 281-41

One of the first painful rewards of meditation will be a better understanding of oneself and the *gradual* growth of a willingness to face oneself.

Through meditation the "inner self," "the higher self," "the oversoul," "the Divine within," is awakened and the energy and power from it pours into the stream of daily activity, providing guidance and a strengthening of the will to choose the "better way."

In preparing the body for meditation it should be recognized that the first step is the creation of a right attitude toward the body itself. This may be begun by becoming better acquainted with the body, its complexity, its beauty, its magnificence. Even a brief study of any organ or function of the body will reveal that it is worthy of being called a "vehicle for the soul." The structure and adaptability of the hand; the composition and movement of the blood; the almost magical formation and operation of the eye, arouse in man a sense of awe and wonder. It is possible to catch a vision of the body as a miniature copy of the universe, and conceive of it as "the part of the soul" which shows in this third dimension. This attitude conceives of the body neither as an object for gratification and adoration nor as something on which to heap debasement and shame. *Through meditation the body becomes not a prison from which to escape but rather an instrument through which the highest spiritual aspirations of the "real self" may be expressed.*

It is easy to lose sight of the purpose of meditation by paying too much attention to physical stimuli such as bathing, diet, breathing, posture. Trying this chant or that incense, keeping this diet or holding that posture, according to someone else's ideas, is not so good as first reaching a point of stillness and light and then choosing that way which seems right. Begin! Later changes in outer techniques can be made according to one's own needs. Cleansing of the body, for example, is a physical parallel to the mental purging which is far more important and more difficult. The readings put it this way:

What is thy God? Are thy ambitions only set in whether ye shall eat tomorrow, or as to wherewithal ye shall be clothed? Ye of little faith, ye of little hope, that allow such to become the paramount issues in thine own consciousness! Know ye not that ye are His? For ye are of His making! He hath willed that ye shall not perish, but hath left it with thee as to whether ye become aware of thy relationships with Him or not. In thine own house, in thine own body there are the means for the approach—through the desire first to know Him; putting that desire into activity by purging the body, the mind, of those things that ye know or even conceive of as being hindrances —not what someone else says! It isn't what you want someone else to give! As Moses gave of old, it isn't who will descend from heaven to bring you a message, nor who would come from over the seas, but lo, ye find Him within thine own heart, within thine own consciousness! If ye will meditate, open thy heart, thy mind! Let thy body and mind be channels that ye may do the things ye ask God to do for you! Thus ye come to know Him. 281-41

The following suggestions are taken from the readings. They were repeated in many variations for literally hundreds of people who sought physical, mental, and spiritual help. Do not be misled by the simplicity of these suggestions. The disciplines are more difficult than they seem.

Select a simple affirmation which describes spiritual ideals and goals. The Lord's Prayer is such an affirmation. Many affirmations were suggested in the Edgar Cayce readings. The oddly worded sentences at times actually help one hold the thought and look for the meaning. The following are examples from the readings:

Father, as we seek to see and know Thy face, may we each, as individuals and as a group, come to know ourselves, even as we are known, that we—as lights in Thee—may give the better concept of Thy Spirit in this world. 262-5

Create in me a pure heart, O God. Open Thou my heart to the faith Thou hast implanted in all that seek Thy face. Help Thou mine unbelief in my God, in my neighbor, in myself. 262-13

How gracious is Thy presence in the earth, O Lord! Be Thou the guide that we with patience may run the race which is set before us, looking to Thee, the Author and Giver of life.[1] 262-24

Select just *fifteen minutes* of the night or day when it is possible to be quiet. This must be a time that can be set aside *daily* until the habit of silence can be established.

Select a place. In the beginning it will be found that it is easier to be quiet in the same place each day. The unconscious mind adjusts

[1]Twenty-four affirmations are given in *A Search for God*, Books I and II (Virginia Beach: A.R.E. Press, 1942 and 1950, respectively).

itself more easily when it accepts the suggestion that it is in a certain place, at a certain time, for a definite purpose.

Sit or lie in a comfortable position. Focus the attention on the affirmation. Do not strain or concentrate. Simply hold the affirmation in consciousness.

You may already be commenting that in fifteen minutes you will not be able even to get started. The Edgar Cayce readings make quite a point of this as one begins. It is better discipline to work *regularly each day* for a few minutes than to attempt long periods of undirected daydreaming. In fact it would be neither desirable nor healthy to force the mind and body until the habit of a short period of control has been established.

Normally some of the following reactions will take place. The body will resist. The chair will be uncomfortable. There will be pressure at one point or another. There may be irritation of the skin or even an uncontrollable desire to move some part of the body. At times thirst will develop. A glass of water will seem absolutely essential to continuing life. In the beginning it will seem impossible not to be conscious of these sensations in the body. Do not pamper them. On the other hand, feel no sense of guilt at being aware of them. Simply return the attention to the affirmation.

As one continues with daily sessions, consciousness will shift from the body to mental activity. All kinds of impressions which have seemingly been forgotten will be remembered. Thoughts of details of the day's activities, plans for tomorrow, or memory of events of a few days past may begin to flicker briefly on the screen of consciousness. Sounds will become more prominent. Noises that have not been heard before will seem disturbing and much louder than usual. Gently but firmly consciousness must be moved back to the affirmation. *This must be done as many times as is necessary.* At the end of the fifteen-minute period one should stop and go about his daily activities. No sense of guilt or disturbance should be felt that the mind is caught literally dozens of times in a fifteen-minute period wandering away from the affirmation.

As the days pass and one persistently keeps the regular time and place for being still, the body and the conscious mind will grow relatively quiet. A new set of images will begin to flood into consciousness. They come from the unconscious. There will be pictures, scenes, faces, colors, designs of all kinds. This may be compared to a very interesting television show. Many individuals stop here to look at these pictures, follow the action in these scenes, and consider this to be meditation. As with attention on the body and the activity of the conscious mind, it is necessary to refocus awareness. Attention should be moved gently but firmly back to the affirmation. The meaning of the words should be re-examined. They should be held up, grasped lightly, but the focus on the words and the meaning of the statement of spiritual purpose which has been chosen should be retained.

As the mind is flooded with fragments of the unconscious mental activity, one may become conscious of what might be called guidance. This is especially true when prayer is substituted for discipline of the body, the conscious and unconscious mind. Such guidance coming as impressions, hunches, even a voice, must be understood for what it really is. The unconscious need not be considered omniscient. If one is taking only the mental activity based on suppression as the basis for guidance, it can be very self-centered and egotistical, when silence and light are ignored. "God's will" for such persons can be as twisted as the guidance of the medieval monk who led the Children's Crusade.

Gradually there will come a quieting of the body. The day will arrive when if asked suddenly to move a foot or a hand, it will be impossible to do so, for one would simply not know where it was. The conscious mind will have grown quiet; the pictures and scenes from the unconscious will have stopped flickering against the wall of the mind. *At this point, an individual is ready to begin deeper meditation.* Longer periods then will be both possible and rewarding. Cycles of activity of the body, the conscious mind, and the unconscious will be repeated. They will remain quiet for periods and then move again with renewed activity. Each time they must be quieted, not by force, nor by pressure, but by simply returning attention to the affirmation. This is a process of releasing by focusing consciousness.

As one approaches the point of stillness, there will be a better understanding of "Be still, and know that I am God." (Ps. 46:10)

At this point of stillness, there will be light. For some this will be a tiny point of brilliant white light. For others it will be a golden speck or a tiny ball. For others it may be a warm, enveloping, penetrating flow of light. Consciousness, at this point, can be moved to the light.

At this instant, there will be a knowing, an awareness, which cannot be described, for the meaning is different for every man. Symbolically, as Jesus may have been explaining in His famous parable, the prodigal son of man's consciousness which has been lost in matter proclaims at this point, "I will return to my Father."

What is to be gained through persistently pursuing the simple discipline of body and mind as outlined above? This light may not come in a day or in a week or in a month. For some it may mean years of work. However, the immediate gains will be many and different for various individuals, according to their needs, their purposes, their development. For some there will come an inner peace arising from release of tension. The quietness achieved, gradually, for mind and body, will begin to show in the daily thought, word, and action. There will come for some a growing sense of balance and poise. Control will seem to come more from within, rather than from without. For others mental activity, such as memory, reason, concentration, may improve noticeably. Creative activity may be extended. Psychic sensitivity may increase. Dreams will become clearer; hunches and intuitive flashes will be more frequent. There will be a greater awareness of the mental and emotional state of others. This kind of "knowing" must not be exploited for selfish ends, either to take advantage or to show authority. Entrance into the unconscious through this doorway makes exacting and challenging demands on an individual. Though it is hard for a Westerner to grasp the full meaning, it is possible to say with the Chinese:

"To concentrate the seed-flower of the human body above the eyes, that is the great key of the human body. Children, take heed! If for a day you do not practice meditation, this Light streams out, who knows whither? If you only meditate for a quarter of an hour, you can set ten thousand aeons and a thousand births at rest. All methods take their source in quietness. This marvelous magic cannot be fathomed."[2]

As meditation is continued, an understanding of what is taking place in the physical body becomes more important. The readings of Edgar Cayce, which insist that the endocrine gland centers are the physical points of expression for the spiritual or soul body, seem more logical.

---

[2] *The Secret of the Golden Flower,* trans. Richard Wilhelm.

In one reading it is stated like this:

Yet it is found that within the body there are channels; there
are ducts; there are glands; there are activities that perform
no one knows what! in a living, moving, thinking being. In
many individuals such become dormant. Many have become
atrophied. Why? Non-usage, non-activity! because only the
desires of the appetite, self indulgences and such have glossed
over or used up the abilities in these directions that they become only wastes, as it were, in the spiritual life of an individual who has so abused or misused those abilities that have
been given him for the greater activity. 281-41

The gonads, the sex glands in the body, are described as the mo-
tor which during meditation raises energy through the cells of
Leydig upward through the other psychic centers to the pineal and
pituitary, the higher spiritual centers of the body.

Besides those mentioned, the adrenals, the thymus, and the thyroid (and parathyroid) are involved. In Eastern teachings the movement of this energy corresponds to the rising of the kundalini.

"The seed blossom of the human body must be concentrated
upward in the empty space," as it is said in a Chinese Book of Life.
And it then continues, "The way leads from the sacrum upward in a
backward flowing manner to the summit of the creative, and on
through the house of the creative; then it sinks through two stones
in a downward flowing way into the solar plexus, and warms it."[3]

In the summer of 1950 we brought seven young men of college
age together in Virginia Beach for a three-week group experiment
designed to test suggestions in the Edgar Cayce readings for increasing psychic perception. Prayer and meditation as described were
given special attention.

A group period of meditation was held from 7 to 7:30 A.M. daily
and for one hour, 2 to 3 A.M., for the last three days of each week.
Participants were urged to spend time alone in prayer and meditation. According to their reports, all of the young men were devoting
as much as two to three hours per day to prayer and meditation by
the end of the first ten days.

---

[3] *Ibid.*

Each of the participants was asked to keep a daily journal in which were noted any reactions to the prayer and meditation periods. These coupled with notes taken at the time of both group and individual interviews are the source of the following comments.

One of these young men indicated that he rarely prayed formally prior to the project. As a child he had not been taught to pray; he had never read a book on prayer; he had never before discussed prayer and meditation with anyone.

For the first four days his journal was blank. Then he began to record a variety of physical reactions which occurred during his quiet periods. He claimed to feel sensations in his spine. There seemed to be a movement from side to side, although he knew there was no actual body movement. A fullness in the head was noticed. Pressure seemed to develop in the chest, making breathing difficult. He felt sexually stimulated. However, after some of the quiet periods the body seemed not to exist.

A variety of mental images were reported as pouring into consciousness. Included among these were triangles, a shepherd's crook, steps with a large ball on top, a white cup out of which a liquid was flowing, a tall mountain in color, etc.

Some of the meditation periods were described as producing strain and irritation. Toward the end of the three weeks the efforts at focusing attention were described as producing relaxation and refreshment.

Here are two selections from this young man's journal. They are interesting, considering the fact that this person had so little background in prayer and meditation.

Wednesday, August 16, 1950, 2:40 A.M.: "I started to meditate, I seemed to be aware that H. L. was in the room watching us. I gradually lost the knowledge of where my arms, legs, back and neck were located. I only knew their general direction–sensation was quite blunt. On thinking of my relationship with God, vibrations that started in the spine, went up to end in a fullness in the head—top and back. I managed to blank them out. I could not see whether the internal field of vision became brighter because the light was on in the room. The mental was more difficult to control. I found that in order to control it, I had to keep thinking of God and man's relationship to him.

The time went astoundingly fast; I meditated for half an hour. When I stopped I had to look at my hands in order to direct them to unclasp themselves. I feel a lot cleaner now."

Saturday, August 26, 1950, 7:30-8:30 A.M.: "I saw a green color upon closing my eyes, then I saw the usual pyramid, then I saw what looked like my big toe and it was white, then the toe got huge. Then I saw the door swing wide open and all a person had to do was to walk across the threshold—and the strong shall carry the lame, that is, carry them over the threshold. The lame are those that cannot walk over the threshold by themselves. The brilliant white light bathed me several times and it was good."

One of the participants who claimed to pray daily, who had been taught to pray as a child, and who had read several books on prayer, was not so expressive in his reports.

There were some physical sensations during the second week, including fullness and pressure in the top of the head and temples, throbbing in lower back and chest, twitching in fingers, and a sense of energy flowing in the body.

A journal extract mentioned stimulation of boyhood memories and a peculiar soreness in heels and lower back.

The physical sensations recorded in the journals seemed to follow a pattern with a few variations. Another of the participants described fullness in the head, excessive saliva flow, constricted breathing, pressure in the middle of the forehead, sickness of the stomach, sweating, throbbing in the chest, and movement from side to side.

This young man's journal contained many entries of "no sensations." Nevertheless, he noted pressure or throbbing in endocrine gland areas, especially in the solar plexus and thymus areas, seventeen times.

The frankness of the following entry written after a 2 A.M. meditation period is reassuring:

Pretty tired from wheeling Miss J. around. [Each of the participants spent at least three hours each week pushing a cripple's wheelchair on the Virginia Beach ocean walkway.] I got up in a daze. I lost my physical consciousness very quickly. I had all I could do to keep my mind focused, though. I was that close to sleep. I would focus on a word and my mind would just stay there—nothing would happen except that the concentration kept me awake. I would find myself off on a tangent and bring myself back with the greatest difficulty. My right nostril started running. My legs up to the hips fell asleep. I found discretion "was the better part of valor" at 2:50—I went to sleep.

In contrast, examine the following description of a seven-thirty prayer period from the same person.

Used Lord's Prayer. Words repeated as at a distance . . . I decided to focus on the individual words, using the idea of the Christ's love. I pulled the words up as high as I ever had before. I continued to push them up via thinking of the Christ-love. Emotions of love started to generate in my own heart. The words went up and up. I used the music to send them higher. I felt fine and loved and was loved; was love. This was not entirely, but a very fine start at breaking down the block . . . at the very end I began to see sparks that popped around in my field of vision. (At various times during the meditation the sunlight was quite strong.) I came out feeling joyous. During the very latter part of the meditation I found myself breathing quickly. Throbbing was continuous. It got more intense. I do not say that this was real love or anything else but it was a greater degree of feeling than I have possessed previously. There was a pulsing sensation in the thyroid, thymus, adrenals and gonads.

Let us look at just one more of the seven journals. This young man recorded very little for six days, then he began to describe such physical sensations as pulsation in the solar plexus, a swaying back and forth, terrific warmth, especially in the forehead, nausea, pulsation in the head, heavy breathing, relaxation, refreshment.

In this account no mental images are described; however, toward the end of the second week two pages are devoted to inspirational self-analysis with a strong religious "flavor." A comment on time is interesting:

No feeling at all except near end when I knew the closing phrases were coming, but it seemed we had just begun and I didn't want to stop. The "whole body" vibration came on these closing words. Each day the period seems to get shorter and shorter. As to the incense—it is *always* pleasing to me and no particular reaction.

It should be kept in mind that the seven participants were asked not to discuss what they wrote in their journals. Group discussions dealt with philosophical subjects. There was no competition to "experience something." In fact, the attitude of all the young men was skeptical, at times cynical and critical. During the three weeks it is true that these boys were subjected to many stimuli to focus on what may loosely be termed "the spiritual life." Service (work) projects, daily group discussions, individual counseling periods, were balanced with dieting, semi-fasting, sweat baths, massages, sand packs, and exercise to cleanse the body.

The report on the project may be used as a guide book in understanding the suggestions from the readings—not as you read them but rather when you test the ideas in your own experience. For meditation, as it is defined in the readings, is *a movement* in consciousness. These seven college students, with widely different backgrounds, who for the most part had experienced little contact with each other, recorded in three weeks very similar physical, mental, and emotional experiences during meditation periods.

Let us return for a moment to the journals. Were the eighty-one physical sensations which were noted in *endocrine areas* indicative of the movement of the spiritual energy which is described in the Edgar Cayce readings? This would seem to be worthy of further consideration.

An explanation in the readings of this movement of energy through the spiritual centers of the body is found in a series of readings on the interpretation of the Book of Revelation as a description of a meditation experience of the author. The seven churches in Asia Minor are described as symbolically connected with the seven endocrine glands which have been named, as are the seven seals which are opened. The chart which appears on the opposite page outlines these suggested relationships.

The description in the Edgar Cayce readings of the forces which are released with the opening of the seals (the four beasts, the four

THE REVELATION
The Book with the Seven Seals—The Human Body

CHURCHES	FAULTS & VIRTUES	LORD'S PRAYER	SEALS	OPENING	FIGURES	ELEMENTS	GLANDS	PLANET SYMBOLS	COLORS
Laodicea	Neither hot nor cold	Father in Heaven	7	Silence			Pituitary	Jupiter	Violet
Philadelphia	An open door	Name	6	Earthquake			Pineal	Mercury	Indigo
Sardis	Hath not been faithful / Hath a name	Thy Will	5	Souls of Faithful Slain			Thyroid	Uranus	Blue (Gray)
Thyatira	Allowed false teachings—Charity-Faith-Service	Evil	4	Pale Horse	Eagle	Air	Thymus	Venus	Green
Pergamos	Hold doctrine of Balaam / Works and faith	Debt (Karmic)	2	Black Horse	Lion	Fire	Adrenal	Mars	Yellow
Smyrna	Blasphemy / Works Have Endured	Temptation	3	Red Horse	Man	Water	Cells of Leydig	Neptune	Orange
Ephesus	Left Thy First Love / Labor and Patience	Bread	1	White Horse	Calf	Earth	Gonads	Saturn	Red

horses, etc.) related these centers to areas of the unconscious, The four lower centers might be said to correspond to the forces of the physical body so ably described by Freud as the "id." The other seals would correspond to higher areas of the unconscious. The meditation experience is a cleansing process. The spiritual (creative) power in man rises upward to the area symbolized by the pineal through which there is a downward flow of universal energy, always available to man, and, as these unite, they move into the pituitary area and overflow to purify and cleanse the lower centers (of the unconscious).

It seems possible that this may be what is meant by the familiar verses from Psalms: " ... my cup runneth over. Surely goodness and mercy shall follow me all the days of my life: and I will dwell in the house of the Lord for ever." (Psalm 23:5-6)

Or, "The light of the body is the eye: therefore when thine eye is single, thy whole body also is full of light ... " (Luke 11:34)

If the endocrine glands can be related even symbolically to the various levels of the unconscious, the stress and importance placed on them in the Edgar Cayce readings become more understandable.

As meditation is continued the cleansing of the mind becomes an important factor. The daily discipline of focusing attention on a statement of spiritual aspiration will automatically stir up and bring resistance from the lower unconscious areas. Thus an individual becomes more aware of the negative attitudes which are held and must consciously begin to deal with them. For example, it is quite common for sexual desires to be stimulated by meditation. A person must be prepared to direct these energies as the urges are brought to consciousness. This is equally true in other areas involving control of attitudes and emotions. The best understood of such relationships may be in the areas of the solar plexus (the adrenals). The same energy which is associated with fear, hate, and anger can become, when converted, courage, persistence, and drive.

Along with meditation there is a need for conscious control of thought. It is undesirable to keep putting into the unconscious barriers of hate, fear, anger, self-pity, arrogance, jealousy, etc., which prevent the flow of creative energy to and from the higher unconscious. The readings stress that mind is the builder. Thought actually takes form in the mental realm. The reality and potency of these forms can easily be demonstrated by getting a person to relive some terrifying experience. The memory can be as disturbing as the actual event.

Is it possible that this is what is meant in Jesus' words, "Therefore if thou bring thy gift to the altar, and there rememberest that thy brother hath aught against thee; leave there thy gift before the altar, and go thy way; first be reconciled to thy brother, and then come and offer thy gift." (Matt. 5:23-24)

The readings are very clear on the kind of mental activity which is necessary:

> Not that some great exploit, some great manner of change, should come within thine body, thine mind, but line upon line, precept upon precept, here a little, there a little. For it is as He has given, not the knowledge alone but the practical application in thine daily experience with thy fellow man—that counts. 922-1

The same thought is continued in the following:

> It is just in living those things in the material manner that are the fruits of the Spirit, that bring with them their reward—which maketh for the understanding within thee. Love ye one another, show forth gentleness, kindness, speak softly, even to those that are harsh, upbraid not, condemn not, be long-suffering. Be patient, but as an activative principle, as an activative experience in thine own self. 922-1

Meditation as outlined here with physical and mental disciplines may seem, at first glance, too simple to be the best doorway to the unconscious. One should not be deceived either as to the importance or the difficulties to be encountered in moving through this doorway. This is the path which has been chosen by the great mystics of all ages. Beyond the short daily period of the search for the silence and the light lie the longer periods of silence through which it is possible to reach the deeper regions of the inner self. These will be opened to him who is persistent in the disciplines of controlled attention and the daily practice of the spiritual laws with which he is familiar. Perhaps it is true, as Evelyn Underhill makes the point in the conclusion of her book, *Mysticism,* that each man in his own small way must eventually find and travel, as he is able, the same road traveled by the great contemplatives.

The Edgar Cayce readings most certainly recommend meditation as the safest and surest way to the higher levels of the unconscious.

8

The Place of the Small Group in the Spiritual Search

"IN THESE PAST two weeks I have come to know, to experience, more love and consideration than I have known since childhood." The man's voice broke. "I don't know how to describe what it has meant for me to try to work with you as members of this group, to feel concern for each one of you, to pray for you, and to know you were praying for me."

Three men and four women shifted a bit in their chairs. Some glanced up quickly at each other. The thought could almost be read in their faces, "What's going on here?" Thoughts flashed back to the day this reserved, almost cold-natured, person had attended the first meeting. He never spoke unless asked a direct question. He seemed critical without putting criticism into actual words. He seldom smiled. This was the person who was "cracking up," whose voice was quavering, whose eyes were filling with tears.

"I feel close to each one of you," he went on. "I don't understand what's happened to me, but I feel able to face myself, to admit my mistakes, yet not condemn myself for the first time in my life. It's wonderful."

He smiled now and words poured out in a torrent. There were confessions of thought about the negative qualities of some who were present; there were admissions of fear of being laughed at or rejected, of being misunderstood. One by one the members of the group began to pray silently. Finally, the man sat down. He was exhausted. He wept uncontrollably. The group leader reached over and clasped the man's hand. For about five minutes there was silence, there was prayer, and then the discussion of "Know Thyself" from *A Search for God,* Book I, continued. There was no group discussion of the outburst.

The man, from that time on, seemed like a different person. Much of the coldness was gone. He smiled, talked freely, and took part in all group activities. A month later he re-established contact with his wife from whom he was divorced and took on more responsibility for his two children which was not required by law. His mother wrote to the group leader that she had never seen such a change in a person. She said that her son had been filled with negative attitudes; that he had no friends and didn't want any; that he actually had cursed her for bringing him into the world. She thanked the group for all it had done for her son.

I watched this change take place in the life of this young man. Later I talked with the mother and others who knew him. The group discussions had pointed the way to self-observation. There had been no special focus of attention on him. Each member of the group had problems. The prayer energy, built up through daily individual meditation and group periods of meditation at each weekly meeting, seemed to flow to the point where it was most needed. The help was in the form of a purging, a breaking down of blocks and inspiration to begin a different kind of life. Neither totally religious nor entirely psychological, the change reached the everyday levels of thought and action on a positive and constructive level.

Work with small groups was recommended in the Edgar Cayce readings as being helpful in turning inward to release greater mental and spiritual energies. Such groups it was suggested should be considered not only as laboratories where experiments in self-observation, disciplines of prayer and meditation, and practice of spiritual law could be shared, but also as healing centers of thought patterns where individuals could find encouragement and protection as they worked together.

I was a member of a group of twelve to eighteen people who received several hundred "group" readings from Edgar Cayce over a period of fifteen years. These readings consisted of short discourses on subjects suggested from the unconscious state. On each of these subjects an affirmation was given which was to be held in attention during a daily period of fifteen minutes' meditation. Group members were urged to test the ideas in everyday life. The discourses, along with the comments and recorded experiences of the group members, were compiled in *A Search for God,* now used by various discussion groups working with the Association throughout the country. Additional pamphlets and reports have been prepared from time to time.[1]

From three to twelve persons may form a group by coming together and agreeing to work with the data from the readings. Meetings are generally held weekly in the homes of group members. The essays are designed to lead from basic to more complex ideas. Discussion leaders rather than teachers are selected on a rotating basis. Reasoning together and reporting on work undertaken are encouraged in favor of lectures or the dispersal of information.

The weekly group session is considered as a laboratory where prayer and meditation not only are discussed but also practiced. In an atmosphere of mutual concern with spiritual purposes and ideals self-observation may be extended through sharing and comparing constructively critical evaluations. The group automatically creates unusual opportunities for practicing patience, kindness, and similar virtues, which, it is suggested, should be the basis for any expansion of consciousness. The group is generally freer of emotional tension than the home, which is, according to the Edgar Cayce readings, man's best spiritual laboratory. Thus, techniques developed in the group can sometimes be used advantageously in the home. In effect the group provides the same kind of atmosphere as technical journals supply for men and women carrying on re-

---

[1]"Handbook for Group Study," "That Ye May Heal" (Virginia Beach, Va.: A.R.E. Press).

search experiments in the physical or social sciences. Dangers of moving too fast and too far are curtailed. Self-delusion is less possible.

The way in which a group may become a laboratory for self-observation may be illustrated from typical meetings. Let us imagine the first two chapters of *A Search for God,* Book I—"Cooperation" and "Know Thyself"—are under discussion. Cooperation has been defined in terms of a relationship with God, of becoming a channel through which creative energy may flow, of being a representative of God in the earth. Each group member is urged to take on a project. Attention is to be focused on establishing friendly, constructive communication with someone with whom there is daily contact but with whom no effort for communication has been made in the past. Prayer and constructive thought are to be followed by words of interest and honest favorable comment. Some simple acts of helpfulness are to follow the mental and vocal communication. Each group member is urged to observe his own and other persons' reactions as this project is carried out. Future group discussions will be augmented by reports on these efforts.

In working with the chapter on "Know Thyself" the stress of the discussion may center for a time on the relation of the physical, mental, and spiritual selves. Oneness or wholeness is the important point for consideration. The discussion is directed to techniques for self-observation which will enable a person to acknowledge this wholeness. Some of the group members may choose to study some particular organ. The complexity of its functions, the uniqueness of its structure, may pave the way for a new attitude toward the body. Other members may wish to report on the latest findings on the mind. A study of conscious functions, such as memory or reason, as well as unconscious action, such as dreams or control of internal, automatic body actions, will open up new dimensions for self-observation. An examination of religious or mystical experiences will enable almost all group members to examine the action of what seems to be a spiritual nature. In all the discussions it is important that the oneness of all of these activities of body-mind-soul be considered. The chapters in the *Search for God* books might be considered as a manual outlining experiments in self-observation which are to be undertaken by each group member.

The emphasis on prayer and meditation provides even better illustrations of the experimental nature of group action. A period of fifteen minutes each day is agreed upon by a majority of the group members. During this time each member focuses attention on the affirmation given at the beginning of each chapter which deals with the core of thought in the chapter under discussion. When the group comes together it holds a group meditation, using the same affirmation. Members of groups have found that the weekly period together has helped many of them with their daily meditation periods. Prayer for each other, as problems arise, as well as prayer for others outside the group who request help, has been found to bring about many rewarding experiences. This work with meditation and prayer seems psychologically sound for group activity.

For many individuals, work with prayer leads to examination of many good books on the subject and rich personal experiences with types of prayer with which they may not be conversant. Prayers of praise of God, worship, thanksgiving, and confession can be added to almost anyone's repertoire with helpful results. Also the study and work with prayer for healing may lead to new concepts of man's relation with the Creative Power of the universe.

It seems to me that the Edgar Cayce readings on group study contain some valuable suggestions for a person concerned with a spiritual search, a venture inward. Individuals seem not only to move more quickly to new levels of consciousness in a group but also to penetrate deeper into "garden rooms," the more beautiful areas of the unconscious mind. Certainly, it is possible to say that from the "readings" point of view the spiritual quest is best pursued not alone, but in the company of others. To paraphrase an old aphorism, "When you enter the gate of heaven you will go in leaning on the arm of someone you have helped." The group study provides a map for the traveler, a flask of water, and opportunities to practice what one knows of spiritual law.

Conclusion

WHAT DO YOU believe about your own place in the scheme of life? Are you merely a physical organism, more complex but like all other animal forms, which begins at physical conception and ceases to exist at death? With this belief you can hold to racial heritage as life's foremost good, hoping that each new generation will be enriched through the genes in the chromosomes of each sperm and egg cell. This is a challenging hope. It demands courage, high ethical standards, sacrifice, and creativity. But in accepting racial heritage as the goal of life, man resigns himself to personal oblivion.

To go further, under this concept all that man knows or can know of matter-time-space-energy must come through the senses of the physical body. This leads naturally to the average person's idea that his conscious self is all there is of him. Under such a pattern of thought any personal relationship with a Creative Force or God becomes remote.

Man has slowly but surely reduced matter to energy. The physical world seems less and less stable and it grows increasingly clear that even the most brilliant scientists are far from even a hazy idea of what the world of matter, much less the world of mind, is really like. It is possible to continue to think in terms of being a peculiarly complex form of energy, part of a stream without goal except to be a part of the stream. Indeed, to many serious thinkers it appears to be the height of audacity to expect to be more than this.

The other extreme is to conceive of man as a special creation, having a peculiar kind and type of job in a planned universe. Under this standard man becomes a spiritual being, a soul, which has taken on a body. Religions based on superstition or revelation cling to this basic concept in a variety of forms. Does man dare claim a direct, personal relationship with God?

Venturing into space will surely extend man's knowledge of the universe. Venturing inward to an equally vast unknown area may bring radical, perhaps even greater, changes in his knowledge and understanding of the universe and himself.

It has been suggested here that Edgar Cayce was a man who ventured inward. He was not the first. Surely, he will not be the last. Through the unconscious he seemed to tap sources of information which lay beyond accepted sense perception. The picture of the nature, extent, and activities of the world of mind which he and others like him have brought to consciousness is as revolutionary in its way as the discovery of the structure of the atom or the new galaxies beyond the range of the first telescopes. The practical applications of Edgar Cayce's new range of perception through the help given people from the physical readings and the measurable evidence of telepathy, clairvoyance, and precognition over a period of many years gives assurance to many of the existence of unexplored areas of mind and spirit. This inner world has been described by mystics and great thinkers of many ages. Again it may be asked, is man mad to dream of and search for mental and spiritual powers which can function beyond the confines of matter?

What are the rewards of this inner search? Powers of mind and spirit may bring a richer life; control of the negative self, which would destroy man, seems possible; belief in life beyond the period of body confinement can become acceptable; the world of matter can be considered as an extension, a projection, of the world of mind; and, finally, personal experiences of the mind and spirit bring a new kind of relationship with one's fellow men and the Force called God. Indeed, God may be said to take over the life and fulfill His purpose in and through man.

In describing his own ability to reach the unconscious minds of individuals who sought his help, Edgar Cayce gave in one reading the following:

> Those that seek, then, attune themselves to that promise which was made to this entity, Edgar Cayce. Then the entity when in that state, that condition where the physical self is laid aside, becomes the channel. Then only SPIRIT-MIND, as may attune itself with the purpose of the seeker, may give that as may be helpful in the experience of those who seek to know better their relationships to their Maker.
>
> Who knows better than the individual himself that which has hindered him from being physically, mentally, spiritually in accord with the divine that IS life manifested in the body?
>
> From whence comes that individual entity's ability to cope with the problems?
>
> Are ye not all children of God? Are ye not co-creators with Him? Have ye not been with Him from the beginning? Is there any knowledge, wisdom or understanding withheld if ye have attuned thyself to that Creative Force which made the worlds and all the forces manifested in same? Thinkest thou that the arm of God is ever short with thee because thou hast erred? "Though ye be afar, though ye be in the uttermost parts, if ye call I will HEAR! and answer speedily." Thinkest thou that this is spoken to another, or to thee?
>
> Open thy mind, thy heart, thy purpose to thy God and His purpose with thee.
>
> As to why this or that information may be indicated oft to individuals through this channel—this may be determined by those who analyze same from a practical, material experience . . . as a psychiatrist, a psychoanalyst. An individual who understands the pathology of a physical body is taken where he is, and is supplied that information which if applied in that condition existent will be helpful in his relationship to that he worships!

God seeks all to be one with Him. And as all things were made by Him, that which is the creative influence in every herb, mineral, vegetable or individual activity IS that same force ye call God—and SEEKS expression! Even as when God said, "Let there be light. For, this is law; this is love.

Hence those who seek in sincerity, in hope, in purpose, to KNOW, receive only to the measure that they manifest their hope, their belief, their desire in a God-purpose through a promise made to a man!

Thus ye have the source. Thus ye have the manner. The seeker answers. For know ye all: Ye give an account unto God for every deed, for every idle word, for every purposeful hope ye have made manifest.

Let not thy heart be troubled. Let it not be afraid. For ye believe in God, then, as His children . . . for thy sake, for thy Lord's sake . . . act like it! 294-202

Perhaps through life in the earth man can learn to purify the dross, quicken the spirit, return to God-consciousness.

One of the greatest obstacles which must be coped with is fear—fear in many forms. Man doubts his fellow man, himself, and his God. Much of this fear may well arise from having become separated from an original state of spiritual consciousness, a Garden of Eden, the Father's House. It seems reasonable that the path of the spiritual quest, the returning to a state of spiritual awareness, must surely at times lead inward, past the dark areas of accumulated guilt and prejudice, fears and frustrations resulting from many false starts, to the lighted areas of the creative or God-mind. Unless we can believe that such areas of the self exist—where we can meet God face to face—we are doomed to a self-created world of confusion and perhaps self-annihilation.

The history of man's progress is the story of those who have found inspiration and guidance from the Creative Power working in and through the innermost recesses of the mind and soul. Each individual according to his own readiness for the search can begin. This is a venture inward.

Bibliography

Part I

A FEW OF THE NUMEROUS
NEWSPAPER ARTICLES RE: EDGAR CAYCE

October 9, 1910. New York *Times* (feature story), "Illiterate Man Becomes a Doctor When Hypnotized."

February 19, 1911. Chicago *Examiner* (feature story), "Psychist Diagnoses and Cures Patients; Ignorant of Medicine, Turns Healer in Trance!"

October 10, 1922. Birmingham *Age-Herald* (feature story), "'Peculiar Gift Has Been Mine Since Youth,' Says Edgar Cayce."

January 4, 1956. Chicago *Daily News*, "Is Previous Life Possible?"

December 21, 1958. *National Enquirer*, "The Miracle Man."

December 28, 1958. *National Enquirer*, "They Called Him Fraud."

April 12, 1959. *American Weekly*, "The Mystery of Edgar Cayce," Maurice Zolotov.

June, July, and August 1959. *The Voice*, "Edgar Cayce, America's Technician in Psychic Research."

March 20, 1960. *Grit* family newspaper, "Mystery Man of Many Miracles" (full-page feature with illustrations, condensation of book).

RADIO PROGRAM RE: EDGAR CAYCE

May 15, 16, 17, 1959. *Monitor Radio Program* (National Hookup, NBC), "The Remarkable Edgar Cayce."

A FEW OF THE NUMEROUS
MAGAZINE ARTICLES RE: EDGAR CAYCE

September 1940. *Magazine Digest*, "Diagnosis by Dream" condensed from *There Is a River.*

September 1943. *Coronet* magazine, "Miracle Man of Virginia Beach," Margueritte Harmon Bro.

1945-'46. *Mind Digest,* monthly section re: Edgar Cayce, including articles: "Akashic Records, Historians of the Soul," Julia Chandler, and "From the Candid Camera of the Cosmos," Gina Cerminara.

September 10, 1946. *Astrology Guide*, "Edgar Cayce and the Blind Man," Gina Cerminara.

December 1947. *Coronet* magazine, "Reilly's Human Service Station," Clayton G. Going.

February 1948. *Tom Breneman's Magazine,* condensation "Story of Edgar Cayce."

February 1953. *Fate* magazine, "Modern Man of Miracles," Paul M. Vest.

September 1953. *Pageant* magazine, "The Man Who Made Miracles," Michael Bakalar.

July 1954. *Fate* magazine, "Visiting Another Life Through Hypnosis," Vaughan Shelton.

Easter 1955. Dr. Norman Vincent Peale's Easter Message booklet.
December 1955. *Fate* magazine, "Edgar Cayce's Window to Eternity," Vaughan Shelton.
June 1955. *Fate* magazine, "Edgar Cayce's Mail Order Miracle," Vaughan Shelton.
July 8, 1955. *Astrology Guide,* "Strange Power of Edgar Cayce," Katherine Breid Holbrook.
August 1955. *Ancient Wisdom,* "Friendly Invasion," Fred Morgan.
May 1956. *True* magazine, "More Experiments into the Unknown," Morey Bernstein, author of *The Search for Bridey Murphy.*
March 1958. *Psychic Observer,* "Psychic Highlights," Lt. Col. Arthur E. Powell.
September 20, 1958. *Two Worlds* (London), "World's Most Amazing Man."
January 1959. *Sir* magazine, "The Miracle of Edgar Cayce," Peter Worlfram.
May 1959. *Horoscope* (Dell Publications), "The Story," G. Cardinal LeGros.
August 1959. *American Mercury* magazine, "In Slumber Deep," Lytle W. Robinson.
May 1960. *Fate* magazine, "Miracles Were My Father's Business," Edgar Evans Cayce.
July 1960. *Pageant* magazine, "The Strange Case of 'Doctor Cayce,' " Arthur Whitman.

BOOKS ABOUT EDGAR CAYCE

There Is a River, Thomas Sugrue. New York: Henry Holt & Co., 1942.
Many Mansions, Gina Cerminara. New York: Wm. Sloane Associates, 1950.
The World Within, Gina Cerminara. New York: Wm. Sloane Associates, 1957.
Edgar Cayce—Mystery Man of Miracles, Joseph Millard. Greenwich, Conn.: Fawcett Publications, Inc., July, 1956.
Edgar Cayce—Man of Miracles, Joseph Millard. London: Neville Spearman, Inc., August, 1961. Same text as above.

BOOKS WITH A SECTION ABOUT EDGAR CAYCE

Stranger in the Earth, Thomas Sugrue. New York: Henry Holt & Co., 1948.
You Will Survive After Death (pp. 91-101), Sherwood Eddy. New York: Holt, Rinehart & Winston, 1950.
In the Name of Science, Martin Gardner. New York: G.P. Putnam's Sons, 1952.
The Search for Bridey Murphy, Morey Bernstein. New York: Doubleday & Company, Inc., 1956.
The Inner Splendor (one sermon on Edgar Cayce), L. L. Dunnington. New York: The Macmillan Company, 1957.
The Healing Power of Faith (pp. 224-229), Will Oursler. New York: Hawthorn Books, Inc., 1957.
Nothing So Strange, Arthur Ford, in collaboration with Margueritte Harmon Bro. New York: Harper & Row, 1958.
First Questions on the Life of the Spirit (pp. 117-118), Thomas E. Powers. New York: Harper & Row, 1959.

A Life After Death (a two-page discussion of E. C.), S. Ralph Harlow. New York: Doubleday & Co., Inc., 1961.
You Can Live Forever, A.T. DeGroot (T.C.U.). Arthur James, no date.

SUGGESTED READING ON REINCARNATION

"The Evidence for Survival from Claimed Memories of Former Incarnations," Ian Stevenson, M.D., *Journal of American Society for Psychical Research*, April 1960.
"How the Case of the Search for Bridey Murphy Stands Today," C. J. Ducasse, *Journal of American Society for Psychical Research*, January 1960.
The Case for Reincarnation. Leslie D. Weatherhead. Surrey, England: M.C. Peto, 1958.
Reincarnation, an East-West Anthology, ed. Joseph Head and S.L. Cranston. New York: The Julian Press, 1961.

Part II: Chapter 1

SUGGESTED READING

A Handbook of Medical Hypnosis, Gordon Ambrose and George Newbold. Balliere, 1956.
Hypnotherapy, A Survey of the Literature, M. Brenman and M. Gill. London: Pushkin Press, 1947.
Time Distortion Under Hypnosis, Linn F. Cooper, M.D., and Milton H. Erickson, M.D. Baltimore: The Williams and Wilkins Co., 1954.

HYPNOSIS USED FOR DEVELOPMENT OF MEDIUMSHIP

Adventures in the Supernormal, Eileen J. Garrett. New York: Creative Age Press, 1948, p. 135.
Nothing So Strange, Arthur Ford, in collaboration with Margueritte Harmon Bro. New York: Harper & Row, 1958, pp. 210-212.

SPLIT PERSONALITY UNDER HYPNOSIS

The Three Faces of Eve, Corbett H. Thigpen and Hervey M. Cleckley. New York: McGraw-Hill, 1957, p. 38.

Part II: Chapter 2

SUGGESTED READING

Human Personality and Its Survival of Bodily Death, F. W. H. Myers. London: Longmans, Green & Co., 1903.
The Belief in a Life After Death, C. J. Ducasse. Springfield, Ill.: Charles C. Thomas, 1961.

Enigma of Survival, Hornell Hart. London: Rider & Co., 1959.

Adventures in the Supernormal, Eileen J. Garrett. New York: Creative Age Press, 1949.

Does Man Survive Death? a symposium from pages of *Tomorrow*–How science, religion, and philosophy view the eternal question of man's immortality, ed. Eileen J. Garrett. New York: Helix Press, 1957.

Part III

SUGGESTED READING

Telepathy and Medical Psychology, Jan Ehrenwald, M.D. New York: W. W. Norton & Co., 1948.

The Dissociation of Personality, Morton Prince, M.D. Cleveland: Meridian Books, 1957.

The Three Faces of Eve, Corbett H. Thigpen and Hervey M. Cleckley. New York: McGraw-Hill, 1957.

Thirty Years Among the Dead, Carl Wickland, M.D. London: Spiritualist Press, 1949.

Beyond the Light, Fay M. Clark. New York: Vantage Press, 1958.

The Sacred Mushroom, Andrija Puharich. New York: Doubleday & Co., Inc., 1959.

Exploring Inner Space, Jane Dunlap. New York: Harcourt, Brace & World, 1961.

The Joyous Cosmology, "Adventures in the Chemistry of Consciousness," Allan W. Watts. New York: Pantheon Books, 1962.

Part IV: Chapter 6

SUGGESTED READING ON DREAMS

The Forgotten Language, Erich Fromm. New York: Rinehart & Co., 1951.

The Meaning of Dreams, Calvin S. Hall. New York: Harper & Row, 1953.

The Twilight Zone of Dreams, André Sonnet. Philadelphia: Chilton Co., 1961.

CONSIDERING THE PSYCHIC CONTENT OF DREAMS

The Mystery of Dreams, William Oliver Stevens. New York: Dodd, Mead & Co., 1949.

"Dreams—The Language of the Unconscious," Hugh Lynn Cayce with Shane Miller and Tom Clark. Virginia Beach, Va.: A.R.E. Press, 1962.

Part IV: Chapter 7

RECOMMENDED READING

A Search for God, Books I and II. Virginia Beach, Va.: A.R.E. Press, Book I copyright 1942, Book II copyright 1950.

The Secret of the Golden Flower, trans. Richard Wilhelm with European commentary by C.G. Jung. New York: Wehman Bros., 1955.

Mysticism, Evelyn Underhill. New York: Meridian Books, 1955.

Conclusion

RECOMMENDED READING
AS SURVEYS OF THE FIELD

Psychics and Common Sense, William Oliver Stevens. New York: E. P. Dutton & Co., 1953.

Psychical Research, Raynor Johnson. New York: Philosophical Library, 1956.

William James on Psychical Research, compiled and edited by Gardner Murphy and Robert O. Ballow. New York: Viking Press, 1960.

The Challenge of Psychical Research, Gardner Murphy. New York: Harper & Row, 1961.

Beyond the Reach of Sense, Rosalind Heywood. New York: E. P. Dutton & Co., 1961.

Index